D1488397

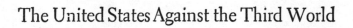

The United States Against the Third World

The United States Against the Third World

Antinationalism and Intervention

Melvin Gurtov

PRAEGER PUBLISHERS
New York • Washington

Published in the United States of America in 1974
by Praeger Publishers, Inc.
111 Fourth Avenue, New York, N.Y. 10003

Second printing, 1975

© 1974 by Praeger Publishers, Inc.

Library of Congress Cataloging in Publication Data
Gurtov, Melvin.
    The United States against the Third World.
    Bibliography: p.
    1. United States—Foreign relations—1945–
2. Underdeveloped areas—Foreign relations.
I. Title.
E744.G86   327.73   73-19436
ISBN 0-275-33470-8
ISBN 0-275-85010-2 (pbk.)

Printed in the United States of America

For friends I love—

Al,
Diane,
Henry,
Marianne,
Warren,
Terry,
Eric,
Marcia

Contents

Acknowledgments

The idea of a book on the themes of antinationalism and intervention in American policy toward the Third World came from the lectures I prepared for two courses in U.S. foreign policy. I felt a need, as much personal as professional, to put the cases of intervention together, examine their linkages, and propose an alternative. Much good work has already been done in reassessing specific instances of American intervention abroad; I hope my broader treatment adds to the respectability of the critical and radical literature.

I wish to thank, first of all, my home campus, the University of California, Riverside, for providing the opportunity to teach and learn, the space to think and write, and two intramural research grants. I used those funds to hire Kathy Krueger as a research assistant; I never made a wiser decision. Kathy did most of the spadework for this book, and if I have been as diligent in my writing as she has been in her research, the reader will be rewarded. Thank you, Kathy.

I am fortunate to have had the help of five persons, friends as well as colleagues, who commented on portions of the manuscript. They are Suresht Bald, Ron Chilcote, Terry Dietz-Fee, George Guess, and Paul Langer. I hope the final product does justice to their suggestions.

MG

Riverside, California

The United States Against the Third World

A government which needs foreign support to enforce obedience from its own citizens is one which ought not to exist; and the assistance given to it by foreigners is hardly ever anything but the sympathy of one despotism with another.

JOHN STUART MILL, 1859

1

The Ideology of
National Interest

Antinationalism and intervention have been conspicuous in American foreign policy ever since the emergence of the United States in this century as a global military and economic power. These themes, as they have appeared in the policies of the four most recent administrations toward the Third World, are the subjects of this study. Primarily, my interest is to explain the circumstances, purposes, and reasoning behind the choice of intervention as one means of coping with nationalism, civil war, and revolution in Third World societies. I am mainly concerned with what American policies reveal about official American understanding of Third World politics and peoples and only secondarily with the decision-making process of intervention.

Eschewing the standard chronological approach, I concentrate on the policies and attitudes of four administrations in four Third World regions: Eisenhower in the Middle East, Kennedy in Africa, Johnson in Latin America, Nixon in Asia. This approach affords an opportunity to treat a critical event in some depth—the interventions in Lebanon, the Congo, the Dominican Republic, and Bangladesh, respectively—while also assessing other interventions that occurred in the same region before or since. A sense of the continuity as well as the constancy of American policy may thereby be provided.

Because this study concentrates for the most part on widely acknowledged cases of U.S. intervention, it does not offer any new definition of "intervention." As I understand this term, intervention is the calculated and partisan use of national power—military, economic, political—to influence the domestic politics of another state. The types of interventions dealt with in this study are those that seek to manipulate the outcome of internal conflict (insurgency, revolution, or civil war) or, through subversion, to precipitate such conflict.

Antinationalism is used in this study to describe an attitude of indifference and sometimes disdain on the part of American policy-makers toward Third World societies and peoples. The special features of a Third World country's history and culture tend to be slighted; rivalries for political power are often mistakenly perceived as ideological struggles between pro- and anti-communists; and the increasingly common interest of Third World governments in self-reliance and self-directedness is ignored. Translated into policy, this attitude eases decisions to intervene by treating Third World countries as cold war symbols and by denying the indigenous roots, hence also the legitimacy, of radical movements and governments. The cases I will examine reflect an American presumption that radical change in Third World politics is inherently inimical to U.S. "interests" and must be prevented or deflected.

Any critical account of U.S. policy, such as this one, gains in value if it can also propose alternatives to the decisions that were made. Therefore, the concluding chapter attempts to synthesize the case studies by addressing the central question they raise: Why intervention? I then propose alternative guidelines for future American policy and suggest how they would reflect different priorities and values in dealing with Third World countries.

Before going on, it is important to give some over-all theoretical setting to the American policies that will be examined. Such a beginning will also establish for the reader my framework for understanding and analyzing U.S. foreign policy. My belief is that American officials assess day-to-day developments abroad on the basis of a reasonably fixed conceptualization of U.S. interests and objectives. Economic gains and losses, and diplomatic or strategic advantage, may be influential in particular decisions. But these and other factors derive ultimately from an identifiable set of principles of American external behavior—principles that, I contend, are generally and widely shared in the upper reaches of a remarkably homogeneous (civilian) foreign-policy establishment.[1]

Americans have been educated to believe that one of the core distinctions between their social system and communist systems is ideology, that while the politics and economies of the socialist states are structured in accordance with Marxist-Leninist theory, in the United States pragmatism, bargaining, and flexibility are the only guidelines of social life. The foreign policies of these two systems, we learn, reflect similar characteristics. Thus, Soviet and Chinese foreign policies are supposedly marked by ideologically inspired dogmatic images and implacable hostilities; single-mindedness of strategic purpose ("two steps forward"—they are always probing for weak spots) and tactical flexibility ("one step back"—they will retreat when faced with superior force); a readiness to exploit conditions of human misery, social change, and political unrest; and an acceptance of violence as a major instrument for promoting change. By contrast, American foreign policy is said to reflect a traditional respect for self-determination and national independence, deep-rooted humanitarian impulses, and dedication to the rule of law. The United States finds itself having to respond to threats by other powers; but it is always (we are told) searching creatively for ways to ease global tensions and avert war, forgoing opportunities to build its own empire, and being receptive to evolutionary, peaceful change. President Kennedy offered a fairly typical official appraisal of the basic contrast between communist and American foreign policies when he said the former seeks to impose a "monolithic world" while the latter seeks a "world based on diversity, self-determination and freedom."[2]

This characterization of the opposing camps is not merely the stuff of July 4 rhetoric but an integral feature of American officials' belief system, regardless of party and administration. The characterization may be put forward in more sophisticated fashion, but it contains the same bedrock assumptions about the way the international system is structured and competition unfolds. Among other sources, these assumptions seem to come from an ethnocentric educational system that makes the "American way" a myth and a mission; from the transference of corporate values, perspectives, and tactics to the foreign-policy arena; and from the formative experiences of four major wars, at least three of which occurred within the lifetime of every major participant in the policy-making process since 1945. The fact that these assumptions have been so frequently and widely articulated by American foreign-policy leaders means to me that there exists a consensus about America's role in the world that amounts to an ideology.

If Marxism-Leninism is the "source" of the foreign policies of the socialist countries, then the "source" of American foreign policy—the ideology or philosophical framework of beliefs that gives focus and direction to policy in particular circumstances—is contained in the doctrine of national interest. I do not mean doctrine in the narrow sense of the Truman, Eisenhower, or Nixon Doctrine, although these are important expressions of the national interest. Rather, I include as doctrine all high-level statements of American policy that, while perhaps explaining or rationalizing governmental behavior in specific cases, also encompass universalistic hopes and ambitions, asserting these to be America's larger purposes in the world. Like the communist countries, America has a grand design that goes beyond the "anti-Communist impulse" for which U.S. interventions abroad have most often been criticized.[3] The fact that this design, or doctrine, is not as insistent, formal, or readily located as the Marxist-Leninist scriptures does not make it any less ideological. Nor is it made less so by its emphasis on conservatism and reformism, in contrast with the radical change called for in most ideologies.

The doctrine of national interest, I suggest, is a perfectly logical expression of a foreign-policy ideology that requires, or sees as inevitable, American involvement in the security and stability of the entire world. That involvement more often is indirect than direct, nonmilitary than military; but it does mean an assumption of American responsibility for the affairs of other societies that often leads to intervention.

The ideology that asserts the necessity of such involvement comprises three axioms:

1. America's domestic tranquility depends on security and stability abroad. The first fundamental rule of American foreign-policy thinking relates the security of American institutions to the prevention of "disturbances" overseas. When President Truman, on March 12, 1947, committed the United States to the protection of all "free peoples" resisting communist aggression, he explicitly applied this rule:

> The United Nations is designed to make possible lasting freedom and independence for all its members. We shall not realize our objectives, however, unless we are willing to help free peoples to maintain their free institutions and their national integrity against aggressive movements that seek to impose on them totalitarian regimes. This is no more than a frank recognition that totalitarian regimes imposed on free peoples, by direct or indirect aggression, undermine the foundations of international peace and hence the security of the United States.

The lesson of World War II for American leaders has been widely accepted to be—in the words of Eugene V. Rostow, an under secretary of state in the Johnson Administration—"that any considerable disturbance in the equilibrium of affairs will threaten our sense of security. We have come finally to understand that we can protect the security of the United States only by actively participating in world politics."[4] McGeorge Bundy, policy adviser to Kennedy and Johnson, has written that "behind every sustained and serious engagement of the United States there lies an express or implied decision that this action is important to the safety and welfare of the United States itself."[5] President Johnson stated the case most succinctly when he said, on April 17, 1965, at Johns Hopkins University, "We fight [in Vietnam] because we must fight if we are to live in a world where every country can shape its own destiny. And only in such a world will our freedom be finally secure."

2. *Security and stability abroad for the forces of freedom depend on America's willingness to carry out the mission and responsibilities entrusted to it.* Every President and senior policy adviser has indicated agreement with President Truman when he said, in April, 1947, that "the free people of America cannot look on with easy detachment, with indifference" to the struggle of other peoples for their rights. "The world today looks to us for leadership. The force of events makes it necessary that we assume that role."[6] John Foster Dulles argued that an American "mission in the world" has been recognized "since the founding of this nation."[7] "History" would not "permit" Americans to live in isolation, John F. Kennedy said. "We are still the keystone in the

arch of freedom, and I think we will continue to do, as we have done in our past, our duty."[8]

Lyndon Johnson, in keeping with his predecessors, also relied on precedent and circumstances when he urged, "History and our own achievements have thrust upon us the principal responsibility for the protection of freedom on earth."[9] One of his, and Kennedy's, chief advisers, Walt W. Rostow, agreed: "We cannot renounce our destiny. We are the trustees of the principles of national independence and human freedom all over the globe; and, given our history, this is a proud and natural responsibility."[10] The price of this responsibility, said Johnson, would have to be paid: "If American lives must end, and American treasure be spilled, in countries that we barely know, that is the price that change has demanded of conviction and of our enduring convenant."[11] Whenever Russia or China "is involved in aggression, or approves it," Eugene Rostow has written, "we *are* the world's policeman, for without our will, and our force, there could be no resistance."[12]

In the Nixon Administration, the rhetoric has been more subdued, but the principle of America's destiny is upheld. Nixon told an interviewer in March, 1971:

> . . . I want the American people to be able to be led by me, or by my successor, along a course that allows us to do what is needed to help keep the peace in this world. We used to look to other nations to do this job once upon a time. But now only the United States plays a major role of this sort in the world.[13]

And, later in the same interview, he elaborated:

> Through an accident of history we find ourselves today in a situation where no one who is really for peace in this country can reject an American role in the rest of the world. . . . The day the United States quits playing a responsible role in the world—in Europe or Asia or the Middle East—or gives up or recedes from its efforts to maintain an adequate defense force—on that day this will become a very unsafe world to live in.

Nixon thus extended the Truman Doctrine into the 1970's.

3. *Fulfillment of America's mission and security responsibilities depends on a willingness and ability to intervene in the domestic affairs of other peoples.* The first two axioms establish the global scope of American interests and the necessity and wisdom of

global involvement. The United States is portrayed as having no choice but to be deeply involved and committed, because threats and acts of "aggression" against "free peoples," "free institutions," and the "Free World" ultimately affect America's survival. Such a conception of the American role leads American policy-makers to subordinate the aspirations and national self-interests of other societies to those of the United States, and to define them in terms that harmonize with American globalism. There is an implicit assertion that the American mission is also *their* mission, and therefore that American involvement in their affairs is as much in their best interests as it is in "ours."

Intervention abroad is an extension of this logic because it is a decisive means of projecting American power directly into another nation's politics. Even in cases where the communist threat is not confirmed and where political violence is the product of purely indigenous social conflict, the presumed right to intervene prevails over the right of each nation to govern itself. President Johnson said, during the Dominican crisis, "Revolution in any country is a matter for that country to deal with. It becomes a matter for hemispheric action only when the object is the establishment of a communist dictatorship." In Johnson's view, as we shall see, the *possibility* of a communist takeover was sufficient grounds for intervention—thus his statement that "the old distinction between 'civil war' and 'international war' has already lost much of its meaning."

Johnson's "doctrine" was not out of harmony with the views of other American policy-makers. "Our common problem, in a world of rapid and often momentous change," Dulles had proposed, "is to insure that necessary changes occur in peaceful fashion without upheaval or war. Violent change is never selective change. . . . Change is beneficent when it is selective, continuing and developing the good while shedding that which is evil, outmoded, or inadequate."[14] Dean Rusk, referring to the American "interest in the orderly progress and political stability of the developing areas," contended that the United States has a "serious national interest" in the peaceful settlement of their disputes, especially because communists might be involved. Although the United States would prefer not playing "peacemaker and policeman," "we just can't ignore these local disputes without increasing the danger to general peace and to our own national security."[15]

How is such logic reconciled with the oft stated American interest in the self-determination of peoples? The typical answer has taken two forms, both of which imply that the United States will judge whether a society is developing politically in ways consonant with its own history and culture. One answer, provided by Walt W. Rostow, is that it is a "legitimate American ideological interest" for the United States actively to promote its version of democracy everywhere. Because "under modern conditions it is difficult to envisage the survival of a democratic American society as an island in a totalitarian sea," Third World nations should "accept as a goal a version of the democratic value judgments consonant with their culture and their history and . . . move toward their realization with the passage of time."[16] Thus, self-determination is acceptable, provided it evolves toward a political system approximating the American model. A second answer accepts the principle but fails to grant its specific application. Dean Rusk, for instance, has remarked, "A principle like self-determination is extremely difficult to apply in detail. In the broadest sweep of national movements it has considerable validity, but it does not lend itself to an exact basis for constitutional construction in country after country."[17]

The ideology formed of these three national interest axioms sets out the logic of American empire. Needless to say, American officials have always rejected the accusation that their objective is a *Pax Americana*. In the same manner as their communist counterparts, they have contended that national power is exerted for strictly unselfish reasons. "It has not been a policy of crusade," Eugene Rostow has written. "All we have sought, and used limited power to achieve, is the acceptance by the Communist nations of a rule of order—an organized and accepted pattern of peace."[18] The United States seeks no advantage for itself when it intervenes —a theme of every policy spokesman when explaining U.S. involvement in Vietnam. Intervention is treated as an altruistic foreign-policy act, as though the objective of a "pattern of peace" favorable to American interests is neutral and agreeable to the rest of the world. Of course, we know that, in private, intervention is not lightly proposed or agreed upon by American policymakers without careful deliberation. But conviction in the doctrine of national interest does mean that intervention is generally regarded in Washington as a *natural* and *traditional,* as well as (from experience) reliable, policy instrument.

By sanctifying intervention, American doctrine creates the disposition to employ it. The doctrine establishes radical political change as a constant threat to American institutions and worldwide relationships. It raises issues of local nationalisms and historic rivalries between small powers to the level of high strategy and international crisis. It expands the scope of American concern to include all actual and potential areas of instability. It does not make intervention inevitable, but the doctrine legitimizes intervention as a means of actively promoting the American version of world order.

2

Eisenhower and the Middle East

Although the adjective "unchanging" has often been used, in Western accounts, to describe the Middle East, it can with greater justice be applied to U.S. policy. Since the late 1940's, when the ideology of American national interest began to justify postwar U.S. leadership of the "Free World," various administrations have pursued essentially the same objectives and had similar concerns. With striking uniformity, they have sought to preserve and strengthen territorial boundaries (in particular, Israel's), to minimize the influence and presence of the Soviet Union, to work with U.S. oil companies in maintaining access to oil under "stable" political conditions, and to contain radical nationalism. Military, economic, and political stability has been the watchword of U.S. policy. Where the United States has seen fit to intervene in the Middle East, its purpose has been to preserve order and prevent undesirable changes of the status quo.

THE EVOLUTION OF U.S. POLICY

In the postwar era, the Middle East became the first Third World region to receive the protective embrace of the containment doctrine. In response to British notification of intention to withdraw military and financial support from Greece, the State Department in early 1947 formulated a $400 million Greek-Turkish aid program. Earlier Soviet-American confrontations over

Iran and the Turkish Straits lent acute urgency to the aid program, and the official rationale for its passage took particular account of the presumed Soviet threat to the Middle East. Presenting the falling-domino logic long before President Eisenhower popularized it, Secretary of State Dean Acheson told leading congressmen that, without the aid, Greece or Turkey, or both, would fall to the Russians, Iran would follow, the entire eastern Mediterranean and Middle East would become vulnerable, and ultimately South Asia and Africa would be open to Soviet penetration.[1] Acheson, Truman, and other senior U.S. officials believed that "a historical turning point had been reached, that the United States must now stand forth as leader of the free world in place of the flagging British."[2] Such was clearly the tone and implication of the Truman Doctrine—the President's aid request to Congress on March 12, 1947—in which he argued that Turkey's "integrity is essential to the preservation of order in the Middle East" and that, with communist control of Greece, "confusion and disorder might well spread throughout the entire Middle East."

Until the Eisenhower Administration, however, Washington was reluctant to supplant the British in the Middle East, even though anti-British feeling, as in Iran and Egypt, made it difficult for the United States to build barriers against the U.S.S.R. An attempt to create a Middle East Defense Organization headquartered in Cairo and with primarily British responsibility failed to gain Egypt's acceptance. Instead, the United States joined with Britain and France to control the Middle East arms balance and preserve territorial boundaries. In the Tripartite Declaration of May 25, 1950, it was agreed that arms for internal security and self-defense would be provided to the Arab states and Israel, and that "the use of force or threat of force between any of the states in that area" would be opposed. This modest effort at Western containment of Middle East tension withered, however, when Gamal Abdel Nasser emerged as the spokesman of Arab nationalism. His assumption of the Egyptian leadership (September, 1953) unfortunately coincided with John Foster Dulles's ambitious plans, in his first year in office, to establish American predominance in the Middle East and save the region from Soviet expansionism.

As recounted by one of his biographers, Dulles, on the basis of a Middle Eastern tour in May, 1953, concluded that anti-Western xenophobia and revolutionary fanaticism were impeding economic development while ignoring the Soviet threat.[3] The United States, he decided, would have to take the leading Western role in the region, overcoming suspicions about U.S. ties to Britain and France and its support of Israel. He was not then prepared to argue for new American security guarantees to demonstrate the U.S. commitment, but he was interested in a more vigorous diplomacy and aid program.

Egypt, and Nasser, proved the great stumbling block. It appears that the Eisenhower Administration, hoping to include Egypt in its containment strategy, used its influence to bring about the Anglo-Egyptian agreement of 1954, which provided for British withdrawal from their Suez base in two years.[4] But the Americans miscalculated Nasser's interest in alignment with the West, and they contributed instead to his alienation. By encouraging anti-Soviet security agreements in the Middle East—between Turkey and Pakistan in April, 1954, between Turkey and Iraq in January, 1955, and the Baghdad Pact (Britain, Turkey, Pakistan, Iran, and Iraq) in February, 1955—the administration cut into Nasser's ambitions for regional leadership, aroused his concern that the United States was bent on replacing Britain as an empire builder in the Middle East, and gave priority to a Soviet threat that Nasser believed was insignificant compared with the threat posed by Israel. In lieu of an American-led collective security arrangement, "Nasser invoked a sort of Egyptian Monroe Doctrine for the Middle East—complete with his own unspoken equivalent of the Roosevelt Corollary. Outside powers must stay out; on the inside, Egypt would undertake to police the area."[5]

American "pactomania" in the Middle East also encouraged closer relations between the U.S.S.R. and Egypt, evidenced most dramatically in the 1955 arms deal with Czechoslovakia. The Eisenhower Administration was alarmed by the implications of Nasser's friendly ties with the socialist world, misreading them as evidence both of the devious character of his "positive neutralism" and of expansionist Soviet aims in the Middle East. A more objective reading of Egyptian and Soviet motives would have seen their relationship as the consequence of an affinity of interests: The Soviet Union sought ways to counterbalance the Baghdad Pact, while Nasser was expressing his independence, emerging pan-Arabism, and concern about Israeli attacks in the Gaza Strip. U.S.-Egyptian relations reached rock bottom when the administration, in July, 1956, withdrew a loan offer to finance construction of the Aswan Dam. Eisenhower and Dulles could no longer tolerate Nasser's procrastination on the offer; Nasser was reluctant to accept what he probably considered an American attempt to buy him away from Moscow. In retaliation, Nasser only days later ordered the Suez Canal nationalized. In the ensuing Suez crisis, Eisenhower refused to support the Anglo-French-Israeli invasion of Egypt, but his action should not obscure either the President's distrust of Nasser or his concern about keeping the Middle East out of Soviet hands. It was precisely in order not to increase Nasser's popularity and to maintain Western unity against the Soviet Union that Eisenhower wound up on Moscow's side in criticizing the invasion.

Suez ended the significance of Britain's role in the region and, by virtue of its own decision not to align with British policy, thrust the United States into a "custodian's" role.[6] Eisenhower accepted that role because, as he told congressional leaders just prior to proposing what became known as the Eisenhower Doctrine, "the existing vacuum in the Middle East must be filled by the United States before it is filled by Russia."[7] In official American thinking, to judge from the President's memoirs, Soviet relations with Egypt made the Russians a direct military, economic, and political threat to U.S. interests throughout the Middle East— even though, the State Department admitted, communists neither controlled any of the region's governments nor seemed about to try to win control.[8]

In his special message to the Congress on January 5, 1957, Eisenhower made clear that the Doctrine's overriding purpose would be to deter the Soviet Union from acting upon its presumed historic interest in "dominating the Middle East." He spoke of the area's immense economic importance to Western Europe and ultimately the United States, and of the "intolerable" situation "if the holy places of the Middle East should be subjected to a rule that glorifies atheistic materialism." The United States, he asserted in keeping with American foreign-policy ideology, would have to assume the responsibility for preserving the independence of Middle East nations—not because it seeks "either political or

economic domination over any other people," nor because it
wants to threaten Russian security ("The Soviet Union has nothing whatsoever to fear from the United States in the Middle
East"), but because the countries of the area need and mostly
want U.S. protection of their cultures, political integrity, and
economies. The President's proposal was therefore twofold: first,
that Congress grant him discretionary power to use up to
$200 million in aid money for the Middle East; second, that Con-
gress authorize him to employ U.S. military forces in defense
against "overt armed aggression from any nation controlled by
International Communism."

House Joint Resolution 117 passed by wide margins and became law on March 9, 1957. So far as the prospect of a U.S.
commitment of armed forces in the Middle East is concerned, the
resolution states that "if the President determines the necessity
thereof, the United States is prepared to use armed forces to assist
any nation or group of such nations requesting assistance against
armed aggression from any country controlled by international
communism." Eisenhower and Dulles seemed to assure questioning legislators that the United States would not intervene in those
situations—civil wars, a communist victory at the polls, or fighting
across local borders—that were not cases of Soviet "aggression,"
and in other cases only if invited to intervene.[9] Despite these apparent constraints, the reaction in the Middle East was hardly one
of warm welcome. As will be noted when discussing Lebanon, the
Eisenhower Doctrine had a polarizing rather than a stabilizing
effect, drawing a line between pro-Western and radical nationalist
governments by injecting the cold war ideological and strategic
contest into the area in a way it had not been previously.

The resolution also marked a watershed in U.S. policy toward
the Middle East because it specified the area as a vital national
interest. While the Truman Administration had treated the area
as though it were vital, it had neither said so publicly nor committed the United States, beyond the vague terms of the Tripartite Declaration, to unilateral armed intervention against Soviet
"aggression" wherever in the area it occurred. Succeeding administrations reaffirmed Eisenhower's objective of containing the
Soviet presence and limiting its penetration. They determined to
prevent Soviet "domination" of the Middle East, to keep conflict

localized, and to avoid a Soviet-American confrontation. They accepted strategic access, economic predominance, and Israel's integrity as basic policy principles. Implicit in these understandings of U.S. interests was (and is) that the actions of radical nationalist movements and governments would be regarded as threats. Should they accept Soviet support or invite a Soviet presence, jeopardize the survival of the oil-producing governments or their neighbors, and challenge Israel's legitimacy or extent of territorial control, they would be regarded as threats to America's goal to keep the Middle East stable and accessible.

THE POLITICS OF OIL

Access to, and exploitation of, the oil wealth of the Middle East has long been an important element of U.S. policy and deserves more than passing mention.[10] Particularly in the last quarter century, American administration have sought to ensure the availability of Middle Eastern oil for the U.S., West European, and Japanese economies, and to deny the Soviet Union opportunities (which it has been presumed Russian leaders would avail themselves of) to cut off the West's access to oil. The fact that American oil corporations dominate the international market adds to U.S. Government interest. Where interventions in the Middle East have occurred, oil has inevitably been of concern to U.S. strategists, whether or not American investments have been directly threatened by the actions of revolutionary movements or governments.

Only about 5 per cent of U.S. oil needs is presently supplied from the Middle East. The figure, however, can be misleading. Not only does it leave out the role and influence of the international oil corporations, it also ignores the dependency of Western Europe and Japan on Middle East oil and the probable increasing energy needs of the U.S. domestic market. Western Europe relies on the Middle East and North Africa for 85 per cent of its oil; Japan for 90 per cent. Despite the development of new sources of oil and energy fuels in the future, their needs, and those of the United States, which already consumes 31 per cent of the world's oil, will surely rise. Recent projections show a growth rate in oil consumption of 84 per cent for the United States, 125 per cent for

Western Europe, and still higher for Japan between 1970 and 1985. During that period, it is expected that oil production will decline in North America but will steadily increase in the Middle East. Clearly, Middle East oil is going to be of even greater importance to the developed capitalist economies over the next few decades than it has been in the past few.

While preserving access to oil for America and its allies, U.S. administrations have also been concerned about the capacity and willingness of the Soviet Union to deny access. Although the U.S.S.R.'s own oil resources have been and for the foreseeable future will be sufficient, a case could be made on political grounds for a Soviet interest in attempting to erode or even prevent Western access to Middle East oil. For the Soviets to act on that interest, however, assumes a congruence of economic purposes and political objectives with the oil-producing governments that has never existed and cannot be foreseen. It further assumes a Soviet ability, if necessary, forcibly to seize and run a Middle Eastern country's facilities, an act that would undoubtedly create far more problems than it would resolve. Where Arab nationalism takes an anti-Western direction that affects U.S. and other oil interests, as has occurred in recent years, it is for economic reasons. Soviet policy may profit from identification with nationalism, but it shows neither the ability nor the determination to control the resources or the decisions of the oil-producing states. After all, regardless of their political leanings, these governments must depend heavily on the oil companies, whose revenue accounts for the bulk of their income and foreign-exchange earnings.

Apart from the strategic and economic need of Middle East oil, U.S. governments have to take account of the heavy investment in it by American oil conglomerates. Five of the seven major foreign oil companies in the region are American (the other two are British), and among them are the biggest U.S. corporations from the standpoints of profits, sales, and net capital assets. The influence these companies may have on U.S. policy derives mainly from the high profitability of petroleum investment—currently, about $1.4 billion a year. Because profits from its overseas affiliates regularly exceed investments, the U.S. petroleum industry has contributed postively to the balance of payments at a time when Washington has had to cope with an over-all and growing imbalance of payments. An "essentially symbiotic relationship" has consequently developed between the government and the oil corporations, one in which the corporations have expected and received government protection and huge tax benefits for their overseas oil interests.[11] And since there has also been "a continuing two-way flow of personnel between the government and the international oil companies," there is further assurance for them that their interests will be adequately represented when policy decisions are made in Washington on Middle East affairs.[12]

When it comes to revolutions and other forms of "instability" in the Middle East, clearly the oil internationals will look to Washington for assistance. Not that the internationals are inevitably going to be prevented by radical nationalist governments from continuing to do business. Rather, these governments, unlike the more traditional ones, "are more likely to resort to expropriation" than to gradual absorption or compromises on the terms of oil concessions.[13] It is no accident, therefore, that U.S. interventions have been undertaken to protect the interests of precisely those conservative states that are the major Middle East oil producers: Iran, Kuwait, and Saudi Arabia.

THE OVERTHROW OF MOSSADEGH IN IRAN

The politics of oil and the cold war together made Western predominance in Iran a high-priority American concern soon after the end of World War II. Iran's oil production, then the highest in the Middle East and fourth highest in the world, was a valuable asset to the West, while the country's geographical adjacency to the U.S.S.R. and its fractionalized politics were believed in Washington to make it an inviting target for Soviet subversion. "Instability" in Iran quickly became an American preoccupation; and in 1953 the Eisenhower Administration, abandoning diplomacy and pressure tactics as methods of coping with Iranian nationalism, resorted to subversion to stabilize Iran's politics and ensure its alignment with Western economic and political interests.

The path to U.S. intervention began in the "crisis" of 1945–46. Mainly as a lever against the Iranian Government, whose oil resources had become the object of British, American, and Russian competition, Stalin kept Soviet troops in northern Iran beyond the date of their promised withdrawal. Moscow found an ally in the minority Azerbaijanis and Kurds, who were pushing for regional autonomy, and in the leftist Tudeh Party. American pressure exerted independently and through the United Nations, and a Soviet-Iranian oil accord (which the lower house of the Iranian Parliament, the Majlis, later refused to ratify), led Stalin to pull out his forces.[14] Washington had thus successfully maneuvered to preserve what President Truman regarded as vital strategic and economic interests in Iran.[15] In the process, it assumed the primary responsibility for defense of Iran's "sovereignty." As the American Ambassador to Tehran phrased it in December, 1946, "Iran is no stronger than the UN and the UN, in the last analysis, is no stronger than the US."[16]

In May, 1951, Prime Minister Mohammed Mossadegh, leader of the nationalist movement to end British dominance of Iran's oil economy—a movement that also drew mass strength and support from the educated middle class because it sought to destroy the power of the wealthy so-called thousand families—gained parliamentary approval to nationalize the Anglo-Iranian Oil Company. The government's act culminated one phase of intense anti-British feeling that grew out of a host of grievances against the company, the most important of which was that Iran was obtaining only a fraction of the company's profits. Mossadegh became the symbol of Iranian nationalism. At the risk of alienating those classes and political factions that were anxious to avoid a confrontation with Britain, he evidently hoped the United States would step in to provide technical help so that Iranians could run the oil industry themselves. In this and other calculations about the Americans, Mossadegh was mistaken. Senior officials in Washington as well as London regarded him as a shrewd demagogue, unreasonable and unpredictable, in Secretary of State Dean Acheson's words, "essentially a rich, reactionary, feudal-minded Persian."[17] These officials preferred dealing with the young Shah, Mohammed Reza Pahlevi, whom they considered moderate and reform-minded. U.S. policy was not prepared to bail out an "extremist" nationalist like Mossadegh, least of all at the expense of Anglo-American amity.

During the remainder of Truman's tenure, Britain and the United States were in accord on the necessity of restoring Iranian oil production under some kind of new agreement. But there were important differences over tactics. The major one was that while the British saw alternatives in Iran to Mossadegh, U.S. officials were concerned that his downfall would open the nationalist movement to control by communists.[18] When British warships and troops were mobilized for a possible intervention in 1951, American pressure led to cancellation of the action.[19] Washington kept urging, against British insistence that nationalization was illegal and that it was vital to be hard-nosed with the Iranians about terms of compensation, that a comprehensive settlement, to include a U.S. loan, was the only reasonable alternative. The Americans were unwilling either to alienate the British totally or to risk a communist takeover. But they also saw opportunities for American oil interests in Iran and throughout the Middle East if a new British-Iranian agreement could be worked out that would bring U.S. oil companies into Iran for the first time. A deal in December, 1950, between the Arabian American Oil Company and Saudi Arabia on a fifty-fifty sharing of profits surely put pressure on Britain to be similarly forthcoming with Iran and prevent the resort to nationalization that occurred soon after.[20] The Truman Administration's thinking would be followed by Eisenhower: encourage U.S. oil companies to get into Iran as a means of holding the line against Russia.

Finding a comfortable position between the often intransigent British and the nationalistic Iranian Government—a position that would also serve U.S. economic and strategic interests in the Middle East—proved a difficult task. Between late 1952 and early 1953, as the new administration was taking office, prospects for a British-Iranian agreement became increasingly remote. The Truman Administration did its part to induce a more flexible position by Mossadegh. It cut off military aid to Iran, severely curtailed economic aid, and cooperated with Britain in a boycott of Iranian oil. Britain did not suffer from the boycott because the sharp decline in Iran's production was more than offset by increased production in Kuwait. But Mossadegh's government did suffer, less economically than politically. His efforts to gain new revenue from the wealthy and to cut into the political and financial resources of the Shah intensified domestic conflict and led Mossadegh to consolidate his power at the expense of both the Shah and the Majlis.

As Mossadegh assumed greater power and snubbed British-American settlement proposals, including a "final offer" in March, 1953, Foreign Secretary Anthony Eden became "certain that the longer Musaddiq stayed in power, the stronger the Communist Party [Tudeh] would grow in Iran. It was an international interest not to give him comfort."[21] For the first several months of the new term, Eisenhower and Dulles disagreed. Eden had to report to Prime Minister Churchill that the President wanted to prevent a rupture with Iran "at any price" and "seemed ready to bring pressure to bear on American oil companies and to go to considerable lengths to keep Musaddiq in power, since he regarded him as the only hope for the West in Iran." The alternative, Dulles told Eden, was possible Russian control of Iran. While sympathizing with the British contention that a "bad" agreement with Iran was worse than none at all, Eisenhower, in Eden's view, "seemed obsessed by the fear of a communist Iran."[22] Like their predecessors, the Eisenhower-Dulles team found Mossadegh's attitude distasteful but were not prepared to take direct action to remove him.

By continuing Truman's policy, however, Eisenhower further promoted the kind of political disruption in Tehran that could only increase opposition to Mossadegh's nationalism, weaken his ability to balance off pressures from the left and right, and ripen conditions for a test of strength. When Mossadegh wrote to Eisenhower on May 28, 1953, to complain of the British-led boycott and to express disappointment that U.S. policy had not changed under the new administration, the President was unmoved. Ignoring Mossadegh's appeal for economic aid, Eisenhower bluntly (and belatedly) responded on June 29 that any U.S. assistance or purchases of oil would have to await the resumption of oil production based on a new U.K.-Iran agreement. Regarding the political situation in Iran, Eisenhower said: "I note the concern reflected in your letter at the present dangerous situation in Iran and sincerely hope that before it is too late, the Government of Iran will take such steps as are in its power to prevent a further deterioration of that situation."[23] Even then, the "further deterioration" was in process: Conflict between pro-Mossadegh nationalists and royalists had paralyzed the Majlis, which in mid-July was declared ended; Mossadegh called for a plebiscite in August, which overwhelmingly (with 99 per cent of the vote) supported dissolution of the Majlis; and the Shah, failing to oust Mossadegh by decree, fled the country.

Eisenhower's reading of these events failed to see that his letter had contributed to Mossadegh's difficulties by making clear to opposition forces in Iran that the Prime Minister could not count on the Americans to replace the British as a true assistant of independent Iranian development. To the contrary, Mossadegh's victory in the plebiscite signified to the President that "Iran's downhill course toward Communist-supported dictatorship was picking up momentum."[24] Eisenhower referred to reports in early August "that Mossadegh was moving closer and closer to the Communists. More and more, he was refusing to crack down on violent Tudeh-party demonstrations in the streets. And, one report said, he was looking forward to receiving $20 million from the Soviet Union" to tide his government over.[25] Overlooked in this perspective was the view of Iranian nationalists, and a number of Tudeh members who left the party, that identified the party with foreign-bred communism rather than with nationalism; the sharp criticism in the Tudeh press of Mossadegh for betraying Iran by seeking U.S. help after getting rid of the British; and the refusal of Mossadegh's supporters to let Tudeh become part of their National Front political alliance.[26] The fact that Mossadegh allowed the Tudeh Party to engage openly in political activities rather than attempt to suppress it was hardly equivalent to "Communist-supported dictatorship." Mossadegh was engaging in a delicate balancing act in which, through lack of American cooperation, he had little alternative but to accept Tudeh support and Soviet aid.

Fear of the consequences of political instability in Tehran drove Eisenhower into the British camp. He now accepted the argument that for an oil agreement favorable to Western interests to be obtained would require acting directly on behalf of the Shah. The President would avoid another Czechoslovakia: Mossadegh would not be allowed to "become to Iran what the ill-fated Dr. Beneš had been in Czechoslovakia—a leader whom the Communists, having gained power, would eventually destroy."[27] In mid-August, a CIA operation was mounted to bring pro-Shah demonstrators into the streets, a show of "popular support" that convinced the army it should oppose Mossadegh.* Within a few days, Mossadegh was under arrest and the Shah was back on top.

In September, Eisenhower received assurances from an unnamed American in Iran that the new leadership would faithfully serve U.S. strategic interests in the Middle East. The Shah was reported willing to bury past differences with Washington and London. "He recognizes now his debt to us and hopes, as he puts it, that we have a realistic understanding of the importance of Iran to us." General Fazollah Zahedi, the new Premier, was reported in the same message to be "fully aware of the importance of the army to the security of his country and is also convinced— as are many members of our military mission—that with the proper help Iran can become a significant link in the Free World's defense."[28] Military and economic aid to Iran, accordingly, was resumed and expanded. During 1955, Iran joined the Baghdad Pact, thus formalizing her participation in the "Northern Tier" defense chain against the Soviet Union.

But it was the American oil companies that earned the biggest windfall from the CIA intervention. Beginning in December, 1953, discussions took place in London among Anglo-Iranian, five U.S. oil giants, French and Dutch companies, and the Iranian Government. By the following August, an agreement had been concluded to set up an oil consortium in which the American companies acquired a 40 per cent interest (8 per cent each), equal to that of Anglo-Iranian. The government of Iran agreed to compensate the company for its claims with a $70 million payment, in return for which it would take 50 per cent of the profits and be paid several hundred million dollars by the companies over several years. The total settlement "marks the entire transaction as the biggest in the history of private business."[29] As interesting is the fact that the administration used the American companies to "save" Iran, even

---

* The fullest account of the CIA's involvement is that of David Wise and Thomas B. Ross, *The Invisible Government* (New York: Bantam, 1964), pp. 110–13. In his memoirs, Eisenhower refers obliquely to covert operations—stating that there were U.S. "representatives on the spot who were working actively with the Shah's supporters," and that "throughout this crisis the United States government had done everything it possibly could to back up the Shah" (*Mandate for Change, 1953–1956* [Garden City, N.Y., 1963], p. 164).

though a Department of Justice antitrust suit was pending against each of them. The Department was persuaded to make an exception for these companies on "national security" grounds, thus allowing them "to become participants in a joint operation which is almost identical in character with that alleged by the Department of Justice in its antitrust suit."[30] It is little wonder that Eisenhower hailed the agreement, in a letter to the Shah, as "the beginning of a new era of economic progress and stability for your country" and as "concrete evidence . . . of our desire that Iran prosper independently in the family of free nations."[31]

INTERVENTION IN LEBANON

An entirely different kind of intervention occurred in Lebanon beginning July 15, 1958, when the first of nearly 15,000 U.S. Marines disembarked on the beaches of Beirut. In three statements the same day, President Eisenhower described the intervention as having the protective purposes of safeguarding American lives—about 2,500 Americans then resided in Lebanon—and securing Lebanese independence.[32] On the surface, the administration's action appears vulnerable to the objection, which critics have often made, that it was motivated mainly by an anticommunist obsession that had been revealed most pointedly in the Eisenhower Doctrine. Upon closer examination, with the intervention placed in the context of other Middle East developments and the Eisenhower-Dulles response to them, the motivation appears to have been as much antinationalism as anticommunism. Eisenhower ordered troops to Lebanon not merely to protect it from "international communism" but also to prevent radical Arab nationalism from extending its influence through revolution.

Nationalism and Revolution in the Middle East in 1957

If antinationalism provides one key to understanding the Lebanon intervention, it is because the U.S. leadership's eyes were fixed, after Suez, on the increasing prestige and influence of Nasser. Having been unable to co-opt him before the canal crisis, as already described, the administration sought to isolate and contain him. He was perceived as a dangerous radical amenable to

Soviet dictates—a caricature that, as Malcolm Kerr has observed,[33] was reinforced by the Israel lobby, the Pentagon, and the oil lobby.

As the Russians began to win the competition for Nasser's favor, his nationalism and regional aspirations became confused with procommunism. His very independence of action was assumed in Washington to increase his susceptibility to Soviet "designs." "If he was not a Communist," wrote Eisenhower, "he certainly succeeded in making us very suspicious of him."[34] Asked about U.S. aid to Egypt, Dulles evinced that suspicion by replying that "we do not want to give such aid if it merely supports governments which are subservient to or sympathetic to international communism."[35] In 1958, Nasser's "exact political leanings were still something of a mystery" to the administration: It couldn't decide, for instance, whether the union of Egypt and Syria in February to form the United Arab Republic (U.A.R.) was communist-inspired or merely communist-supported![36] The fact that the communist party was outlawed in Egypt, and that one of Nasser's conditions for union with Syria was that all political parties be abolished there, evidently carried little weight in Washington.

These misperceptions of Nasser disposed the Eisenhower Administration to intervene in inter-Arab politics, beginning in Jordan in the spring of 1957. At the beginning of the year, King Hussein's government had satisfied Nasser's concern about Jordanian independence by terminating British subsidization of his army and a 1948 treaty that had permitted a British military presence. But Hussein was wary of coming within Cairo's orbit, and in April he angered Nasser by appointing a new, conservative government. Violent demonstrations against the dismissals of pro-Egyptian officials broke out throughout Jordan, and when Hussein charged that Cairo was behind them, a war of words began. Believing that Hussein needed encouragement, Eisenhower, in his first action under the Doctrine, ordered units of the Sixth Fleet into the eastern Mediterranean. Hussein successfully resisted his opponents, for which he was rewarded with a U.S. economic aid grant of $10 million.

The President's decision, however, seems to have done far more harm than good. It showed how readily military power would be used to help stabilize an entirely domestic political conflict. It seemed to ignore the question of relevancy: What purpose would gunboat diplomacy serve when the challenge to Hussein's authority stemmed from pan-Arabism, not communist interference? Hussein himself seemed to recognize the dilemma, because despite the U.S. action and subsequent aid, he refrained from associating Jordan with the Eisenhower Doctrine. This first application of the Doctrine, then, did not demonstrate its appropriateness; rather, it may have emboldened the administration to believe that a timely show of force could resolve the complexities of Middle East politics in America's favor.

The next test of the Doctrine came in Syria in the summer of 1957. Washington had been concerned about political developments in Syria since Suez, when it became apparent that radical nationalism, influenced by the Baath party's identification with Nasser's policies, was moving the country leftward. Seeking to cut short this movement, the United States in the fall of 1956 had joined with Iraq and Britain in an unsuccessful attempt to impose a more responsive Syrian government.[37] No doubt Syria's subsequent interest in Soviet economic aid and arms and alignment with Egypt was greatly increased by the abortive invasion, which indicated that the Baghdad Pact powers posed a threat to Syrian security. And when Jordan accepted U.S. support in April, 1957, it meant that Syria was surrounded by hostile governments.

The conjunction in Syria of increasingly strident nationalism and anxiety about external threats made Western influence rather unwelcome. Rather than seek to understand the sources of Syrian concern, however, Washington again attempted to eliminate the "problem" through subversion—an amateurish CIA plot, uncovered in August, 1957, that led to a formal Syrian complaint to the U.N. Security Council.[38] Syria's conclusion of aid agreements with Moscow and the appointment of a pro-Nasser army chief of staff were enough to prompt Eisenhower's "suspicion . . . that the Communists had taken control of the government."[39] Washington's Middle East allies were eager for military action against Syria, and Eisenhower, while hesitant to endorse it until Syria "provoked retaliation," agreed that a communist takeover of Syria "would soon be complete" unless additional steps were taken.[40]

The President's decision to encourage a confrontation with Syria accepted the possibility of a major Middle East war. He assured Turkey and other allies of U.S. support and protection if they decided to make a "defensive" reply to anticipated Syrian "aggression." U.S. aircraft and the Sixth Fleet were ordered forward, and the Strategic Air Command was put on alert. A special envoy was dispatched to Turkey and Lebanon, after which new arms shipments reached Lebanon, Jordan, Iraq, and Saudi Arabia.[41] Eisenhower made a simple calculation: A major war was worth risking because "the alternative . . . —to do nothing and lose the whole Middle East to Communism—would be worse."[42]

Much to Eisenhower's surprise, however, all the U.S. allies except Lebanon and Turkey began backing out of a showdown battle with Syria. Historic rivalries and self-interest surmounted concern about Syrian "communism." The Turks increased their already substantial forces along the Syrian border to 50,000 men, prompting Soviet threats of intervention if Turkey committed aggression.[43] Eisenhower came to Turkey's defense; but it was the "defection" to Syria's side of Saudi Arabia's King Saud that broke the tension. Saud, who Eisenhower "hoped might eventually rival Nasser as an Arab leader,"[44] and whose country's oil resources and leasing of an air base to the United States made him a valued ally, suddenly came out in support of Syria against attack.

The easing of the Syrian crisis represented a substantial victory for Nasser. Syria's integrity was preserved, as was its radical political orientation. For Washington, on the other hand, the crisis was another setback to the Eisenhower Doctrine. Hostility to Nasser was not strong enough to produce the collective intervention the Americans were willing to support. A "communist" Syria was clearly more dangerous in Washington's eyes than in the eyes of its Middle East partners. The episode should have convinced the administration that Arab unity and the separate interests of the Arab states had more decisive impact on the policy-making of the region's governments than the "threat" of a "pro-Soviet" takeover. Yet in Lebanon, where the question of communism was moot, and where support for a U.S. intervention from Arab allies was even less likely, the lesson of Syria was ignored.

The Intervention

The American tendency toward a military response to political realignments in the Arab countries forms one element of the background to the Lebanon intervention. Two others may now be introduced: Lebanon's domestic and international politics in 1958, and further divisive changes that year in the Arab world.

The Lebanese Situation. The intrusion of Arab nationalism and American cold war ideology into the Middle East in the mid-1950's was bound to have upsetting consequences for a nation as delicately balanced politically as Lebanon. Its population of roughly 1.5 million divided almost evenly between Christians and Moslems, with the latter group holding a slight advantage because of the recent arrival of a few hundred thousand Palestinian refugees. To maintain political harmony, Lebanese politicians had agreed in 1943 that the presidency would always be held by a Christian, the prime ministership by a Moslem, and other senior offices by similar numbers of both religions. Political stability therefore required that, domestically and internationally, the Lebanese Government avoid identifying itself closely with either the West or the Arab world.

Lebanon's political balance began to be disrupted in early 1957 when President Camille Chamoun, in anticipation of parliamentary elections, decided to move for a constitutional amendment that would enable him to gain re-election (his six-year term was due to end in September, 1958). To succeed in that unprecedented act, Chamoun would need strong support in the Chamber of Deputies, which he secured in the ensuing elections. Several notable figures in the Moslem opposition lost their seats, and this circumstance, together with Chamoun's appointment of political hacks to high offices, aroused increasingly intense hostility.[45]

What made the situation so explosive was that Chamoun's domestic machinations were coupled to increasingly open alignment with the United States. During the Suez crisis, Chamoun had refused to break relations with Britain and France. In 1957, when a Presidential representative toured the Middle East with the clear purpose of buying support of the Eisenhower Doctrine with U.S. aid, only Lebanon responded affirmatively. A joint communiqué endorsed the anticommunist theme of the Doctrine and promised that the United States would consider a Lebanese request for U.S. military assistance to combat a communist aggression. Thereafter, Chamoun favored U.S. intervention in Jordan and Syria. To Chamoun's opposition, which was predominantly Moslem but included prominent Christians, his course was threatening to overturn the country's political traditions. Even Eisenhower, while welcoming Chamoun's endorsement of the Doctrine, regarded his second-term plans as "a political error."[46]

Matters came to a head in early April, 1958, when the government asked for a parliamentary vote of confidence. It won the vote, 30 to 1; but before it was taken, seven of the eight opposition deputies walked out, angered at the government's defense of its pro-American policies. Within a month, rioting, violence, and strikes occurred; a United National Opposition Front was formed; and, on May 12, insurrection began with the setting up of barricades in the Moslem section of Beirut. Christians generally flocked to Chamoun's side; but the opposition Front, while mainly Moslem, "enjoyed intersectarian support at the highest level."[47] The Front's support was, moreover, geographically dispersed: Rebels controlled the Moslem quarter of Beirut, the center of Tripoli, most of the northern border area with Syria (held by Shi'i and Druze tribespeople), and the south.[48] At the time of the U.S. intervention, about 70 per cent of Lebanese territory was in rebel hands.[49]

There is little doubt that the rebellion had encouragement from Egypt and Syria; Chamoun's continuation in office was an obstacle to Arab unity, and his vigorous support of U.S. policy made Lebanon a threat to radical nationalist governments. Since Lebanon, moreover, was receiving U.S. hardware and propaganda support from clandestine CIA radio stations,[50] Nasser probably had few compunctions about sending the rebels arms, money, and men across the Syrian border or about using Radios Cairo and Damascus to make anti-Chamoun broadcasts. But the Lebanese civil war was from start to finish pre-eminently a domestic political contest between, on one side, an ambitious Christian president and, on the other, a host of political leaders and the Moslem masses who found Chamoun's actions intolerable. Nowhere was this circumstance more clearly recognized than at the top level of the Lebanese Army.

General Fuad Chehab, the Christian commander in chief of the small (perhaps 8,000-man) army, was fully aware that "the fighting was a protest by a mass of the citizenry against a presidential renewal and not an attempt to subvert Lebanese independence."[51] Asked time and again by Chamoun to suppress the rebellion, he refused, and instead used the armed forces defensively in patrolling, securing government and military facilities, and containing the fighting. Chehab feared that since the army itself was interdenominational, its involvement in the civil war would split it and probably destroy the nation as well.

From Washington's vantage point, the political complexities of the Lebanese situation were reducible to the communist threat.

> Behind everything [wrote Eisenhower] was our deep-seated conviction that the Communists were principally responsible for the trouble, and that President Chamoun was motivated only by a strong feeling of patriotism. He was the ablest of the Lebanese politicians and would undoubtedly agree not to be a candidate again for the Presidency if only he could be assured of a strong and sincere pro-Western successor.[52]

The President saw the Soviets "pushing everywhere" in the Third World, abetted in the Middle East by Nasser. When Chamoun, on May 13, contacted Eisenhower to ascertain "what our actions would be if he were to request our assistance," Eisenhower was already prepared to entertain a request for U.S. intervention.[53] The U.S. Ambassador in Lebanon, Robert McClintock, was immediately authorized to inform Chamoun

> that although Lebanon should not invoke American assistance unless its integrity were generally threatened and its own forces were not sufficient for the protection of the state, nevertheless the United States was prepared, upon request both from the President and the government of Lebanon, to send certain combat forces which would have the dual mission of protecting American life and property and of assisting the government of Lebanon in its military program for the preservation of the integrity and independence of the Republic.[54]

The Lebanese request would be met *not* under the Eisenhower Doctrine (since it was not claimed that Egypt or Syria was "controlled by international communism") but, as Secretary Dulles indicated on May 20, under the stipulation in Joint Resolution 117 that each Middle East nation's independence is "vital" to the U.S. national interest.[55]

From Eisenhower's account it is apparent that Dulles was prepared to engage in "direct action" during May.[56] The President was more cautious. Although the Soviet response to intervention did not worry him, he acknowledged the probable adverse reaction throughout the Middle East, a possible blockade of the Suez Canal, destruction of oil pipelines running across Syria, and domestic pressures against friendly governments in Jordan and Iraq. He was therefore willing to wait, but not to remain passive. Once more the Sixth Fleet was moved eastward, army airborne units in Europe were put on alert, and additional military aid was airlifted to Lebanon. Joint planning with the British military was begun, and a new military command for the Middle East was created. Nearly two months before the intervention, the gears for it had been set in motion.

An additional condition of U.S. intervention, Chamoun had been informed on May 14, was that Lebanon bring its case against the U.A.R. before the U.N. Security Council. This was done June 6. On June 11, the Security Council voted to establish an Observation Group in Lebanon (UNOGIL) "to ensure that there is no illegal infiltration of personnel or supply of arms or other material across the Lebanese borders." Between the time of its arrival on June 19 and the U.S. intervention of July 15, UNOGIL issued two main reports that did much to debunk Chamoun's accusations and confirm the primarily domestic character of the Lebanese civil war.

The UNOGIL staff was headed by a Norwegian, an Ecuadorian, and an Indian, with an American as executive officer. Its principal findings, issued July 30, were (1) that the infiltration of arms from Syria "cannot be on anything more than a limited scale, and is largely confined to small arms and ammunition," and (2) that "in no case have United Nations Observers . . . been able to detect the presence of persons who have indubitably entered from across the border for the purpose of fighting."[57] To be sure,

UNOGIL's mission was performed under adverse conditions that inevitably raised questions about the reliability of its conclusions. For instance, the group only belatedly gained access to rebel-held territory along the Syrian border; it had limited means for policing the lengthy border; it arrived after infiltrations of men and supplies from Syria had been well under way; and most of its observations were conducted during daylight hours. Accepting these deficiencies, however, and accepting, therefore, that infiltrations were occurring across the border, need not alter the crucial implication of UNOGIL's reports, which was that the U.A.R. was not guilty of the "massive" intervention charged by Chamoun. Eisenhower was disappointed; but he assured Chamoun that U.S. intervention would not require U.N. approval.[58]

Of greater consequence is that the establishment of the Observation Group in Lebanon was creating conditions for a settlement when the U.S. intervention occurred. Nasser, whose government had not objected to UNOGIL when it was formed (a circumstance Eisenhower found "puzzling"), contacted Washington with a proposal that General Chehab succeed Chamoun at the end of his term, with the rebels to be granted amnesty. This "not wholly unreasonable" idea (in Eisenhower's words), which became a reality after the intervention, was passed on to Chamoun. But despite having officially declared on June 30 that he would not seek re-election, Chamoun "did nothing to follow up" Nasser's proposal.[59] The U.A.R. thus had little incentive to stop assisting the rebels. Even so; by mid-July UNOGIL had so sufficiently improved its ability to patrol the border and detect violations that Eisenhower reported the cross-border traffic was reduced and "the situation in [Lebanon] was moving toward a peaceful solution."[60] As UNOGIL reported, the effect of the U.S. intervention was to obstruct and set back its work in rebel-held areas just when it had finally succeeded in gaining unimpeded access to them.[61] Whatever chances for a Lebanese settlement through U.N. diplomacy might have existed in mid-July were thus shattered by the precipitate action of the United States.

The Middle East on the Eve of Intervention. In and of itself the Lebanese civil war, even though viewed in Washington as somehow related to international communism, probably would not have led to direct U.S. military intervention had political circumstances in nearby countries been less tumultuous. Though poised to act with force, Eisenhower saw prospects for a settlement among the Lebanese factions and between the governments of Lebanon and Egypt. Perhaps he believed that the same sort of gunboat diplomacy that had helped Jordan's King Hussein to retain power in 1957 would turn the tide for Chamoun as well. But continued division in the Arab world during 1958, culminating in the Iraqi coup of July 14, seems to have pushed Eisenhower into Dulles's corner. Anxiety about communism became linked to paranoia about Nasserism.

This new round of internal upheaval was touched off by the merger of Egypt and Syria on February 1, 1958. It was a marriage that Nasser entered into with considerable misgivings, since Egypt had enough domestic problems without having to add those of Syria. But the political conditions of association—including removal of the Syrian Army from politics and dissolution of all parties—were agreeable to Nasser, as was the pan-Arabism and anticommunism of Syria's dominant party, Baath. Perhaps above all else in importance to him was that Egyptian control of Syria's defense and foreign policies would ensure Syrian loyalty at a time when Iraq and Saudi Arabia were still seeking to lure Syria into their pro-Western camp.[62] Formation of the U.A.R. thus did not mean the extension of communist influence in the Middle East but, rather, another impediment to it.

Two weeks afterward, on February 14, King Faisal of Iraq and King Hussein of Jordan announced the federation of their countries as the Arab Union, with Iraq the senior partner. The union had "some State Department encouragement"—as Nasser must surely have guessed.[63] It was an obvious response to the U.A.R., and it meant that "to all intents and purposes Jordan had effectively joined the Baghdad Pact."[64] The one benefit Nasser derived from the Iraq-Jordan agreement was that it put King Saud under great pressure to identify either with it, and thus with the pro-Western forces, or with the Cairo group. Saud's choice, which took the form of covert plotting against Egypt and Syria, helped to weaken his already tenuous position. On March 24, the King was forced to turn over full powers to his brother, a Nasser sympathizer. "King Saud's usefulness was temporarily, at least, at an end," wrote Eisenhower.[65]

In mid-July, 1958, consequently, the Middle East lineup showed Egypt and Syria on one side and Lebanon, Jordan, Iran, and Iraq on the other, with Saudi Arabia uncommitted. Then, on the morning of July 14, an element of the Iraqi Army under Brigadier Abdel Karim Kassem took advantage of an unexpected security lapse to overthrow the government and assassinate the King, the Premier, and a number of others. Kassem became Prime Minister of the new radical regime. Nasser quickly recognized it. Although, as much as he welcomed a new partner, he had no advance knowledge of the coup,[66] Washington acted as though Nasser not only knew about it beforehand but also had instigated it with Soviet support.

The Decision to Intervene. The coup in Iraq triggered Eisenhower's decision to intervene in Lebanon. When the President met with his advisers after hearing the news, his "mind was practically made up" that the United States would have "to move into the Middle East, and specifically into Lebanon, to stop the trend toward chaos."[67] Chamoun, Hussein, Saud, and Israel's Ben-Gurion were said to be alarmed at the turn of events in Iraq, and Chamoun had already made a request for U.S. intervention within forty-eight hours.[68] Eisenhower thus had the formal invitation he wanted before acting. The CIA could not say for certain that Nasser was responsible for the coup, but Eisenhower was aware that the Iraqi Army and the new government were headed by pro-Nasser people. The public reaction in the Middle East to a direct intervention would be mostly bad, Dulles said, and it would not resolve the basic instabilities in the area. But the intervention, Eisenhower reasoned, would be legal, the Soviets probably would not respond with force, and the alternative of doing nothing was no alternative at all: "In Lebanon the question was whether it would be better to incur the deep resentment of nearly all of the Arab world (and some of the rest of the Free World) and in doing so to risk general war with the Soviet Union or to do something worse—which was to do nothing."[69] One may wonder what could be worse than the Arab world's resentment and war with the U.S.S.R. Eisenhower did not say; his main concern was to take the first step toward restoring "reasonable stability to the Middle East."[70]

A desperate need to "do something" to contain Nasser's influence was not Eisenhower's only motive. Another, which he stressed in his public statements explaining the intervention, was that Soviet communism was behind the trouble. Eisenhower said "Lebanon was selected to become a victim" of "the same pattern of conquest with which we became familiar during the period of 1945 to 1950." It was another in "the Communists'" long string of "indirect aggressions."[71] While other high-ranking Americans, such as the Deputy Under Secretary of State and Middle East troubleshooter, Robert Murphy, doubted that communism was the main issue in Lebanon, Eisenhower had no doubts.

Since both Cairo and Moscow were seen to be challenging the Eisenhower Doctrine, the President regarded Lebanon as a test case of American willingness to respond to provocations and help friends. Just prior to being dispatched to Lebanon to serve as liaison between the American Embassy and the military, Murphy was briefed by Eisenhower on the purposes of the intervention.

> He said that sentiment had developed in the Middle East, especially in Egpyt, that Americans were capable only of words, that we were afraid of Soviet reaction if we attempted military action. Eisenhower believed that if the United States did nothing now, there would be heavy and irreparable losses in Lebanon and in the area generally. He wanted to demonstrate in a timely and practical way that the United States was capable of supporting its friends.[72]

Faith in the "word" of the United States was at stake, Dulles reportedly argued before leading congressmen on July 15. Failure to act now would result in the "loss" of the Middle East, its oil, Africa, and eventually Asia.[73] Vice-President Richard Nixon likewise pointed to the "chain reaction" effect of the Iraqi coup had the United States not stepped in. Our friends and allies "from Morocco . . . clear over to the Pacific area" would have become panic-stricken.[74] It was, in essence, the domino reasoning of Truman and Acheson all over again, with Lebanon replacing Iran as the place to draw the line against the enemy's expansionism.

On the afternoon of July 15, Eisenhower summoned twenty-two senior congressmen of both parties to discuss Lebanon. He reportedly told them that "no decision has been made. . . . You see you are not being called in here after a decision has been reached."[75] In fact, the decision to land troops *had* been made and was probably already being implemented, as evidenced by the landing of Sixth Fleet Marines within twenty-four hours of Chamoun's request.[76] Eisenhower was certain that "we had to go in," even though none of the congressmen present was enthusiastic about doing so.[77] Indeed, he had "warned" them two months earlier "that he might have to run the risk of war by intervening with military force in Lebanon without prior discussion in Congress. 'In this case, if there has to be a public debate about the course of action, there would be no use in taking it at all,' he said."[78] The President believed he already had the authority to act under the Joint Resolution; and since the "defense" of Lebanon could further be rationalized under Article 51 of the U.N. Charter (which recognizes the inherent right of collective self-defense), he decided that an explanation before the Security Council could await the start of the landing.

A notable feature of the intervention was that U.S. firepower was massively deployed in a small nation whose own army was unwilling to attack the rebels and very nearly fought the disembarking Americans instead. Washington had been concerned about the reaction of General Chehab's forces, but this did not keep the President from initially deploying several thousand Marines (who soon outnumbered the entire Lebanese army), backed up "with tanks, armoured amphibians, and self-propelled atomic howitzers, although no nuclear weapons were unloaded."[79] Their arrival was greeted not with public applause but with word that Chehab was about to carry out a coup against Chamoun, who was anxiously telephoning the U.S. Ambassador to "send Marines with tanks quickly." The ambassador had to warn Chehab of "most disagreeable consequences" if the coup were attempted.[80]

Events of the next few days, July 16–18, had all the ingredients of a comic opera, made deadly serious by the fact it was a military intervention. A direct confrontation of Marines and Chehab's army was narrowly avoided, as was an attack on the Marines by the Lebanese Air Force. Eventually, the Marines, their vehicles, and their commanders were escorted into Beirut from the beaches by Lebanese army jeeps, the commanders riding in the ambassador's Cadillac with General Chehab alongside.[81] When Robert Murphy arrived in Beirut he found that President Chamoun was virtually a prisoner in his official residence, afraid to go outdoors or near a window for fear of being assassinated.[82] To complete the picture, the President of the Chamber of Deputies wrote in protest against the intervention to Eisenhower and the Security Council.[83]

By mid-August, 1958, the United States had nearly 15,000 soldiers in Lebanon. Additionally, there were Marine, naval, and air units offshore and on alert for possible further movement to Iraq and Kuwait. About 2,200 British paratroopers, moreover, were landed in Jordan on July 17, presumably to bolster Hussein's confidence. The stage was set for American politicking to re-structure the Lebanese situation in ways that would "stabilize" it. Murphy was the key man.

Murphy recognized that the resolution of Lebanon's difficulties required the holding of new elections to replace Chamoun. He moved toward that objective by assuring the rebel leaders that U.S. troops were not in Lebanon to promote Chamoun's re-election. The news was a relief to them, as it probably was to Nasser. Chamoun acceded—he had little choice—and on July 31 General Chehab was elected to succeed Chamoun at the end of his term in September. One of the more moderate rebel Moslem leaders, Rashid Karami, became Premier. With order thus restored, U.S. troops began to depart; the withdrawal was completed on October 25. Murphy went on to visit Cairo and Baghdad for talks with Nasser and Kassem. Both were pleased to learn that the United States had not intervened in Lebanon as the prelude to an attack on Iraq, and Nasser asserted he looked forward to friendly rela-tions with the new Lebanese Government.[84] For a while, there would be relative tranquility in the Middle East.

An Evaluation

The Lebanon intervention "worked"; but should it have been undertaken? No lives were lost, the Soviet leadership declined to go beyond verbal condemnation of the intervention, and politics in Lebanon returned to normal. Nevertheless, the circumstances and purposes of the intervention need to be critically reviewed; sending military forces to become participants in another country's political life cannot be condoned simply because the results were those the administration desired. The United States intervened in a country where the issue was not communism but local and Arab politics; where the army was more eager to fight the Marines than to subdue its own countrymen; where the countryside and most of the major cities were controlled by the rebels, not by forces loyal to the President; and where an opportunity was let pass to achieve a settlement without intervention on the same terms that were accepted after the intervention.

Looking back, Eisenhower saw the intervention as having convinced Nasser "that he could not depend completely on Russia to help him in any Middle East struggle, and he certainly had his complacency as to America's helplessness completely shattered."[85] Why Eisenhower was so certain that Nasser counted on getting Soviet commitments, and considered the United States weak and indecisive, is not clear. Nasser had already seen the United States make shows of force in 1957 without Soviet counteraction to influence events in Jordan and Syria. But because the President believed that Nasser was responsible, along with the "Communists," for Lebanon's civil war, he was eager to convince Moscow and Cairo of America's toughness. The coup in Iraq gave him the opportunity.

To the extent that Lebanon's troubles were external in origin, Eisenhower misplaced responsibility for them. It was the Eisenhower Doctrine and U.S. strategic planning that had divided the Arab states, added to Nasser's pan-Arabic appeals, encouraged interest in Soviet assistance, and thus set the stage for Chamoun's incessant pleas for intervention, first in Jordan and Syria, then in his own country. In selecting Lebanon as a test case, the Americans acted as though Nasser's appeal and the success of Soviet diplomacy could be stifled by introducing U.S. troops into the Middle East. Little, if any, consideration seems to have been given to the notion that Nasserism could impede the growth of communist parties (as in Egypt, Syria, and Kassem's Iraq), or that every American show of strength only reinforced Nasser's (and the Soviet Union's) argument that the United States was the clearest danger to Middle East independence, or that even within those states (including Lebanon) that rejected Nasser's ambitions for regional leadership there was widespread sympathy with his interest in eliminating great-power manipulation of the region.

Seeing Lebanon as a test case also led the administration to slight the significance of General Chehab's refusal to involve the army deeply in the civil war, and to underestimate the potential danger of direct U.S. involvement in the fighting. The general understood, as Washington did not (or not very well), that President Chamoun's ambitions and divisive politics were primarily responsible for the civil war. By intervening in that situation, the United States inevitably became a principal actor in Lebanese politics. It ran the risk of fighting Chehab's army at a time when he was emerging as Chamoun's likely successor; it might have been forced to take Chamoun's side in a larger conflict; and it eventually undertook responsibility for new elections held during a U.S. military occupation. The appropriate way to deal with Chamoun was to dissociate the United States from him, not to intervene at his invitation.

The opportunity to bring about a settlement in Lebanon without intervention occurred in early June, 1958, with President Nasser's proposal that Chamoun step down at the end of his term in favor of Chehab. Not only was that the outcome of the intervention, it also became the American objective. Where once the United States had claimed to be intervening to secure Lebanon's independence, after Robert Murphy's arrival it became evident that only when Chamoun stepped down would civil order be restored. When, in 1959, the Moslem Premier, Karami, visited Eisenhower and suggested that Murphy's arrival, without U.S. troops, would have been sufficient, the President disagreed. But Eisenhower "could not completely smother the thought that if our visitor's statement had been true, every one in my administration could have been saved a lot of anxious hours."[86] Indeed, had Eisenhower either indicated to Chamoun his support of Nasser's proposal or sent Murphy to tell Chamoun he could not have U.S. troops to bail him out of a domestic political dispute, for American policy-makers there would have been no Lebanese crisis.

Finally, the Lebanon intervention reflected an underlying antinationalism in American policy that continues to the present. Like Mossadegh and Kassem, Nasser was treated as a front man for Moscow whose aspirations for Arab unity were inseparable from presumed Soviet ambitions to "dominate" the Middle East. Chamoun, like Hussein and Saud, was a patriot, meaning he supported American objectives and would cooperate with Washington against Nasser and his friends. In the American perspective, Nasser and Chamoun had one thing in common: They were important not for what they represented in their national settings but for their degree of cooperativeness with U.S. political, economic, and strategic interests regionwide.

The Lebanon intervention, in consequence, was intended to stabilize the "chaotic" Middle East in the sense of preventing another success for radical Arab nationalism. For, as has been argued in behalf of the intervention,[87] had the United States not sent troops, quite possibly the traditional equilibrium of Lebanese politics would eventually have been tilted in favor of the Moslem rebels. Chehab, even if elected to succeed Chamoun, might have been forced to give way to a radical leadership responsive to Cairo's policies. After Syria and Iraq, another such victory for Nasser was intolerable to Eisenhower and Dulles. No price, not even the outside chance of a confrontation with the U.S.S.R., was too high to pay to keep the Lebanese from determining their own political fate.

Eisenhower was the first of four Presidents to misunderstand Nasser and end up as his antagonist. Kennedy and Johnson tried to domesticate Nasser with a large economic aid program that, in the Americans' judgment, was inefficiently used. Sentiment in Washington against Nasser mounted anew, abetted by a civil war in Yemen that broke out late in 1962 in which Egypt and Saudi Arabia became heavily involved. Most of the U.S. aid was not renewed in mid-1965. A chance to revive the aid program the next year failed, one reason apparently being that when Saudi Arabia's King Feisal proposed an "Islamic pact," Nasser took it to be another made-in-America plan for surrounding the radical Arab states. The resumption of Egyptian-American hostility, symbolized and reinforced by the Yemeni civil war, in important ways set the stage for the Six Day War of 1967. For by then "Nasser felt desperately in need of a dramatic success at the expense of the United States and its friends; . . . the United States, not having Nasser's ear, was in no position to urge restraint upon him; and . . . the Israeli government, upon receiving American counsels of restraint, had little reason to take them very seriously."[88]

Through the Six Day War and the conflict of October, 1973, U.S. support of Israel, moderated mainly by the need to appease the conservative oil-producing states (Iran and Saudi Arabia), has been the great obstacle to normalized U.S. relations with Egypt and its allies. Although the independence of the radical Arab governments from Soviet control has long since been accepted in Washington, intervention to keep their influence from spreading, and thus threatening access to oil, remains a major feature of U.S. policy. In September, 1970, for example, when Syrian tanks crossed into Jordan in support of Palestinian guerrillas contesting the authority of King Hussein, the Nixon Administration replayed the gunboat diplomacy of the Eisenhower years. The Sixth Fleet was deployed to the area and Marine units were alerted for involvement on the King's behalf. Hussein and the Palestinian leaders agreed to a cease-fire, but once again American power had been projected into regional politics in the name of stability. American diplomacy in the Middle East has yet to accept the legitimacy of the Arab nationalism which Nasser stood for and which continues to motivate his successors, the heads of the other radical Arab states, and the Palestinian movement.

3

Kennedy and Africa

INTRODUCTION

In the political history of Africa, decolonization stands out as the principal development of the post–World War II period. Between 1952 and 1962, thirty new nations were established, and by the close of the 1960's, only nine territories were still colonies. As has often been remarked, however, the attainment of independence was, for many of these "newly emerging nations," only the first step toward genuine statehood. Colonial rule had imposed technical and market dependency on the European metropoles that left many new states with little choice except to remain tied to the French community or the British Commonwealth. European bureaucrats, technicians, and in some cases military officers had to be retained. There were also imposing obstacles within the new states to the exercise of full sovereignty. Central governments had limited economic and administrative resources to impose and carry out authority in rural areas; they were beset with demands by tribal minorities for greater autonomy, politically, economically, and culturally; and they had inherited parliamentary institutions and norms that frequently proved unsuitable to tribal- and personality-oriented political cultures.

Each of these problems had implications for American policy, particularly toward the end of the 1950's, when it became clear that there would soon be a quantum jump in the number of newly independent African states. African governments, regardless of their colonial past or their new leaders' philosophical inclinations, could all agree on the necessity of economic independence no less than political independence. Economic independence might mean the sudden nationalization of European enterprises, a turn against Western offers of aid, a turn to the Soviet Union (and later China) for technical assistance, or a willingness to have trade relations with countries outside the Anglo-French-American bloc. Considering how vital African raw materials and unmanufactured foodstuffs had, by 1960, become to America's allies in the North Atlantic Treaty Organization (NATO); considering that while trade with, and investment in, Africa was not vital to the American economy, certain precious minerals (such as uranium, copper, and cobalt) were important; and considering, too, that the significant growth of U.S.-African trade and investment relations after the world war promised an increasing U.S. stake in access to African economies,[1] developments of the kinds mentioned might be of concern to U.S. officials.

Political independence in Africa meant that the immediate postcolonial period was likely to be marked by sharp criticisms of the colonialist powers and their allies, by a surge of solidarity among the Afro-Asian states, and by their first efforts to translate this new national and international identity into political influence. The Afro-Asian Conference held in Bandung, Indonesia, in early 1955; the attraction of numerous governments to the nonalignment principles and strategy of Nehru, Nasser, and Tito; and the presentation of Afro-Asian resolutions in the U.N. General Assembly demanding the immediate end of colonial rule were some of the manifestations of political independence. For American leaders, who prided themselves on a national tradition favoring self-determination, and who had been instrumental in introducing into the U.N. Charter guidelines for the social improvement and political progress of dependent peoples (Chapters XI–XIII of the Charter), trends such as nonalignment, anticolonialism, and independence movements (which might involve revolutionary violence) were a real challenge. They put squarely the issue of American priorities: In a choice between self-determination and the oft-proclaimed need for North Atlantic unity against international communism, which way should U.S. policy go?

The domestic difficulties experienced by newly independent African states also were relevant to U.S. policy, or at least, as time would show, were thought to be. If African governments neglected or were unable to satisfy the diverse demands of their constituents, or if the delicate balance of tribal, class, regional, and occupational representatives in these governments should be upset, rebellion, insurrection, and coups d'état were likely to erupt. And wherever political violence might occur, there was the possibility of exploitation by leftist radicals linked somehow with Moscow. In the process of upheaval, even if the danger of a communist takeover was slight, ultranationalism might make it difficult for the United States to maintain naval or air bases on African territory.

During the Eisenhower Administration, the American response to Africa was one of studied neglect, from the minuscule U.S. aid program to the small cadre of Foreign Service specialists on Africa. Yet Africa was considered to have economic significance for the United States. It had precious minerals to which the United States required access, and to which the communist nations should be denied access.[2] Africa was a large and growing market for American enterprise, Vice-President Richard Nixon reported after a three-week trip. "It can truly be said that the welcome sign is out for investment of foreign private capital in Africa." The government, he advised, should "draw the attention of private American capital" to appropriate investment opportunities.[3]

The best—that is, the cheapest—way of protecting U.S. access and investment was to support continued African ties to the European powers, as Nixon's report also urged. Such ties would lighten the American aid burden, complement U.S. investments, provide some insurance against radical change (by creating dependency on Western finances and trade), and thus solidify the "Free World's" position. As Eisenhower's Assistant Secretary of State for African Affairs stated in May, 1959:

We support African political aspirations where they are moderate, non-violent and constructive and take into account their obligations to and interdependence with the world community. We also support the principle of continued African ties with Western Europe. We see no reason why there should be a conflict between these two concepts.[4]

Moderateness and orderliness were the desirable qualities of African politics, for, as Secretary of State John Foster Dulles said, "precipitate action [toward independence] would in fact not produce independence but only transition to a captivity far worse than present dependence."[5] Consistent with that projection, which saw communism as the ultimate winner in any revolution, the Eisenhower Administration's treatment of Africa reflected far more concern about the cold war competition than about the issues surrounding anticolonialism. Nixon's report to the President was a case in point. Another was the administration's action in 1960 when the General Assembly voted on the first major Afro-Asian resolution against colonialism: It abstained along with the European colonial powers.

The administration's choice of siding with the NATO colonialist powers rather than take a chance on identifying with independence movements or radical nationalist governments was also dictated, it appears, by fear of losing strategic access to Africa and the Mediterranean. The United States had jet bases at three locations in North Africa and in the Portuguese Azores, had invested large sums in air and port facilities there and along the African coastlines, and had made arrangements with the colonial powers to use port facilities in sixteen locations for repair, refueling, and submarine stations.[6] To maintain access required not only that Washington avoid offending its NATO partners—the major exception, U.S. opposition to the Anglo-French invasion of Suez in 1956, was based on American strategic and tactical calculations, not on a different interpretation of colonialism—but also that it do nothing to exacerbate racial and other tensions between Africans and Europeans. As a House subcommittee report advised:

> Should any nations in Africa have racial disorders, these might result in the loss of the use of these bases by the United States or other free Western forces. It is to the American interest that the people in the areas where these bases are located have a peaceful government friendly to the United States and its interests. Thus, the colonial problem should be settled in such fashion as to increase the peaceful economic well-being of the colonial peoples around these bases.[7]

In a series of lectures on Africa and American policy that, given the anticommunist fervor of the times, was quite enlightened, Chester Bowles, who would serve for a year as John F. Kennedy's

Under Secretary of State, was critical of the Eisenhower Administration's neglect of Africa. Bowles's theme was that if American political tradition (self-determination and anticolonialism) and economic achievement (the capitalist model) were to have meaning in Africa, and if the United States wished to maintain access to strategic bases and resources, the United States would have to do a much better job of identifying with African nationalism and the movement toward independence. Treating Africa as a problem of containment and supporting the colonialists in the United Nations had to end. "The most powerful nation in the world, which asserts that it is leading a global coalition for freedom, cannot declare itself to be a nonparticipant in the affairs of a continent boiling with change, without abdicating its position of leadership."[8]

To what extent Bowles helped to shape Kennedy's approach to Africa is uncertain, since the new President took office with many of the same convictions. What is significant about Bowles's views is that they called for a revision of tactics, not objectives. Bowles was arguing that Eisenhower wanted the right things—vital minerals, protection of investments, bases, the minimization of communist influence—but was going about getting them in the wrong way. He thus set the stage for Kennedy's so-called new Africa policy, under which the revolutionary potential of African nationalism was to receive American recognition, and movements for self-determination were to be endorsed. The real challenge, however, was to transform rhetoric and sympathy into policy, a challenge that required discarding or sharply modifying the strategic and economic imperatives of Eisenhower's program. The Congolese civil war showed how the Kennedy Administration, with a very different perspective on Africa, ended by pursuing similar policies of intervention. Before examining those policies, however, it is important to see them against the background of Kennedy's over-all approach to African nationalism.

KENNEDY AND NATIONALISM

"In no part of the third world did Kennedy pioneer more effectively than in Africa." So begins Arthur M. Schlesinger, Jr.'s chapter on the Kennedy Administration's policies in Africa.[9] Not only former advisers but also critics of Kennedy's foreign policy have accepted Schlesinger's conclusion. Reassessment of Kennedy's rhetoric and action on African affairs, especially regarding the Congo, indicates otherwise. The strong impression Kennedy created of devotion to the principles of self-determination and anticolonialism is contradicted by his, and his advisers', overriding concern about Africa's strategic and economic value, which posed for them the constant danger of a "power vacuum" that the Soviet Union could and would exploit. The policy that resulted was protracted intervention in the Congo under the U.N. flag.

Perhaps no President entered office with higher marks for avowed sympathy with revolutionary nationalism than did John F. Kennedy. It was Kennedy who, in the spring of 1954, as a very junior senator from Massachusetts, challenged the Eisenhower Administration's Indochina program on the basis that further military involvement in support of the French would be reckless and, more fundamentally, would not alter the disaffection of the Vietnamese people for colonial rule. Still more forthright, and certainly more attention-getting, was his Senate speech of July 2, 1957, on Algeria, which he delivered not long after joining the Subcommittee on Africa of the Foreign Relations Committee. At a time when official Washington was desperately trying to maintain a hands-off, no-comment position on Algeria, Kennedy charged that the administration's silence and military assistance to France were contributing to the continuation of a repressive colonial war. He urged that Washington use its influence toward a cease-fire and settlement, recognizing the legitimacy of the revolutionaries' demands for self-determination and independence. "Instead of abandoning African nationalism to the anti-Western agitators and Soviet agents who hope to capture its leadership," Kennedy proposed, "the United States, a product of political revolution, must redouble its efforts to earn the respect and friendship of Nationalist leaders."[10]

The quotation, however, betrays a basic dilemma in Kennedy's approach to Africa that has long been characteristic of American policy in the Third World. Put in question form, the dilemma is: Should the American Government, even at the expense of alienating its North Atlantic allies, seek the friendship of nationalist leaders, and identify with their objectives, because of a basic affinity of interests and out of a sense of human solidarity? Or should the United States identify with nationalism in order to edge out local and international communism and win strategic points for the "Free World"? Kennedy's speech on Algeria, so laudable in proclaimed sentiment, was throughout couched in traditional cold war terms: If the United States failed to move with the tide of Algerian self-determination, "Soviet imperialism" would. Although, in another speech, he cautioned that merely because Soviet activities in Africa constituted a "threat" the United States should not treat Africans "as pawns in the Cold War,"[11] the tenor of his talks on Africa suggests that the cold war was foremost in his thinking.[12]

Nor was concern about competition with the Soviet Union the only qualification of Kennedy's pronationalist credentials. His speeches on Africa suggest that domestic politics, personal stature, and American economic access to Africa were also involved. Arthur Schlesinger, commenting on Kennedy's motivations for making the speech on Algeria, writes that the senator "had just come on the Senate Foreign Relations Committee and no doubt wanted to move into foreign affairs in a way that would at once be arresting and useful and demonstrate a basic liberalism."[13] Calling for Algerian independence from France, and linking it to the need for better American relations with the colored peoples of the Third World, got Kennedy the public notice he wanted.

Kennedy's interest in Africa also extended to concern that newly independent nations, though influenced by the American Revolution, might look elsewhere than to the United States for the solution to their economic and political problems. Independent Africa posed a challenge if Americans wished "to maintain our relative political or economic position."

> They [the Africans] believe that their poverty, squalor, ignorance, and disease can be conquered. This is their quest and their faith. To us the challenge is not one of preserving our wealth and our civilization—it is one of extension. Actually, they are the same challenge. To preserve, we must extend. And if the scientific, technical, and educational benefits of the West cannot be extended to all the world, our status will be preserved only with great difficulty.[14]

In the preceding and other speeches, Kennedy indicated how the United States should "extend" its "wealth and civilization" to

Africa.[15] Since the American goal, "for the good of Africa, for the good of the West, is a strong Africa,"[16] the United States should substantially increase Africa's share of the foreign aid budget (it was under 3 per cent in 1959), augment development capital appropriations and technical assistance, establish an Educational Development Fund for Africa, and in any other feasible way provide the training, resources, and capital to ensure "sound, orderly economic development for Africa."[17] Kennedy's proposals, actually not very different from those urged by Eisenhower toward the end of his tenure, amounted to the traditional American approach to Third World instability: Win the dollar battle with the communist powers, move economic planning in a capitalist direction, increase Third World economic dependence on the West, and thus create conditions of "development" that will reduce the attractiveness of socialist alternatives.

"We can no longer think of Africa in terms of Europe," Senator Kennedy observed in 1959. "We dare not think of Africa in terms of our own self-interests or even our own ideologies."[18] But as President, Kennedy learned, or was persuaded, to sing a different tune. He frequently permitted European interests and the North Atlantic alliance to take precedence over Third World sympathies —the same choice he had so vehemently criticized Eisenhower for having made on Algeria. The gap between Kennedy's charm and impressiveness when dealing on the personal level with African diplomats—so deftly described in Schlesinger's memoir—and his decisions could often be enormous.

On the positive side, in 1961 and 1962 Kennedy approved American support in the United Nations for resolutions that called on Portugal, a NATO ally, to move toward ending colonialism in Angola, Mozambique, and Guinea-Bissau. But it is a considerable overstatement for Schlesinger to write that the U.S. vote "liberated the United States from its position of systematic deference to the old colonial powers."[19] As will be discussed later in this chapter, the administration, partly because of developments in the Congo but mainly because of concern about losing air force facilities in the Portuguese Azores, capitulated to Lisbon's pressure and voted against, or watered down, other Afro-Asian resolutions that entailed sanctions against Portugal.

Curiously, Kennedy's reluctance to confront the nationalism

issue squarely—a reluctance that would seem to relate directly to his priority concern, manifested as senator, about Africa's place in the cold war competition—did not prevent his administration from adopting flexible policies toward radical *governments*. He was "perplexed" and annoyed when Ben Bella of Algeria visited Castro's Cuba and there criticized U.S. policy in Vietnam and called for U.S. forces to give up the Guantanamo base.[20] But the President went ahead with an aid program of about $50 million annually (it had been drawn up before Algeria's independence). And he authorized the start of PL-480 surplus wheat deliveries at a time when Algeria badly needed wheat imports. Kennedy's willingness to ignore the Ben Bella government's radical nationalism and increasingly friendly relations with the Soviet Union was in sharp contrast with policy under Lyndon Johnson. The PL-480 program was nearly ended in 1965, a U.S. Information Service branch office was closed down on charges of engaging in subversion, the claims of Americans for nationalized properties could not be settled, and finally relations were broken after the start of the Arab-Israeli war in 1967.[21]

Similarly in the cases of Guinea and Ghana, Kennedy had to overcome resistance within the AID and State Department bureaucracies in order to push through assistance programs to the radical nationalist governments of Sékou Touré and Kwame Nkrumah.[22] In Guinea, the administration stepped in after an inefficient and interventionist Soviet aid program led to the ouster of Moscow's ambassador in December, 1961. In Ghana, Kennedy waited almost a year before giving final approval to U.S. Government loans of about $40 million to finance the Volta Dam project. Considering the unfortunate precedent of Eisenhower's cancellation in 1956 of aid for the Aswan Dam in Egypt, Kennedy's decision was all the wiser.

Kennedy's flexibility on relations with radical nationalist governments thus stands in marked contrast to his response to revolution and civil wars, a response motivated by political expediency, considerations of economic advantage, and the imposition of a cold war framework around Third World political turmoil. Not that politics, economics, and ideology were absent from Kennedy's dealings with Ben Bella, Touré, and Nkrumah. Rather, these factors do not appear to have prevented Kennedy from treating their countries with a compassion and creativity that would be absent in his Congo policy.

CIVIL WAR IN THE CONGO

The Eisenhower Inheritance

As would be the case in Laos, Vietnam, and Cuba, Kennedy's Congo problem was a holdover from the Eisenhower years. In all these instances, however, the new administration was not so committed to past policies that it could not seek to create new opportunities for itself. The main reason no such search took place is that Kennedy shared Eisenhower's evaluation of the risks facing the United States, and the national interests at stake, in the Congolese civil war.

The Republic of the Congo, on June 30, 1960, became one of seventeen African nations to achieve independence that year. Belgium, anxious to avoid "another Algeria," granted independence far ahead of the schedule it preferred. In the Belgian view, the Congolese were not ready for self-rule; and having kept higher education and administration from qualified Congolese, Belgian officials could prove their point. As one colonial administrator put it to Robert Murphy, in 1960 the U.S. Ambassador to Brussels: "Our system, unlike the British and French, avoids creating a discontented group of men who cannot get work for which they think they are qualified."[23] The Belgian Government evidently expected that its paternalistic tutelary system would ensure Congolese dependence on colonial administrators, technicians, and military officers for a long time to come.

In a country such as the Congo, where the tensions of long-term colonial rule were augmented by tribal, linguistic, and regional differences, the potential for violence after independence was high. Within one week, fighting began among the tribes; Congolese soldiers revolted against their Belgian officers and went on a rampage in Léopoldville, the capital, causing most of the European civilians to flee the country; and, on July 11, Moise Tshombe declared the secession of Katanga province from the republic. The Congolese Government's Vice-Premier, Antoine Gizenga, requested direct U.S. military assistance on July 12 to help put down the secession, which Belgian troops, in violation of a friendship treaty with the Congo signed June 29, were supporting. Gizenga's appeal was refused. The same day, therefore, Premier Patrice Lumumba and President Joseph Kasavubu jointly requested the U.N. Secretary General to assist in ending Belgian "aggression," which they clearly distinguished from "aid . . . to restore [the] internal situation in [the] Congo."*

Meeting on July 14, the U.N. Security Council approved a Tunisian resolution to provide the Congo with military assistance. American logistical support, which was to be critical to the U.N. operation throughout the crisis, was authorized by President Eisenhower. By the third week of August, the United Nations Force (UNF) had about 15,600 troops, mostly African, for which the United States supplied airlift, equipment, food, helicopters, reconnaissance planes, and jeeps. Eisenhower also ordered the stationing of "an attack carrier near the mouth of the Congo River" and obtained an extra $100 million appropriation from Congress for the Mutual Security Contingency Fund.[24]

Eisenhower's unhesitating support of U.N. intervention was prompted by several considerations. The most important one was, as he wrote, that "with a position of leadership in the Free World, we did not want to see chaos run wild among hopeful, expectant peoples and could not afford to see turmoil in an area where the Communists would be only too delighted to take an advantage."[25] Eisenhower saw in the Congo "a restless and militant population in a state of gross ignorance—even by African standards,"[26] which may explain in part his administration's abstention on the Afro-Asian anticolonialism resolution in 1960. For Eisenhower, as for Kennedy, "chaos" and "turmoil" had to be contained and then channeled in a pro-Western direction.

The danger Eisenhower saw in the Congo was that the "Communists" might manipulate the chaos for their own ends. He viewed Patrice Lumumba as a "Soviet tool," "radical and un-

---

* "The essential purpose of the requested military aid," said the cable, "is to protect the national territory of the Congo against the present external aggression which is a threat to international peace." A clarification sent the next day by Kasavubu and Lumumba said: "The purpose of the aid requested is not to restore internal situation in Congo but rather to protect the national territory against act of aggression posed by Belgian metropolitan troops." U.N. Security Council, Document S/4382, July 13, 1960.

stable," whose influence was bound to grow—a characterization only slightly different from Ambassador Murphy's.[27] Since, even before the outbreak of violence in the Congo, Eisenhower had concluded that the United States should no longer stay out of the affairs of African colonies or newly independent countries,[28] he was determined to prevent Soviet inroads. To avoid a direct confrontation, which Gizenga's proposal for direct U.S. aid might bring about, the administration decided to make the United Nations the instrument of U.S. policy.

A second major American objective in the Congo, related to, but distinct from, the strategic interest, was to ensure that the incomparable mineral wealth of the Congo, in particular the resources of Katanga province, would remain accessible to the Western powers and not fall into hostile hands. "Sixty percent of the world's cobalt, 70 percent of its industrial diamonds, and about 10 percent of its copper and tin come from the Congo," one writer reported in 1960.[29] Katanga, which provided between 45 and 60 per cent of the Congo's revenues, was then the fifth largest producer of copper in the world. The province also produced all of the Congo's cobalt, 16 per cent of the world's germanium, 5 per cent of its manganese, and nearly all its radium.[30] And it was a major source of zinc, gold, cadmium, and, until 1960, uranium.

The Congo's and Katanga's mineral production benefited mainly Belgium and West European financial interests. Five major holding companies dominated the Congo's economy, of which by far the largest, the Société Générale de Belgique, controlled a variety of Katanga enterprises. The main one, Union Minière du Haut-Katanga, was Tshombe's principal financial supporter, funneling revenues from its mines to keep his resistance alive. Together, these conglomerates reaped a tremendous profit from the Congo, on average (between 1947 and 1958) at least twice as much as firms that invested in Belgium.[31] Thus, while a Senate subcommittee report found, in mid-1960, that a complete break between Belgium and the Congo would "have a relatively small effect" on Belgium's economy over-all, it also pointed out the importance of the Congo for Belgium's balance of payments, the airlines and maritime industries, jobs, and public finance.[32] Omitted, of course, was the specific impact if the major holding companies of the Congo, or Katanga, were taken over by an unfriendly government.

While official Washington could not fail to ignore the "loss" of the Congo's resources to West Europeans, it had also to take account of American economic interests. Direct American investments in the Congo were small at the time: only about $10 million to $12 million, compared with $3.5 billion by Belgians.[33] The biggest U.S. investor, ARMCO International Corporation, manufacturer of steel products, sought government protection for its half-million dollars of assets,[34] but it seems doubtful that investments were a major U.S. concern. Rather, the administration may have been motivated in its Congo policy by the prospective loss of copper and zinc supplies, the major U.S. imports that made the United States, by 1958, the leading market for Congolese products. Union Minière companies were the chief producers of both metals; and, until its uranium deposits were reportedly exhausted in April, 1960, it had for about fifteen years been a principal supplier of atomic materials for bomb production.[35]

At first glance, U.S. strategic and economic interests in the Congo in 1960 might seem to have dictated alignment with Tshombe and Katanga rather than intervention behind the United Nations to help preserve the Congo's unity. There were pressure groups in Washington, led by Connecticut senator Thomas Dodd and an unofficial Katanga lobby, that argued unsuccessfully in Tshombe's behalf, claiming he was an ardent anticommunist and that U.N. involvement played into the hands of Russia and the neutralist "cryptocommunist" governments. Needless to add, the Belgian, British, and French governments also supported Katanga's cause. Washington, however, rejected such advice, *not* because of unconcern about the communist threat or the Western economic stake in Katanga, but because the Eisenhower Administration was convinced "that the former Belgian Congo could be a proper self-supporting state if it included Katanga Province, but that the infant Republic would become a bankrupt derelict, susceptible to Soviet domination, if deprived of Katanga."[36] Washington and its European partners were at odds over means, not ends; what they were willing to see happen—the breakup of the Congo—Washington believed it could not "afford."

In coming to the conclusion that the United Nations's mission in the Congo should be to reimpose order and restore unity, the Eisenhower Administration made two highly questionable assessments—about Lumumba and about Tshombe—that were to have lasting impact on U.S. policy. First, the administration, as previously noted, believed that Lumumba was susceptible to Moscow's influence, if he was not a communist outright. Yet, on the eve of independence, the Premier accepted the continuing need for Belgian technical assistance and said an appeal for "outside help" would not be made "unless an amicable agreement [with Belgium] proves absolutely impossible." Condemning "reactionary nationalism," Lumumba said he sought "a Belgo-Congolese nationalism which will unite Belgians and Africans in the defence of their common patrimony."[37] The initial appeal for U.S. military aid was, in fact, from Lumumba's closest supporter and eventual successor, Antoine Gizenga. To be sure, Lumumba was radical in his nationalism, but radical in the sense of wanting to establish a Congolese identity and of being vigorously anti-imperialist and anticolonialist, not in the sense of following Moscow's orders or faithfully observing Marxist-Leninist protocol.* Lumumba drew his strength from his charisma—"a rare ability to sense and articulate the demands of his public," whatever its language or tribe.[38]

The American disaffection for Tshombe sprang from the equally mistaken belief that Katanga's secession was entirely the product of Union Minière's financing, and that Tshombe's position on secession was inflexible. The secession clearly could not have been sustained without Belgian support; but "a host of factors—ethnic, linguistic, geographical, economic, and political—have conspired to create a feeling of separateness in Katanga."[39] Like his Belgian backers, Tshombe was reluctant to share Katangan mineral wealth with the rest of the Congo; unlike them, he

---

* As Lumumba said in August, 1960: "You see, gentlemen, they are trying to distort your focus when they call our government a communist government, in the pay of the Soviet Union, or say that Lumumba is a communist, an anti-white: Lumumba is an African. The government of the Congo is a nationalist government that doesn't want any imported ideologies, but which demands nothing except the total, complete liberation of the Congo." From a speech reprinted in Wilfred Cartey and Martin Kilson (eds.), *The Africa Reader: Independent Africa* (New York: Random House, 1970), p. 87.

was prepared to bargain with Léopoldville if Katanga were granted substantial autonomy as part of a loose confederation. By supporting the UNF's effort to end the secession, both Eisenhower and Kennedy deeply involved the United States and the United Nations in a civil dispute based on longstanding tribal, economic, regional, and political differences.

Failing to comprehend either Lumumba's nationalism or Tshombe's separatism, Eisenhower initiated support of a U.N. military involvement that was itself of dubious legality. The July 14 Security Council resolution, unanimously approved, authorized the Secretary-General (Dag Hammarskjöld)

> to take the necessary steps, in consultation with the Government of the Republic of the Congo, to provide the Government with such military assistance, as may be necessary, until, through the efforts of the Congolese Government with the technical assistance of the United Nations, the national security forces may be able, in the opinion of the Government, to meet fully their tasks.[40]

The resolution did not condemn Belgian "aggression" but did instead "call for" the withdrawal of Belgian forces, which by then had been reinforced and had moved out from their two bases to restore order. To meet that situation, a second unanimous Security Council resolution, adopted July 22, again urged Belgian withdrawal, authorized "the Secretary-General to take all necessary action to this effect," and requested all states not to interfere in the Congo or "impede the restoration of law and order and the exercise by the Government of the Congo of its authority."[41]

The principal effect of these two resolutions *should have been,* in keeping with the initial Lumumba-Kasavubu request for U.N. action, to facilitate the withdrawal of (by then) some 10,000 Belgian troops. Although Lumumba would later turn away from the United Nations because it failed to move decisively to end Katanga's secession, his first cause for hostility toward Hammarskjöld and Washington was that the Belgians were not expelled. He insisted on several occasions that order would return to the Congo "five minutes after Belgium's withdrawal"; but, with the exception of the Soviet, Ceylonese, and Tunisian representatives in the Security Council, none supported his position.[42] Instead, Hammarskjöld, in line with American preferences, used the UNF as a peacekeeper and guarantor. The meaning of these missions was that the U.N. command, not the Congolese Government, would determine the departure of the Belgian troops, and that the restoration of law and order (including efforts to disarm the Congolese Army) would precede such withdrawal.*

Because the United Nations did not immediately act to ensure the Belgian withdrawal, yet also (and correctly) refused to march on Katanga, Lumumba, in mid-August, declared that the government had lost confidence in the Secretary-General. By then, part of a second province had seceded, and Lumumba felt compelled to act on his own. Responding to his aid appeal, the Soviet Government dispatched 10 Ilyushin transport planes for Lumumba's troops, about 100 trucks, and an estimated 200 technicians and 100 other diplomatic, news, and medical personnel.[43] The military operation, coupled with the arrival of Soviet aid in early September, proved Lumumba's undoing in more ways than one. The operation itself resulted in considerable bloodshed, without subduing the secessionist provinces; the U.N. Secretariat came to regard Lumumba's forces as a more immediate threat to the peace than the Belgians or even Tshombe's mercenaries; and Lumumba's closeness to Moscow prompted President Kasavubu to announce, on September 5, that Lumumba had been removed from office.

Just as the events of early July had raised questions about the propriety and practicality of U.S.-U.N. involvement in the war, the dismissal of Lumumba raised the question of direct U.S.-U.N. entry into Congolese politics. Lumumba's reply to Kasavubu's action—convening the cabinet, dismissing Kasavubu, and calling for army and public support of his government—meant that Hammarskjöld and Washington would either have to choose between the two leaders (in which case the choice was preordained) or disengage from an increasingly complex civil conflict. Constitu-

* Belgian withdrawal was personally negotiated by Hammarskjöld with Tshombe in August, 1960. But not until September, 1961, when about 230 officers and men attached to Tshombe's army departed, was the withdrawal completed. Thereafter, French, South African, and Rhodesian mercenaries fought on Katanga's side. See Ernest W. Lefever, "The U.N. as a Foreign Policy Instrument: The Congo Crisis," in Roger Hilsman and Robert C. Good (eds.), Foreign Policy in the Sixties: The Issues and the Instruments (Baltimore, Md.: Johns Hopkins Press, 1965), p. 145, and Lefever's Crisis in the Congo (Washington, D.C.: The Brookings Institution, 1965), pp. 33–34.

tionally, under the *Loi Fondamentale* (Fundamental Law) that had been drawn up before independence with the Belgian constitution as the model, Kasavubu had the right to dismiss his Premier. But the two Congolese Chambers, charged with "authoritative interpretation of laws," voted that both revocations, Kasavubu's and Lumumba's, were illegal.[44] The United Nations, instead of letting the Congolese decide the issue, even if that meant continued fighting, chose to take sides.

In what one former U.N. official has termed "Mr Cordier's anti-communist *coup*,"[45] an American representing the United Nations in Léopoldville, Andrew W. Cordier, ordered seizure of the airport and radio station, a move approved by Hammarskjöld in a statement before the Security Council on September 9. Not only was this act an obvious and calculated effort to break the constitutional impasse by throwing U.N. (and U.S.) support to Kasavubu, the "moderate"; it also contradicted Hammarskjöld's explicit assurances that the UNF would not become involved in Congolese politics and, more specifically, violated a Security Council resolution of August 9 that "reaffirms that the United Nations force in the Congo will not be a party to or in any way intervene in or be used to influence the outcome of any internal conflict, constitutional or otherwise."[46]

The "coup" was a major escalation of U.N. and American intervention in the Congo. It was also an important victory for the so-called Congo Club, of which Hammarskjöld was "chairman" and Cordier the representative of American funding and support (without which no U.N. mission was possible), and from which the Soviet Union was excluded.[47] Lumumba's position was undermined, compelling him in October to establish an alternative government in Stanleyville. The Congolese leadership was thus moved in the pro-Western, nonradical direction desired by Washington. Under the Secretary-General's direction, the UNF was enlarged. President Eisenhower, speaking before the General Assembly on September 22, endorsed Cordier's action, promised more money for the U.N. program in the Congo, condemned external intervention in African affairs, and equated the United Nations's effort "against outside pressures" with previous involvements in Iran, Greece, Korea, Suez, and Lebanon. As his administration's term ended, civil disorder in the Congo had become transformed into an anticommunist intervention in which the United States could count on the United Nations's full cooperation.

Kennedy's Congo Policy

The linchpins of Kennedy's Congo policy were precisely those of Eisenhower's.[48] The Soviet threat to central Africa would have to be deterred, using the United Nations as the instrument of deterrence.[49] If deterrence failed, the Soviets would take advantage and, before too long, "would spread [their] tentacles over this newest of continents."[50] The specter of falling dominoes in Africa brought to Kennedy's mind two parallels:

> Kennedy did not want the Congo to become another Laos, draining American energies and goodwill in a jungle war against Communist-supported local troops. Nor did he want it to become another Cuba, providing Communism with a strategically located military base, vast natural resources and a fertile breeding ground of subversives and guerrillas.[51]

Working through the United Nations would prevent "another Laos"; supporting a military effort to bring Katanga back into the fold would prevent "another Cuba." It is noteworthy that the same Kennedy who had dismissed the Cuba analogy when some State Department "Africanists" had applied it to Ben Bella's Algeria should have so readily adopted it when dealing with the Congo.

Kennedy's perception of the Soviet threat, which, as will shortly be seen, was shared and reinforced by key individuals in the State Department, evidently stemmed in part from the ideological labels some of his chief aides attached to the Congolese radical nationalists. For example, Harlan Cleveland, Assistant Secretary of State for International Organization Affairs, told a House committee in April, 1961, that while Lumumba—who by then had been arrested and murdered—was "a locally bred nationalist" and Gizenga was "trained as a Communist" but had probably been a disappointment to Moscow, both men were threats to Congolese independence. Cleveland reasoned from the Laos case, which he interpreted as a situation in which the Pathet Lao "can be turned on and off from long range," that is, from Moscow. In similar fashion, Lumumba and Gizenga either were already or would become Soviet tools, willing to turn the Congo into a Soviet-run totalitarian state ("witness Castro, let us say").[52] As in the past, no explanation of Gizenga's initial appeal to the United States for aid was offered; no implication was drawn about Lumumba's popularity; and no attention was devoted to the expeditious, last-ditch nature of the radicals' "alliance" with Moscow.

Linked to the strategic issue in American thinking was an equally strong political issue, made explicit in Cleveland's testimony: "The ultimate political issue in the Congo," Cleveland asserted, is "whether the Congolese are going to be governed by themselves or whether they are going to be governed from elsewhere."[53] In his view, it was part of "American doctrine" and "interest" "to make sure that people everywhere have some opportunity to participate in decisions affecting their own destiny." Or, in the words of George W. Ball, Under Secretary of State, the "long run" U.S. aim was a "stable society under a stable and progressive government." It might be nonaligned internationally, "but it should be strong enough and determined enough to safeguard its real independence," by which he clearly meant close ties with the United States and Western Europe.[54]

These views were not confined to the Department of State. Like the strategic calculations, they were shared by the President, for whom "stability," "viability," and "law and order" were synonymous with anticommunism.[55] It was only a short step from such thinking to the belief that the United Nations, which had so successfully acted in behalf of U.S. interests on previous occasions, should be in the vanguard role, *both* preventing "communist" domination and ending the secession in order to stabilize Congolese politics.

The broad strategic and political objectives of Kennedy's policy, which encompassed concern about Western access to the Congo's economic resources,[56] seem to have complemented the aims and ambitions of the U.N. Secretariat. For the Americans, Katanga's secession had to be ended in order to preserve a pro-Western Congo. For the U.N. leadership, first under Hammarskjöld and then (after his death in a plane crash in September, 1961) U Thant, Katanga was a threat to the organization itself, in that a failure to keep the Congo unified would be a failure for the United Nations as a peacekeeper. An "unspoken bargain" thus emerged, Conor Cruise O'Brien relates from his personal involvement, among the Secretariat, Washington, and those Afro-Asian governments that regarded secession as a threat to their own territorial integrity.[57] In the self-interest of each group, radicalism needed to be contained in central Africa through what Harlan Cleveland aptly termed "sanitary intervention" by the United Nations to provide the Congo with a long-lasting "steel understructure."[58]

"Sanitary intervention" became the new ingredient the Kennedy Administration added to the Congo policy of Eisenhower. And, again, as in Laos, Vietnam, and Cuba, Kennedy made an inherited policy very much his own, beginning in the Security Council. The American delegation headed by Adlai Stevenson adroitly pushed through a lengthy resolution on February 21, 1961, that substantially broadened the UNF's mandate.[59] Responding to the deterioration of order in the Congo after Lumumba's murder, the resolution "urged" that the UNF "prevent the occurrence of civil war" by all means, including "the use of force, if necessary, in the last resort." The UNF was further directed to assure the withdrawal of Belgian and all other "mercenaries" (a provision that probably accounts for the Soviet Union's abstention rather than veto), and to "reorganize" and "control" the Congolese armed forces. The Congolese Parliament was urged to reconvene. While all states were requested not to interfere in the Congo's affairs, the UNF prepared, "if necessary," to reunify the Congo by force of arms.

On the basis of its amplified directive, the UNF helped bring about a settlement between Stanleyville and Léopoldville that led, on August 1, 1961, to agreement on Cyrille Adoula, a qualified "moderate," as Premier and Gizenga as Vice-Premier. But by late 1962, Adoula's authority was in jeopardy; the U.N. Plan for National Reconciliation that he supported had failed to obtain Tshombe's consent, and a parliamentary motion of censure had narrowly failed. Tshombe's rejection of the plan and his announcement, in December, 1962, of a "scorched-earth" policy rather than compromise, played into the hands of those in Washington (and elsewhere) who, for a year, had been urging quick military action to end the secession and prevent a "communist" takeover (that is, Adoula's fall) in Léopoldville.⁶⁰

With a rationale for resort to force, the UNF, transported by American aircraft and using American trucks, armored personnel carriers, and other equipment delivered by the administration, successfully moved into Katanga. (At about the same time, in October, 1962, the United States began a program of direct military aid to the Adoula regime that would seem to have violated the February 21, 1961, Security Council resolution barring outside interference.)⁶¹ In January 1963, Tshombe's resistance came to an end.

The fact that the U.N.-U.S. intervention succeeded should not preclude critical analysis of its legal, moral, and political implications for American policy.

Kennedy entered office with an opportunity to contract the Eisenhower commitments on two fronts, namely, support of Kasavubu over Lumumba (as reflected in Cordier's "coup") and support of U.N. intervention to restore order. Instead, Kennedy reaffirmed the first and expanded the second, both on questionable legal and practical grounds. At the very least, Kasavubu's dismissal of Lumumba was legally questionable; and it was certainly politically foolish, considering Lumumba's large personal following and the intensified fighting his removal was bound to occasion. Quickly, however, at a February 15, 1961, news conference, Kennedy came out in Kasavubu's favor. The President thus chose to take sides in a civil dispute and, like Eisenhower, put a cold war face on it.

Kennedy also might have sought to restore the UNF's role in the Congo to its original and sole legitimate purpose: to expedite the Belgian withdrawal in conformity with the "opinion" (the word used in the July 14, 1960, resolution, which remained operative) of the government of the Congo, represented in Patrice Lumumba as well as Joseph Kasavubu. It is therefore astonishing to read interpretations of the Lumumba-Kasavubu request by senior State Department officials under Kennedy, who said it authorized the UNF to restore Congolese unity, protect it against outside threats, and rebuild the Congo's institutions.⁶² It was because the U.N. command, with American support, performed precisely those

tasks *without* invitation that the more radical nationalist governments of Africa and Asia, including Ghana, the United Arab
Republic, and Indonesia, shouted "neocolonialism."

The United Nations and, through it, the United States could
not take upon themselves the duty to reintegrate Katanga by force
—to engage, as Sorensen puts it, in a "precedent-setting role as a
nation-builder."[63] Whether self-determination should, as Senator
Dodd and others believed, have applied to the secession of a
province with a minority of the national population would ultimately have to be decided by the Congolese. (Since not one
government ever recognized Katanga, it is evident Tshombe's
cause had no African or international sympathy.) But Dodd was
on the mark in insisting that the United Nations was setting a
dangerous precedent by intervening militarily, "upon the request
of any central government, to prevent the secession of any national minority or grouping."[64] And, as Tshombe's subsequent
agreeement, in 1964, to return as Premier of the Congo showed,
Katanga's secession was revocable, provided the terms of continued federation could deal satisfactorily with tribal rivalries and
diverse economic interests.

What of the American decision-making process that produced
Kennedy's determination to lend moral, material, and political
backing to the U.N. effort? As the accounts of Roger Hilsman
and Schlesinger show, Congo policy divided the executive bureaucracy along lines similar to those that had developed over the
colonialism votes in the United Nations and U.S. aid to radical
nationalist governments. The "Africanists," architects of the
"new" Africa policy under Kennedy, were centered in G. Mennen
Williams's Bureau of African Affairs and the U.N. Mission. They
viewed the termination of Katanga's secession as vital to the
viability of the Congo, to the prevention of secessions elsewhere
in Africa, to the tenability of the new policy they believed they
were promoting, and (in at least one case) to the security of the
United States.[65] Kennedy quite plainly sided with this group,
adding to its arguments the "big picture" of "another Laos" and
"another Cuba." On the other side were the "Europeanists," who
argued that using force to end Katanga's secession was not worth
the price of alienating NATO allies. But these men, mostly in the
Bureau of European Affairs and the Pentagon, were neither so

enamored of Tshombe's cause nor so opposed to Congolese unity that they were willing to resist all forms of U.S.-U.N. intervention.

The first and principal point to note about this division of opinion in Washington is that there was no authoritative spokesman or bureaucracy for the alternative of disengagement and noninvolvement. To be sure, a few members of the White House staff reportedly argued that the Congo conflict was an internal affair and that the Soviet threat was not yet evident.[66] But they had neither the personal nor the institutional power to make an impressive case. As a result, the only choice posed for Kennedy by his advisers was between more or less, faster or slower intervention in Congolese affairs.

Secondly, the notion that Kennedy and the "Africanists" were responsive to African anticolonialism and self-determination needs qualification. Kennedy's primary objective was to block Soviet influence while avoiding either a protracted guerrilla war ("another Laos") or the establishment of a communist base for subversion outside the Congo ("another Cuba"). To the extent that anticolonialism was influential in Kennedy's opinion, it provided a convenient rationale for intervention, since most of the Afro-Asian governments wanted to see Katanga's secession ended and Belgian forces ousted. Self-determination was fine, one official let on, only so long as (in Washington's opinion) Moscow remained uninvolved.[67]

In like manner, American officials judged Congolese nationalists by the company they kept, which ruled out Lumumba and Gizenga as useful partners. To be "genuinely" independent, the government in Léopoldville would have to be "moderate" and "broadly based," meaning—as in the case of the 1961 Adoula cabinet—some, but limited, representation to the radicals.[68] (The parallel to official American requirements for an acceptable coalition government in South Vietnam is striking.) The maintenance of such a "progressive" administration in power could then be used to legitimize further intervention, as occurred late in 1962, when Adoula's government seemed on the verge of collapse. Identification with African nationalism, in short, depended on the willingness of African nationalists to identify with U.S. interests.

These features of policy-making on the Congo—the lack of pressure for the alternative of noninvolvement, and the distortion of the colonialism and nationalism issues to serve the end of deterring "communism"—came together in the final months of 1962, when a decision had to be made whether to escalate the use of force against Tshombe. Negotiations had failed to bring about reunification; the United Nations would have no authority to maintain troops in the Congo beyond 1962; the Indian forces, backbone of the U.N. operation, might have to be withdrawn; and a U.N. embargo of Union Minière's mineral exports was not compelling Tshombe to acquiesce. According to Hilsman, who participated in drawing up a new plan of action for the President, "Our conclusion was that the only thing that would move Tshombe was a *credible* threat of military coercion, and that the only way to make the threat credible was actually to decide to do it."[69]

Why was disengagement not considered preferable to an all-out, U.S.-assisted assault on Katanga? The overriding reason, once again, had little to do with African nationalism or anticolonialism. Rather, it was that disengagement carried unacceptable "risks"— Hilsman's word—of increased Soviet involvement and influence. He has written:

. . . given the increasing signs of Soviet activities, including attempts to woo even the moderates in Léopoldville, we estimated that the Communists would parlay our disengagement into a position of considerable influence, through a military aid program which their representatives in Léopoldville were offering anyone who would listen. One could easily foresee that from a base in the Congo, the Communists could play hell with affairs in much of Central and Southern Africa.[70]

"The greatest risk," Hilsman goes on, was of "full engagement" against a bigger menace later. And it was on this reading of events that Hilsman's two colleagues, Under Secretary Ball and Robert C. Good, Director of the Office of Research and Analysis for Africa in the Bureau of African Affairs, changed their positions and backed the use of force to compel unification.

The "risks," then, were to U.S. interests, narrowly conceived as keeping communist influence out of Africa. Being in violation of the U.N. Charter's principle (Article 2/7) of nonintervention in the domestic affairs of member states was obviously not considered, since it was the administration's contention that the Congolese civil war ultimately posed a threat to "international peace and security," thus permitting U.N. involvement. Yet in other circumstances—for example, concerning African demands for the application of sanctions against South Africa and Portugal —Article 2/7 was in American interests to uphold. The moral and political risks of American involvement in a potentially very destructive military operation, in which U.S. aircraft would be dropping bombs on African villages, were also slighted. So, finally, was the possibility that, as would happen in South Vietnam, a small commitment of U.S. power might have to be followed by a larger, more direct one—although Kennedy seemed prepared to accept deeper U.S. involvement.*

In the judgment of the State Department specialists who lent their support to a military solution, the risk of expanded Soviet influence outweighed that of the U.N. operation's destructiveness. This assessment can be challenged on two counts. Casualties may have been relatively light and Tshombe did not carry out his threatened "scorched-earth" policy. But had the operation become prolonged and had Tshombe proved as irresponsible as his critics charged, Katanga could have been left in a shambles. The very effort to "save" a reunited Congo might have ended by making the Congo less "viable" than before. As for the Soviet threat, it is clear that the United States acted on the basis not of a major Soviet presence in the Congo, but of the presumed Soviet *potential* to form an alliance with Congolese politicians. The only "evidence" of Soviet subversion was that Moscow was offering aid to the Léopoldville government. The extent of Soviet activities was "blown up . . . to quite unjustified proportions," Hilsman acknowledges.[71]

The UNF's operation, in short, was *preventive intervention* rather than a response to an existing threat. Believing that the

* In December, 1962, the State Department proposed, and Kennedy eventually agreed, to lend jet fighters to the U.N. command on request, apparently without U.S. pilots. (Cf. Arthur M. Schlesinger, Jr., A *Thousand Days: John F. Kennedy in the White House* [Boston, Mass.: Houghton Mifflin, 1965], p. 578; and Theodore C. Sorensen, *Kennedy* [New York: Harper & Row, 1965], p. 638.) The success of the Congo operation, however, removed the need to send the planes. But, as Schlesinger recalls (*ibid.*), Kennedy "was ready, if necessary, to go very far down the military road to secure a unified Congo."

Soviet Union would ultimately be able to parlay a military assistance program into a base from which to penetrate central Africa, Kennedy wound up going far beyond the level of involvement reached by Eisenhower. Apparently, none of Kennedy's close advisers raised doubts about Soviet ability to manipulate Congolese politics any better than American or U.N. officials had been able; none challenged the prevailing assumption that Moscow would have reliable ideological allies among the radical nationalists, or saw the real parallel to Laos in the inability of Western intervention to bring stability to an internally fragile young nation.

Although it is unfair to argue with the benefit of hindsight, a summary of events in the Congo after Tshombe's surrender is enlightening. Early in 1964, soon after Lyndon Johnson assumed the Presidency, rebellion against Léopoldville's authority mounted anew, with some support from Moscow and Peking. With the UNF's departure in mid-year, the United States stepped into the breach. The UNF's equipment was turned over to the central government, and the U.S. military mission, set up late in 1963, provided training, T-28 jet fighters and technicians, vehicles, and communications equipment.[72] The T-28's were flown against the rebels by "two or three Americans recruited by the Central Intelligence Agency," and when the State Department grounded them, Cuban exiles took their place.[73] But the rebel forces gained in strength and territorial control, capturing Stanleyville in August, 1964. The embattled Kasavubu, in a remarkable turnabout, invited the exiled Tshombe to take over the premiership. Without pausing to appreciate the irony, which was compounded by Tshombe's hiring of white mercenaries to fight the rebellion, Washington added transport planes, helicopters, three B-26 bombers, and a 100-man contingent (including 40 paratroopers) to its aid program.[74]

Put on the defensive, the rebels warned they would hold about 1,300 foreigners in Stanleyville as hostages; and they tortured and killed a large number of people, perhaps 20,000.[75] In November, 1964, the United States launched a successful air rescue operation named Dragon Rouge, using 545 Belgian paratroopers.[76] But they did not stop at that; they joined forces with Tshombe's mercenaries to topple the Stanleyville regime. A humanitarian effort had turned, much like the initial U.N. effort in 1960, into a political operation dominated by whites. And in both cases, too, the alleged American objective of acting in response to African nationalism became submerged in the greater determination to quash African radicalism. The parallels are, however, not unusual, because the intervention of 1964 had its roots in American intervention during the three previous years.

American Alternatives

Kennedy's decisions on the Congo evolved from a selective reading of African politics. He and his "Africanist" advisers reportedly were aware that the anti-imperialism and anti-neocolonialism of the radicals in Stanleyville stemmed from nationalist sensitivities and not from rigid Marxism.[77] But the Americans suspected the radicals' ultimate loyalties, feared that Western access to the Congo would be in jeopardy, believed they were susceptible to Soviet subversion, and thus followed in Eisenhower's footsteps by focusing on the Soviet threat and working for the removal of Lumumba's successors. Aware, too, that the majority of African (and concerned Asian) governments differed widely in their preferences regarding the structure and political leadership of a unified Congo, the administration nevertheless used the Security Council's mandate to intervene to remold a unified Congo along pro-Western lines.

In pursuit of containment and stability, of pacification and nation-building,* U.S. officials neglected two fundamentals of African, and indeed Third World, politics. One is that while the African governments could all agree about the necessity of extirpating all vestiges of colonialism, they had quite different points of view about communism and radical nationalism. Secondly, the extraordinary mixture of personalities, motives, social programs,

---

* These two words, "pacification" and "nation-building," are not my invention. To "pacify" the country is given by Sorensen (*Kennedy*, p. 636) as the Kennedy Administration's objective in the Congo; and "nation-building" is one of the American missions listed in the essay by G. Mennen Williams (in Helen A. Kitchen [ed.], *Footnotes to the Congo Story* [New York: Walker, 1967], pp. 154, 158) as well as by Sorensen (p. 637). The similarity of vocabulary between the Congo and Vietnam is, it should by now be evident, not coincidental.

"ideologies," and international affinities that is the fabric of political life in black Africa means that external intervention from any source cannot for long manipulate politics in the manner of the colonial powers.

An alternative American policy in the Congo that proceeded from the above two points would have meant a strict interpretation of the first Security Council resolution of July 14, 1960. It would have recognized the ease with which a military operation can slide into political partisanship, and would therefore have eschewed using force in the civil war or interposing the United Nations in factional disputes. In line with the request of Lumumba and Kasavubu, the UNF would have sought only to expedite the evacuation of Belgian troops and all mercenaries; to convene negotiations between Tshombe and the Léopoldville government (as well as between radicals and conservatives); and to establish an observation mission to monitor and report violations of a cease-fire if requested by the government. The American role would then have reduced to providing humanitarian relief (which was Kennedy's first action), helping to bring about a settlement of the civil war (which could best be accomplished by influencing the Belgian withdrawal), and declaring support for Congolese territorial integrity and noninterference by all foreign governments.

Limited U.S. involvement would not have satisfied several African states or the U.N. Secretariat, which by the time Kennedy took office had already moved in Kasavubu's favor. Full-fledged civil war might not have been prevented, although the withdrawal of foreign troops from Katanga would have removed Tshombe's chief means of resistance. The Congo Government might well have turned to Moscow anyway for assistance to move on and occupy Katanga, ignoring pleas to negotiate a settlement. The toll in African lives and property, not to mention European assets, might have been much higher than it was under the U.N. operation.

On the other hand, limited involvement directed at obtaining Belgium's withdrawal, not ending Katanga's secession, would have been consistent with American proclamations of sympathy for anticolonialism and self-determination. It would have avoided meddling in Congolese politics, the fruits of which were alignment with Tshombe and his mercenaries in a second military intervention in 1964 that aroused the anger of many African governments. It would have preserved the United Nations as an instrument for preventing foreign engagement in civil wars rather than used it as an instrument of U.S. foreign policy and active participant in domestic disputes.

Finally, such a policy would have accepted the risk, so-called, of increased Soviet involvement in the Congo. Had the Soviet Union refused to heed U.N. and American appeals not to take sides in the dispute, the appropriate American attitude was that Moscow should be given enough rope to hang itself. Intervention in Congolese politics entailed more responsibilities and pitfalls than opportunities. Subsequent events in the Congo and throughout Africa would demonstrate the ultimate futility of major power interference.

CIVIL WAR IN NIGERIA

Not long after fighting in the Congo had died down, officials in the Johnson Administration were again faced with civil war in Africa. On May 30, 1967, the leadership of the eastern region of Nigeria declared its secession and the formation of a Republic of Biafra. The Nigerian Government in Lagos promptly took steps to seal off Biafra from access to the outer world. The ensuing war lasted thirty months, until January, 1970. The American response, unlike during the Congo civil war, was to maintain "neutrality" throughout the fighting. But the issues posed by the secession were different in Nigeria, American interests in "stability" did not require involvement, and the war was not internationalized as quickly or as broadly as it had been in the Congo. "Neutrality" served the U.S. interest in seeing Biafra fail.

Like the Congo, Nigeria, which gained independence in October, 1960, brought together tribal peoples representing vastly different cultures, economies, and politics. British rule had been the cement of the Nigerian nation; as Nigerian spokesmen recognized, the country was a British creation, not a natural expression of political, geographical, or cultural unity. When the British departed, the deep-seated fears and suspicions between tribes and regions—in particular, between the north (dominated by the

Hausa-Fulani group) and the south (mainly the Ibo)—resurfaced. Since colonial administration emphasized regionalism rather than national integration, it may be that the disintegration of Nigeria in 1966 and 1967 was in large measure a direct consequence of British policy.

Biafra's break with Lagos occurred after over a year of political turmoil and inability of Easterners and Northerners to compromise their differences.[78] The north, dominant in size and population at the time of independence, held political sway until a military coup on January 15, 1966, brought a primarily Ibo government under Major-General Ironsi to power. Ironsi was kidnapped and murdered; his army chief of staff, Lieutenant-Colonel Yakubu Gowon, seized power on July 29 and launched a pogrom against Easterners, first in the army and later outside it. Between 10,000 and 30,000 Easterners were killed, many more were injured, and perhaps 2 million began to return to their home region from other parts of the country. Despite these developments, regional leaders met late in 1966 and early in 1967 to debate structural alternatives to the federal system of government, with the east holding out for a confederation formula favorable to greatly increased regional autonomy. But the continuation of assaults on Easterners, the burdens placed on the eastern government by the refugees, and the widespread belief among the Ibos that Gowon's government would never accept any diminution of northern power increased pressures to secede. By March, 1967, secession seemed inevitable when a government decree expanded central military authority and the east issued "survival edicts" to assert control over formerly national trade, judicial, educational, and other institutions within its boundaries.

Gowon at first declared the war a purely internal Nigerian matter and called upon all nations to refrain from interfering. But in August, taking advantage of Russian opportunism—the West's refusal to supply arms—he secured Soviet arms, jet fighter planes, and technicians. Biafran forces, though numerically far inferior, were rapidly advancing upon Lagos. (At the high point of their offensive, in September, 1967, the Biafrans were within 100 miles of the capital.) The British Government thereupon reversed policy, evidently in the belief that the shorter the war, the better Britain's prospects of maintaining her influence in Nigeria and limiting that of the Soviets. Arguing further that Britain was left with no other choice, Whitehall mounted a major supply effort that eventually outpaced Russian deliveries.[79]

These arms deliveries to Nigeria, the position taken by the Organization of African Unity against the secession (and also against U.N. involvement), and the respect accorded the Nigerian blockade by most nations greatly decreased Biafra's prospects. Only four African states—Tanzania, Zambia, the Ivory Coast, and Gabon—recognized the republic, on the basis, however, of the justness and evident popularity (in the east) of the secession, not of Biafra's right to self-determination.[80] Of these four states, the latter two, formerly French colonies, served as transit points for French aid, which was the major source of Biafra's external arms support. The assistance was hardly sufficient to overcome the logistical and manpower advantage of the government forces. By early 1968, if not before, the Biafrans were being pushed gradually backward; and when an armistice was arranged on January 12, 1970, the republic had been reduced to about one-tenth of its original size.

The American choice of "neutrality" during the civil war was based on practical calculation rather than adherence to legal or moral principle. The Congo precedent must surely have preoccupied the administration. There was no eagerness to undertake another intervention, especially since Vietnam had first priority. British and Soviet arms were going to the same side, moreover, and the threat of a communist-instigated domino effect in Africa such as had weighed heavily in decisions of the early 1960's was nonexistent in Nigeria.

Above all, "neutrality" was an easy choice because the British were standing in for American interests. Washington, in turn, sought to ease Britain's intervention by arguing publicly that British arms sales were justified—and Soviet sales were not—since London was a traditional supplier of Nigeria. The two governments shared a concern about the disorderly impact of a successful secession on other tribally heterogeneous African states, even without communist involvement. They also seemed to believe the Soviet deliveries *had* to be matched—an almost automatic response similar to that in the Congo conflict, although on that occasion London and Washington took different sides—in order to preserve Western influence. Finally, both powers may have been disturbed at the prospect of having their access to Nigerian oil deposits upset by the war. Nigeria was known to have immense oil resources that were largely untapped, and the newest oil fields were in the eastern region's coastal areas.[81] The oil companies at first negotiated with the Biafrans on payment of revenues, but backed out when Lagos imposed a blockade on tankers and the fortunes of war turned against Biafra. With the Suez Canal closed because of the Six Day War, Britain needed Nigerian oil and could not "afford" to dicker with a rebel government.[82] Hence, for political, strategic, and probably economic reasons, American "neutrality" anticipated and quietly supported a British-assisted Nigerian defeat of the Biafran revolt.

And what of the Biafran cause? At the time of the war, Biafra, like Katanga, represented a minority of the national population (about 30 per cent). But Biafrans had a stronger claim to self-determination based on historic regional and tribal differences, the breakdown of negotiations on a new political order, the pogrom against Easterners, territorial control and popular support, and, once the war began, widespread starvation in the east that, Biafrans contended, was a deliberate Nigerian policy. Being in the minority, however, Biafra could not expect support from many African states or from the major powers. What her leaders *had* a right to expect was that all governments would refrain from intervening, directly or indirectly, to tip the scales further in Nigeria's favor. Had the Soviet Union and Great Britain stayed outside the conflict, the results might have been quite different. At most, the Biafran forces might have succeeded sufficiently to prompt further regional defections from the federation, as was their goal. At the least, they could have fought a defensive, guerrilla-style battle against Nigerian forces for a protracted period.

The United States was clearly in no position to prevent other governments from taking sides in the civil war. But American neutrality might have proceeded from an effort to judge the specific issues in the contest, including moral and humanitarian considerations. In that case, Washington would not simply have refrained from selling arms to Nigeria or Biafra, it would have criticized those who were so involved, it would have sympathized with the motivations behind Biafra's decision to secede, and it would have urged a cease-fire and negotiations, in contrast with the Nigerian Government's position. The defeat of the Biafran revolt and the restoration of order in Nigeria made American policy appear eminently sensible. But the narrow "realism" on which that policy was based proved appropriate only because the alignment of external forces favored an eventual Nigerian victory. As we shall see in the case of Bangladesh, a similar policy could as readily lead to stunning defeat.

Preserving the Status Quo in Southern Africa

"Self-Determination" in Portuguese Africa

The Congo story shows how strategic and economic imperatives can take precedence over nationalism in American policy-making. U.S. policy toward Portuguese Africa is a similar story. Although the components of American thinking, and the manner of U.S. involvement, may appear at first glance to bear little similarity to those in the Congo crisis, the essence of the policy—to act in accordance with American self-interest, most narrowly construed, rather than on the basis of proclaimed American principles— brings the two cases close together. Policy toward Portuguese colonialism is another case of collaborative intervention, this time against independence movements.

There was a brief moment at the start of the Kennedy Administration when, notwithstanding the alliance with Portugal in NATO and the Azores bases, the American Government cast votes in the United Nations against Portuguese colonial interests. The first vote came after the start of widespread rebellion in Angola (March, 1961). (The rebellions in Guinea-Bissau and Mozambique broke out in 1962 and 1964.) The American action was a rude awakening for Lisbon, whose argument that colonial matters were within the domestic jurisdiction of Portugal (the colonies were declared to be provinces of the metropole in 1951), hence not subject to U.N. debate or interference, had been good enough for Eisenhower. To compound the agony for the Portuguese, the commercial sale of arms was banned and U.S. military assistance was reduced from $25 million to $3 million in 1961.[83]

By 1962, however, the administration had begun to shift gears on Angola, showing that, contrary to Schlesinger's conclusion quoted earlier, the March, 1961, vote had not "liberated the United States from its position of systematic deference to the old colonial powers." Military aid to Portugal increased and a long-term loan was floated by American banks.[84] The Berlin crisis seems to have been the chief reason: The Azores bases were important in 1961 for airlift and refueling (they had been used before in the Lebanon intervention), and they would be needed in case of another showdown with the Russians.[85] Events in the Congo may also have been influential, partly for bureaucratic reasons,* partly because of the administration's continued anxiety about falling dominoes in Africa (Angola being next door to the Congo), and perhaps partly because of the Angolan revolutionaries' radicalism. No longer was self-determination the guideline of U.S. voting in the United Nations. Although the American delegation, then and since, has paid lip service to aspirations for independence in the colonies, occasionally chided Lisbon for failing to carry out social and political reforms, and even expressed an interest in sending a U.N. mission to investigate, it began in 1962 to reject or abstain on every Afro-Asian resolution that condemned Portuguese rule or called for the application of sanctions against Portugal. The consistent message of American spokesmen has been that the United States *believes* in self-determination and *encourages* understanding between Portuguese authorities and Africans, but *declines* to interfere in the affairs of an ally. The Portuguese suppression of liberation movements in Africa has been deemed not a fit subject for U.N. action, much less independent U.S. pressure.

Outside the U.N. chambers, indirect American military and economic support of Portugal's struggles to maintain her empire have also, and rightly, drawn the fire of African spokesmen. For at the same time as American delegates have expressed hopes for

---

* Having resisted the advice of the Europeanists in the State Department on Congo affairs, Kennedy may have found it difficult to turn them away again on Angola and the Azores, especially since their position had the military's strong support. Moreover, since Congo policy was dictated by concern over a Russian base in central Africa, an anti-Portuguese policy that would favor the revolutionaries may have been considered inconsistent with, and ultimately capable of undermining, the administration's effort to bring a "moderate" pro-Western government to power in Léopoldville.

Portuguese-African solidarity, the United States in a variety of ways has been paying Portugal's way in Angola and the other colonies. Through bilateral military assistance, compensation for use of the Azores, military training programs, the guarantee of private investments in Angola, trade with the colonies, and U.S. Government approved sales to Portugal of "commercial" items having military uses, Washington has greatly, perhaps critically, contributed to the survival of Portuguese rule.

In 1961, President Nkrumah of Ghana asserted that "Portugal is only able to wage a colonial war because fundamentally she has the backing of the North Atlantic Treaty Organization. If this backing were withdrawn tomorrow and Portugal was excluded from NATO, Portugal's colonial rule would collapse the day after."[86] If the statement is an exaggeration, it is only slightly so, since, without American and European support, the already severe strain on Portugal's budget caused by the colonial wars would probably become unbearable. Although American officials have rarely admitted that Lisbon diverts U.S. aid for NATO purposes to the colonies, the diversion is so substantial that, like covert American operations in Southeast Asia, it is an open secret. Evidence of the diversion has been systematically compiled, and a U.N. Special Committee investigation in 1962 confirmed Portugal's "extensive" use of NATO arms in Angola.[87] Perhaps the clearest proof is that about 130,000 men of Portugal's armed forces of approximately 218,000 are stationed in Angola, Mozambique, and Guinea-Bissau.[88] Along with the equipment these forces require, a major portion of Portugal's defense budget, part of which is subsidized by U.S. military aid,* must go to their maintenance.

* The total U.S. military assistance program for Portugal in fiscal years 1950–70 has been reported as $319.7 million, of which $310.2 million was delivered before FY 1964. In FY 1969 and FY 1970, the program's value was just under $1 million a year. (U.S. Senate, Committee on Foreign Relations, Subcommittee on United States Security Agreements and Commitments Abroad, *Hearings: Spain and Portugal*, 91st Cong., 2d Sess., part 11, March 11, April 14, 1969 and July 17, 1970 [Washington, D.C.: Government Printing Office, 1970], p. 2406.) Pointing to the decreased value of the program in recent years, the State and Defense departments have argued (*ibid.*, p. 2404) that it is not relevant to Portugal's ability to fight the three-front revolution in Africa. But the argument ignores the arms stockpile that earlier U.S. military aid enabled the Portuguese to build. It also fails to take account of the many other ways American sources contribute to the Portuguese budget (discussed

The transfer of such funds and equipment is in clear violation of both the North Atlantic Treaty, which does not cover the colonies, and U.S.-Portugal defense agreements since 1951, which state that American assistance is to be used solely to promote defense of the North Atlantic area.

Portugal also benefits from military equipment and other funds given it by Washington to use the Azores air and naval facilities,* as well as NATO naval facilities in Lisbon. The precise value is difficult to pin down, since payment (actually, rent) occurs in a variety of forms. For example, the total should include expenditures by the U.S. military—over $19 million in Fiscal Year 1970[89] —to maintain the bases and forces stationed there; deliveries of warships, military supplies, and aircraft; and Export-Import Bank credits and straight economic assistance that, under the December 9, 1971, Executive Agreement, were part of a $436 million package deal.[90] The United States also conducts a military training program for Portuguese officers, in Portugal and in the United States. And, despite the 1961 embargo, which Nixon Administration officials maintain still is in effect "against the shipment of U.S. arms and military equipment for use in these territories," government-backed loans have enabled Lisbon's state-owned commercial airlines to purchase Boeing jets that officials admit can carry military passengers.[91]

While U.S. military equipment, funds, and training are being used against the independence movements, American investors are putting millions of dollars into the colonies' mineral and offshore

---

below), thereby directly supporting counterinsurgency and colonial rule or indirectly supporting it by freeing funds the Portuguese Government might not otherwise have available.

* After 1962, when the initial base agreement expired, the Azores were used by the United States under a unilateral Portuguese extension that Premier Salazar insisted upon because of unpalatable U.S. voting in the United Nations. In 1971, the Nixon Administration chose the device of an Executive Agreement that extended the agreement for five years. The administration claimed it did not need to seek Senate approval, since the agreement was merely an implementation of the North Atlantic alliance treaty. The real reason for using an Executive Agreement apparently was to avoid the kind of full-scale airing of American policy toward Portugal and the colonies that submission of the Azores accords as a treaty would surely have entailed.

petroleum resources. Over thirty U.S. companies were established in Angola and Mozambique by 1970. The total value of their investments is at least $200 million, and a U.N. study in 1965 concluded that the revenues thus provided were helping perpetuate colonial rule to the detriment of the African inhabitants. Since then, the Portuguese authorities have actively sought out foreign investors by liberalizing their tax and profit regulations. With the United States guaranteeing corporate investments against "political risk" through AID's Overseas Private Investment Corporation, the incentives for private American investment are substantial. The colonial authorities clearly want U.S. and other companies of the NATO nations (especially Britain) to develop a stake in Portuguese African "stability" and make the colonies self-sufficient. American business, backed by the government, seems quite willing to help Lisbon in both regards.

Just as American corporate revenue sustains Portuguese rule— as one example, the major U.S. company in Angola, Gulf Oil, had invested about $130 million by 1969[92]—American trade with the territories, especially Angola, also redounds chiefly to Portugal's profit. The United States is an important market for Angolan coffee (the major export), of which it buys over 50 per cent; overall, the United States accounts for about 12 per cent of Angola's imports and nearly 24 per cent of its exports, in both cases second only to Portugal.[93]

There are compelling reasons why the United States should eliminate all the above sources of support of Portuguese colonialism in Africa. The Azores, in spite of their usefulness to the United States during the 1973 Middle East war for shipping arms to Israel, are not vital for U.S. strategic or tactical purposes. The primarily logistical functions of the air and naval facilities there, as congressional testimony by Pentagon officials has acknowledged, can be carried out at alternative locations (though at greater cost), and may soon be superseded by improvements in long-range airlift and sealift capability. Fears that Portugal might pull out of NATO, or that the alliance itself might be shocked into disrepair, have little substance. Portugal contributes negligibly to NATO (since there are so few of its forces stationed on the continent), and some, perhaps most, of the NATO partners would welcome ending their politically embarrassing association with colonialism and of Portuguese claims on NATO's military resources.*

American officials have also contended over the years, *inter alia*, that support of Portugal is important as an alternative to violence. President Nixon stated: "We are convinced that the use of violence holds no promise as the solution to the problems of southern Africa."[94] What the President meant, and what U.S. officials have consistently supported, is the preference for colonialism over revolutionary nationalism, *especially* in the white minority–run countries of southern Africa, where the American economic stake, in trade and investments, far exceeds that in the rest of Africa.[95] The installation of radical nationalist governments in Angola and Mozambique would heighten racial tensions in South Africa and Rhodesia. Considerable pressure would be exerted on the ruling white elites to relax their stance on black political and social rights or face externally supported insurgency. Neither regime would necessarily be in danger of extinction; but the "instability" that Portugal's departure would create has always seemed to disturb American businessmen and officials alike. South African, Rhodesian, and Portuguese authorities have played on their concern by equating a nationalist victory with the extension of communism.

The appropriate counterargument to the fear of revolution must be that identification with it will serve U.S. interests, whether conceived in moral, political, or economic terms, better than opposition to it. Eventually, the independence movements in Portuguese Africa will succeed—the Guinea-Bissau movement declared itself an independent government in September, 1973—and the Portuguese will be thrown out. When the day comes, one year or ten years from now, where should the United States find itself? It is not necessary and it is not desired that Washington become an active partner of the insurgents. What is essential is that, in the case of Portuguese Africa or any other anticolonial struggle (that of the Viet Minh against France is an obvious parallel), the

---

* It is by no means certain, moreover, that a complete embargo on military aid to Portugal would result in termination of the Azores agreement. The threat is there; but American refusal to pay more blackmail money might force Lisbon officials to conclude that they need the money Americans invest in the Azores in spite of the embargo.

United States *not support the colonialist power,* directly or in-directly.

Morally and *humanistically,* such a policy would square espousal of self-determination and anticolonialism with preparedness to honor the government's own embargo. American training, funds, and military hardware would no longer be playing a part in the repression of African peoples. It is unacceptable to contend, as the State and Defense departments have, that U.S. aid to Portugal is a small fraction of the total Portuguese budget and that Portugal can procure arms elsewhere. If U.S. allies in Europe are willing, as in the past, to sell arms to Portugal, that should not be a pretext for American complicity. The same guideline should apply to American trade and private investment: Washington is in a position to bar the former and discourage the latter.

Politically, American association with Afro-Asian proposals to enact sanctions against Portugal would, as happened in 1961, hearten all black African governments (some of which, through the OAU, have long been sending military assistance to the revolutionaries) and do much to counter charges of U.S. neocolonialism. Cutting off aid to Portugal should also facilitate contacts with the revolutionary leaders, whose alienation from the West surely deepens with every year of American and NATO support for Lisbon. Such contacts would enhance the prospects for healthy relations between the United States and the postrevolutionary governments, including equitable, mutually beneficial trade relations, private investments, and technical assistance programs. The longer Washington delays acceptance of the nationalist credentials of the independence movements, the more radicalized, anti-American, and dependent (for political and military support) on Moscow or Peking they are likely to become. The violence Nixon and past Presidents have feared seems destined to sharpen rather than abate if American policy remains wedded to the colonialists.

"Peaceful Pressures" in South Africa and Rhodesia

Since American policy toward the Portuguese territories has been related as intimately to South Africa and Rhodesia as to NATO politics, some further word seems in order about recent developments in U.S. relations with those two white racist regimes.

Speaking of Africa, Richard Nixon reported in 1971: "To an unusual degree, our conception of the current realities is unencumbered by the weight of previous undertakings."[96] In fact, U.S. policy is significantly weighted down by the past—by the traditional belief that "diplomacy and peaceful pressures" rather than uncompromising sanctions and isolation are the best means of inducing change in the racist policies and attitudes of Johannesburg and Salisbury; and by continuation of profitable business relations with both countries in the belief (or on the pretext) that the United States thereby maintains a constructive dialogue with them.

Like previous administrations, Nixon's has acquiesced in sanctions authorized by the international community (led by the Afro-Asian nations) but has not strictly applied them nor initiated pressures of its own. On the one hand, the government does not recognize the Smith regime in Rhodesia, condemns *apartheid* in South Africa, supports a (1970) Security Council arms embargo and other measures to weaken South African control over Namibia (South West Africa), and maintains it respects an embargo on arms shipments to South Africa as well. On the other hand, certain types of business transactions with Rhodesia continue—the sale of assets by U.S. firms, and, by congressional legislation (the Byrd Amendment), the importation of chrome ore, despite a U.N. sanction voted in 1972. Condemnation of *apartheid* has not kept American businesses from importing goods produced by forced labor or investing in and developing South African industries that favor the technical skills of Europeans.[97] Nor has it affected the government's Export-Import Bank credits for exports to South Africa, its maintenance of a satellite tracking station that reportedly discriminates against blacks, or its unwillingness to appoint a black American to a diplomatic post in South Africa.[98] The embargo on arms for South Africa was stretched under Nixon to permit the sale of spare parts for old types of military aircraft, as well as of commercial jets with potential military uses.[99]

Policy toward southern Africa, like policy during the Congolese civil war, has thus been short-sighted, deceitful, and self-deluding. It has failed to acknowledge and come to terms with radical nationalist movements and popular aspirations for self-determination. It has conspired with minority colonialist leaderships to prolong their authority, all the while proclaiming support for independence, sanctions, and social justice. And, in the name of stability and peaceful change, it has contributed to the likelihood of more intense and widespread violence in Africa—violence that encourages racial polarization and perpetuates armed confrontation between the white regimes and their black neighboring states. No doubt, simple bureaucratic inertia and the resistance to change of entrenched interest groups form part of the explanation of American unwillingness to match policy with principle. But strategic, economic, and ideological interests and anxieties have also been responsible. So long as these elements continue to exert influence, intervention in some form—as in the Congo and Portuguese Africa—and support of the forces of reaction—as in South Africa and Rhodesia—will be the characteristics of American policy in Africa that many Third World governments will keep foremost in mind.

4

Johnson and Latin America

THE "SPECIAL RELATIONSHIP"

Political and Military Dimensions

All great powers have traditionally considered the areas adjacent to them to be their special preserve, usually for a combination of military, economic, and political reasons. At the close of World War II, this spheres-of-influence concept was very nearly formalized in the Churchill-Stalin understanding of October, 1944, that, on Germany's defeat, Britain and the United States would exercise predominant influence in Greece, while the Soviet Union would have "50%" to "90%" of foreign influence in Rumania and Bulgaria (Yugoslavia and Hungary being evenly divided). President Roosevelt found the understanding distasteful, but developments at the war's end led to its implementation. Stalin's thinking that the Balkans and Eastern Europe were properly within the Soviet sphere, that Western Europe and Greece belonged to the Anglo-French-American sphere, and that Latin America (plus Japan later on) was rightfully America's became a reality.

In Eastern Europe, Soviet governments have consistently maintained the right to intervene in order to prevent the evolution of circumstances inimical to Russia's political system, military security, or economic well-being. The so-called Brezhnev Doctrine of 1968 merely articulated, with unusual bluntness, a long-standing premise of Soviet relations with its neighbors, one that had led to intervention in Hungary, Poland, and Czechoslovakia. In Latin America, rules of the game with similar purposes have been established by the United States. One is that access to Latin America by U.S. diplomats, public and private enterprise, and a range of other "contacts" (from CIA agents and military attaches to trade union officials and professors) must be preserved to the broadest extent possible. A second is the obverse of the first: Access to the region by hostile influences should be limited or denied if they threaten (or appear to threaten) American security, political and economic paramountcy, and access. Fidel Castro's social revolution in Cuba was a seminal event in U.S.–Latin American relations because it violated these rules. The 1965 Dominican intervention, which is the main study of this chapter, was a direct outgrowth of successive U.S. failures to contain, subvert, and weaken Castro, who had suddenly denied the United States access to Cuba, accepted a Soviet presence instead, and threatened to infect other countries with his antihegemonic "disease."

American governments throughout this century have considered the *domestic conditions* as well as the foreign policies of Latin American countries to have a direct bearing on U.S. access. They have therefore propounded a third rule: that the independence of Latin American governments is qualified to the extent they are unable to maintain political stability, promote public order against subversive forces, and protect American lives and property. The United States reserves the right to act to secure that independence, on its own behalf and on behalf of the Latin American community. Within its sphere of influence, like the U.S.S.R. in Eastern Europe, the United States claims the powers of chief arbiter and upholder of law and order. In contrast with interventions elsewhere in the Third World, U.S. administrations have had broader congressional support on Latin America and have not felt as constrained by the views of nonhemispheric allies, the possibilities of Soviet or Chinese counteraction, or international law.

The sources of these three rules run deep in American history. It was to preserve U.S. influence and access that the Monroe Doctrine (December, 1823) declared: ". . . we should consider any attempt on their [the European colonial powers'] part to extend their system to any portion of this hemisphere as dangerous to our peace and safety." The corollary of Secretary of State

Richard Olney in July, 1895, was bolder: "To-day the United States is practically sovereign on this continent, and its fiat is law upon the subjects to which it confines its interposition." Theodore Roosevelt extended America's "fiat" to cover the political and social stability of Latin American societies. In his corollaries of 1904 and 1905, Roosevelt referred to "the exercise of an international police power" as a part of the U.S. obligation under the Monroe Doctrine in cases of "chronic wrongdoing," uncivilized behavior, "wrong actions" toward America or Americans, and inability to maintain justice and order by the region's governments.

The assumptions of American pre-eminence that lay behind these pronouncements underpinned a protracted period of U.S. "interpositions" in the Caribbean area. Beginning in Cuba in 1898, after the end of Spanish rule, the period did not come to a close until 1934 and the withdrawal of American forces from Haiti. (In all, according to a House Committee on Foreign Affairs publication, Presidential employment of U.S. forces in Latin America occurred over one hundred times between 1806 and 1933.)[1] The purposes of these interventions were similar to those in Guatemala, Cuba, and the Dominican Republic in recent years, leading one writer to propose "that the United States has historically acted as an outlaw with respect to civil strife in Latin America."[2]

One purpose of these earlier interventions was to acquire economic or military privileges for American public and private concerns. The 1903 Platt Amendment tied Cuba closely to the United States and secured a naval facility at Guantanamo on long-term lease. U.S. aid and encouragement to Panamanian revolutionaries against Colombia in 1903, after Colombia had rejected a U.S. proposal to begin construction of an interoceanic canal, enabled Roosevelt to obtain sovereign U.S. rights "in perpetuity" over the Canal Zone from an independent Panama. Military intervention in Nicaragua in 1912 quelled a revolution that threatened to upset American ambitions for rights to a second interoceanic canal route—rights that were granted two years later in the Bryan-Chamorro Treaty.

A second basic American purpose in intervening was to establish order, thus securing the assets and safety of U.S. corporations and citizens. Such was the case when Secretary of War Taft became provisional governor of Cuba from 1906 to 1909 in the wake of a political upheaval; when fiscal and then military authority was imposed on Haiti in 1914 and 1915 (a protectorate was established by treaty in 1916) to restore financial and political order, which took about twenty years; and when another revolution in Nicaragua in 1927 led President Coolidge to dispatch marines (they stayed until 1933) to protect U.S. investments and canal rights, and to reinstitute order and "good government."

A closely related reason for U.S. intervention was to prevent internal warfare from leading to revolution and economic chaos. President Taft's application of Dollar Diplomacy to Nicaragua in 1912 was intended, in his words, to remove "at one stroke the menace of foreign creditors and the menace of revolutionary disorder." Military intervention in, and occupation of, Santo Domingo in 1916 under Wilson was to protect growing U.S. sugar interests and stabilize customs revenue collection. American administration of the Dominican customs, which had begun in 1907, continued until 1940, while the occupation lasted until 1924. And for a third time in Cuba, from 1917 to 1923, U.S. troops were dispatched following a disputed presidential election. The American presence protected U.S. business interests, reformed Cuba's national finances, and enabled the government in power to avoid a possible revolution.

Finally, U.S. interventions have had a demonstrative purpose: to show a willingness and ability to use force to assert American supremacy, and thus preserve U.S. "honor" and freedom of action in the region as a whole. When, for instance, the Mexican leader, General Huerta, refused to order a twenty-one gun salute in apology for the arrest of American sailors at Tampico in 1914, President Wilson ordered forces across the border. The Mexican people, said Wilson, "are entitled to settle their own domestic affairs"; but the United States must act "to keep our great influence unimpaired for the uses of liberty, both in the United States and wherever else it may be employed for the benefit of mankind." President Coolidge made a similar distinction concerning the Nicaragua intervention in 1927, arguing that while it was not America's "desire" to become involved in Nicaragua's domestic affairs, "the stability, prosperity, and independence of all

Central American countries can never be a matter of indifference to us."

Franklin Roosevelt's Good Neighbor policy represented a temporary turning away from traditional interventionism. In part, the very success of interventionism during previous decades made abandoning it feasible,[3] though without renouncing the principles of Monroe, Olney, and Theodore Roosevelt. The main reason for the shift, however, was the Nazi threat. Pledges at Montevideo (1933), Buenos Aires (1936), and Lima (1938) of nonintervention in Latin American affairs were the *quid pro quo* of regional solidarity and joint action to keep Nazi influence out of America's sphere.[4] This much became apparent in the postwar period, when international communism replaced Nazism as America's major foreign opponent. Under Truman, Roosevelt's concept of collective defense against external aggression was expanded even as the nonintervention principle was reaffirmed. The "deal" that was struck entailed renewed promises of North American respect for Latin domestic sovereignty, defense assistance under the Mutual Security Program, military cooperation in an Inter-American Joint Defense Board, and technical assistance under the Point Four program. Latin American governments would provide a hospitable climate for U.S. investment, subscribe to the anticommunist containment strategy, build up their defense forces, and broaden their interpretation of the meaning of (communist) "aggression" so as to increase the latitude for (U.S.-led) collective action.[5]

The legal underpinnings of this arrangement were the Inter-American (Rio) Treaty of Reciprocal Assistance of 1947 and the 1948 Bogotá Charter of the Organization of American States.[6] The Rio Treaty establishes "an armed attack by any State against an American State" as the basis of collective action; but it also provides for immediate consultation to decide on joint measures in the event of "an aggression which is not an armed attack," including "any other fact or situation that might endanger the peace of America." These latter clauses, because of their open-endedness, were useful to the United States in two respects. They helped to focus attention on communist subversion, as in Resolution 32 agreed upon at Bogotá. It declared "international Communism . . . incompatible with the concept of American freedom" and urged the member states to take steps against foreign-sponsored propaganda and threats.[7] And these clauses effectively nullified the U.N. Security Council's authorizing power (under Article 53 of the Charter) in cases of regional collective action. A Soviet veto, such as would have been exercised in the Cuban and Dominican cases, could be avoided.[8]

Presumably, most of the Latin American singers of the Rio pact felt protected against arbitrary U.S. intervention by two articles of the OAS Charter. The Charter, while reiterating the above principles of Rio, states in Articles 15 and 17:

> No state or group of States has the right to intervene, directly or indirectly, for any reason whatever, in the internal or external affairs of any other State. The foregoing principle prohibits not only armed force but also any other form of interference or attempted threat against the personality of the State or against its political, economic and cultural elements.

> The territory of a State is inviolable; it may not be the object, even temporarily, of military occupation or of other measures taken by another State, directly or indirectly, on any grounds whatever. No territorial acquisitions or special advantages obtained either by force or by other means of coercion shall be recognized.

As the Guatemalan, Cuban, and Dominican cases would show, nonintervention has been acceptable to American administrations only so long as Latin "instability"—the "communist threat"—has not jeopardized U.S. business and political interests. At that point, American officials have consistently put the need of "collective" defense ahead of the nonintervention principle. For example, Adolf Berle, a key State Department official on Latin American affairs in both the Roosevelt and Kennedy administrations, wrote in 1962 that the principle of individual or collective self-defense "is necessarily supreme and overriding," meaning that an "attack" on a Latin American state would give the United States the "right" both of self-defense and defense of the "attacked" state.[9] And since, as Secretary of State Acheson had testified some years earlier,[10] an internal communist-supported revolution would be considered an "armed attack" within the meaning of the Rio Treaty, it would rest with the American Government to decide whether to intervene, notwithstanding Articles 15 and 17. After all, an Eisenhower Administration official proposed, "nonintervention can only be a reality so long as an adequate collective system of security is available to all States."[11] But it was left to President Kennedy to draw the limit of nonintervention in boldest terms:

> Should it ever appear that the inter-American doctrine of noninterference merely conceals or excuses a policy of nonaction—if the nations of this hemisphere should fail to meet their commitments against outside Communist penetration—then I want it clearly understood that this Government will not hesitate in meeting its primary obligations, which are to the security of our Nation.[12]

In short, both at the time the treaties were signed and thereafter, Washington reserved the right of intervention under the collective defense principle. The Latin American governments were either persuaded or hoped that in defending them against "communist aggression," the United States would not repeat the "interpositions" of the past in their domestic affairs. They underestimated the possibility of "protective" or pre-emptive interventions by the United States in their name.

The Economic Dimension

U.S. policy has been to make Latin America dependent on the United States not only for its supposed external security needs but also for its economic well-being. American economic penetration takes such forms as assistance grants, bilateral and multilateral development loans,[13] private investment, trade, and government-funded trade unions that promote the capitalist anticommunist ethic supportive of overseas business.[14] In the Eisenhower years, these were regarded principally as methods of shoring up the Latin economies in the belief that the bigger their foreign trade, the stronger the American (hence, the entire Free World's) economy. Not until the Kennedy-Johnson years and the Alliance for Progress did economic penetration also become a specifically strategic weapon. By greatly expanding U.S. economic aid, vigorously promoting private capitalism, and condoning the trade union movement's collaboration on occasion with the CIA[15]—all while shifting military assistance to emphasize internal defense, so that Latin armies would turn from making coups to civic action and counterinsurgency—Kennedy added new dimensions to containment. The Alliance for Progress was meant to be an alternative to U.S. military intervention in keeping the Americas free of communist subversion, in large part by making them more open to U.S. corporate profit-making.

The Alliance for Progress was launched in August, 1961, at the Punta del Este (Uruguay) Conference. The program's ten-year commitment of $20 billion in public and private funds to economic growth, agrarian reform, education, and a variety of "social development" projects probably would not have received Kennedy's concerted support had Fidel Castro not existed. Indeed, Kennedy's announcement of the Alliance in March, 1961, came only a month before the Bay of Pigs invasion was launched. He posed for a hesitant Congress the choice of either funding the Alliance or risking "a grave danger that desperate peoples will turn to communism or other forms of tyranny as their only hope for change. Well-organized, skillful, and strongly financed forces are constantly urging them to take that course."[16] The task force he assembled after his election had earlier reported to him that Latin communism "resembles, but is more dangerous than, the Nazi-Fascist threat of the Franklin Roosevelt period and demands an even bolder and more imaginative response."[17] A new program, it was therefore recommended, should seek to identify with the democratic ("progressive") left and land reform, deny recognition to dictatorships and regimes that had come to power by coup, and emphasize—in the later words of Dean Rusk—"the prospects of peaceful change through constructive, democratic processes as an alternative to change through the destructive extremism offered by the Communists."[18]

The notion of social revolution by evolution, thus placing a premium on stability, specifically meant enlarging opportunities for American private enterprise. One of the chief architects of "development" as an anticommunist strategy, Walt W. Rostow, would write with respect to the Alliance that foreign capitalist expansion needed "scope for real initiative and creativeness, a real basis for collaboration with governments, and a way of demonstrating to all the people its inherent virtues."[19] Yet Kennedy found in 1961 that U.S. private investment in Latin America had declined by about a billion dollars since 1957. The business community, especially after Castro's victory, was reluctant to invest in unstable societies and was putting pressure on Washington "to talk less about social reform and more about private investment. They had a point," Arthur Schlesinger comments, "since all the Alliance's capital requirements presupposed an annual flow of $300 million of United States private funds to Latin America."[20]

Through legislation passed in Kennedy's tenure and added to later on, the climate for investment improved significantly. In the 1960's, as Table I shows, private and government investment became increasingly profitable. By 1965, of U.S. assets and investments world-wide, about 17 per cent (over $18 billion) were in Latin America.[21] Investment and tough conditions on U.S. loans

TABLE I.
U.S. INVESTMENTS IN LATIN AMERICA:
INCOME ADVANTAGE (RECEIPTS LESS PAYMENTS)*

(in millions of dollars)

	1960	1965	1970
Direct private	$720	$991	$1,059
Private long-term holdings	100	147	107
U.S. Government	64	116	150

* Source: *Statistical Abstract*, 92d ed., 1971, p. 754.

to Latin governments were the linchpins of an essentially counter-radical strategy, a Latin Marshall Plan to "channel the revolution . . . in the proper direction and prevent it from being taken over by the Sino-Soviet bloc."[22]

Trade was, and still is, an important component of that strategy. Although it is frequently maintained that U.S. corporations and the government require raw and strategic materials from Latin America, such as sugar, oil, and copper,[23] the over-all picture of Latin American dependence on the United States as an export market and supplier (primarily of manufactured goods), as well as the principal source of investment capital, may be more relevant to understanding U.S. policy. While certain U.S. businesses and the government, in other words, may have need of particular

Latin commodities, none would seem to be so critical (that is, unavailable elsewhere) as to account for, say, the persistent U.S. interventions in Latin affairs. From an economic standpoint, U.S. interventions may be motivated less by the need for specific commodities than by the determination to maintain Latin dependency and to show by example that local government actions hostile to U.S. economic interests will not be tolerated. The U.S. share of Latin America's world trade has, as the figures in Table II show, declined slightly in recent years; but it remains quite imposing and gives Washington great leverage over Latin domestic policy-making.

TABLE II.

U.S.–LATIN AMERICA TRADE*

(in billions of dollars)

	L.A. exports to U.S.	L.A. exports world-wide	U.S. exports to L.A.	World-wide exports to L.A.
1955	$3.5	$8.0	$3.3	$7.5
1960	3.6	8.6	3.6	8.3
1966	3.9	11.7	4.2	10.6
1969	4.1	13.5	4.9	13.2

* Sources: *UN Statistical Yearbook,* 1964, p. 464; 1967, p. 394; 1970, p. 402; 1971, p. 412.

There is another political dimension to the U.S.–Latin America economic relationship that is often overlooked. Doing business with Latin America, especially private enterprise, will always be important to Washington, because capitalism's "presence" promotes the kind of "development" that makes communism a threat to local governments and entrepreneurs. K. H. Silvert has put the issue well:

Adolf Berle is correct in saying that economically the United States can live without Latin America. But is there here also an implication that we can live as well culturally if a potentially major group of Western nations chooses developmental paths that may isolate the democracies of European orientation conceptually and ideologically more than they need to be? Latin America is the largest readily available reservoir of recruits to Western modernism in the world.[24]

The North American development model, to the extent it is emulated or adopted by Latin societies, complements the security aspect of containment.

The economic and strategic calculations that prompted the Alliance for Progress became increasingly irrelevant by the early 1970's. The insurgent threat from Cuba was generally seen as diffuse and remote; revolutionaries, to the limited extent that they could attract a following, seemed to be turning from rural to urban guerrilla warfare; the democratic left failed to demonstrate a commitment to reform, while the military continued to show an interest in coups; the increased U.S. capital flow to the region did not spark an economic takeoff; and anti-American nationalism found renewed expression in expropriations of corporate property. As one writer summarized the state of the Alliance in 1970,

> The key premise of the Alliance—the simultaneous compatibility of all its objectives: economic growth, social equity, political stability, constitutional democracy, the promotion of U.S. national security —has been continuously undermined since 1961. It has become clear instead that each of the Alliance's objectives is difficult to achieve, that they may be impossible to accomplish simultaneously (at least in the short run), and that U.S. security may not be threatened in any immediate sense even if none of the other goals is attained.[25]

Accordingly, the economic half of the Nixon Administration's Latin America policy has reflected a banker's caution about how much economic growth, political pluralism, and internal security really can be bought with aid and investment. Much more aid than before is being channeled through international and regional institutions. The President promised to reduce barriers to the expansion of Latin American exports. And he ordered the removal of many restrictions on the ways in which U.S. assistance loans could be spent.[26] But the administration remains firmly in control of the levers of economic influence. As a believer in the "vital role" of private enterprise abroad, Nixon took steps to improve the investment climate for American business and to stimulate the development of local private capital.[27] Bilateral U.S. economic assistance to Latin America was $762 million in fiscal year 1970. U.S. aid via the Inter-American Development Bank and the

World Bank was considerably more (about $1.5 billion),[28] and the extensive U.S. contributions to those institutions give it considerable control over the allocation of their funds. As U.S. relations with Chile in 1971 indicated, multilateral as well as bilateral aid would continue to be used, at Washington's discretion, to undermine governments whose domestic or foreign politics it considered undesirable.* The comparative aloofness of Latin America in official U.S. thinking in the early 1970's hence neither detracts from the U.S. capacity to use its influence for political and economic ends nor promises a major alteration of the practice of economic containment.

COUNTERREVOLUTION IN GUATEMALA

In the postwar period, Guatemala was the first test of Washington's commitment to the containment of radical leftism and the protection of American economic interests in Latin America. The punishing power of the "collective defense" doctrine, unilaterally implemented, was shown to have greater relevance to U.S. policy than the nonintervention principle. Speaking several years later, Eisenhower recalled "a very desperate situation . . . in Central America, and we had to get rid of a Communist government which had taken over, and our early efforts were defeated by a bad accident and we had to help, send some help right away."[29] He was referring to a CIA-engineered operation begun late in 1953 and successfully concluded in June, 1954, to overthrow the government of Jacobo Arbenz Guzman.

The Arbenz Government

The threat that Arbenz was believed to pose for American interests in Latin America was his inauguration of a social revolu-

* When the socialist government of Salvador Allende came to power in Chile, it nationalized the vast holdings of American copper mining companies without making significant compensation. Using this circumstance as its rationale, the Nixon Administration imposed a credit blockade to prevent Allende from obtaining economic aid from international, regional, and private U.S. sources, and from renegotiating Chile's debt to the Export-Import Bank and the Agency for International Development. (See James F. Petras and Robert LaPorte, Jr., "Chile: No," *Foreign Policy*, Summer, 1972, pp. 132–58.) At the same time, the United States doubled aid to the Chilean military, which overthrew Allende in 1973.

tion, which had major implications for Guatemalan politics and foreign policy. Elected in 1950, Arbenz, in a much more concerted way than his predecessor, Juan José Arevalo, took dead aim at the privileged classes and foreign capital that dominated the economy. Departing from Guatemala's century-old tradition of ruthless dictatorship, Arbenz sought to open up politics and the economic system—through constitutionally guaranteed civil liberties, the legalization of trade unions, literacy and school programs, political party competition (including the Communist Party, the PGT, legalized in 1952), and, most important, the Agrarian Reform Law of 1952. Guatemalans in the early 1950's, especially if they lived in rural areas, experienced a new dignity as well as purely economic betterment.[30]

By February, 1954, land reform had resulted in the distribution of over 180,000 hectares to about 56,000 peasants.[31] Troubling to the U.S. State Department, however, was that the 1952 law enabled the expropriation of idle banana plantation land belonging to the United Fruit Company, the major American investor in Central America. About 240,000 acres were expropriated in 1953 and another 174,000 acres in 1954. The Guatemalan Government offered compensation in bonds based on the company's own earlier valuation of its land for tax purposes. United Fruit rejected the bonds, valued at about $1.2 million, and, with State Department support, demanded $15 million.[32] The conflict was not resolved until Arbenz's overthrow, because Arbenz was clearly determined to break the hold of United Fruit and its affiliates on a major sector of the Guatemalan economy.*

In focusing land redistribution on the vast unused holdings of United Fruit, Arbenz had a powerful political issue with which

---

* United Fruit at the time had an investment of about $50 million in Guatemala (and $400 million in Central America). The company owned about 43 per cent of International Railways of Central America (IRCA), the only main-line railroad in the country and owner of the only pier at Puerto Barrios, the major port. In 1953, about 87 per cent of Guatemala's exports (by volume) and 44 per cent of imports moved through this port— and then inland on IRCA cars, at rates far below those for United Fruit's rivals. Daniel James, "Guatemala's Warning to U.S. Business," *Fortune*, July, 1953, pp. 73, 169; and Richard Allen LaBarge, "Impact of the United Fruit Company on the Economic Development of Guatemala, 1946–1954," in LaBarge *et al.*, *Studies in Middle American Economics*, Middle American Research Institute, Tulane University, New Orleans, 1968, pp. 14, 16–17.

nationalists of differing persuasions could readily identify. Yet it was the PGT that benefited most from land reform. Here lay the seeds of America's discontent, for the combination of radical nationalist leadership, rapid social change, and communist party activity in Guatemala was seen in Washington as being amenable to Soviet manipulation and direction. Inevitably, Guatemala would become the first communist state in the hemisphere. This view ignored the fact that the growth of the Guatemalan communist movement was directly occasioned by local circumstances:[33] politicization of the rural population due to land reform helped the PGT to expand its mass base; the PGT's cohesiveness, seeming incorruptibility, and staunch support of land reform contrasted with the dissension and indecisiveness characteristic of other parties; Arbenz, opposed by the Church, landowners, business, and the urban middle class, needed the PGT's support as part of a coalition (which also embraced the government bureaucracy, the army, and the PGT-dominated labor unions and peasant organizations) to carry out his programs. The communists received Arbenz's favor, in short, because they were in the vanguard of the social revolution that was central to his leadership, and because, more than any other party, they represented the demands for change of the antitraditional, newly mobile classes.

After 1952 the PGT, though having only 2,000 to 4,000 members, was rewarded with several key government posts and control of major government agencies.[34] Several party leaders visited Moscow and attended international conferences of leftist organizations. The party consistently endorsed Soviet policy positions; Arbenz himself established friendly relations with several of the socialist governments. On the basis of these facts, Washington concluded that the PGT was subordinate to the Soviet party and, being the most influential party in Guatemala, was either coming to control Arbenz or (if Arbenz was himself a communist) was in league with him on the U.S.S.R.'s behalf. Eisenhower recalled that Arbenz "by his actions soon created the strong suspicion that he was merely a puppet manipulated by Communists."[35] Secretary Dulles, reciting the reasons for U.S. opposition to Arbenz just prior to his overthrow, said he "was openly manipulated by the leaders of [world] communism. . . . It was not the power of the Arbenz government that concerned us but the power behind it."[36]

The American Ambassador to Guatemala, John E. Peurifoy, who had previously served in Greece during the civil war, was convinced Arbenz was an outright communist: "Well, Mr. Chairman, I spent 6 hours with him [one] evening, and he talked like a Communist, he thought like a Communist, he acted like a Communist, and if he is not one, Mr. Chairman, he will do until one comes along. . . . as far as I am concerned, he had all the earmarks."[37] In Peurifoy's view, it was wrong to make any distinction between local and international communism, or between economic and political Marxism. To him, the only difference between Greece and Guatemala was in the "ways [Soviet] agents operated"; the general pattern was the same.[38]

Not only did these interpretations denigrate the nationalism of Arbenz and distort the reasons for the success of the Guatemalan communists, they also exaggerated the PGT's strengths and ignored its weaknesses, several of which were mentioned in the State Department's own white paper on Guatemalan communism.[39] The paper pointed, for example, to the party's "dependence on the good will of the Guatemalan Government, particularly of the President, and at least the neutrality of the Guatemalan Armed Forces." It also noted the party's lack of trained personnel, relatively inexperienced leaders, distance from Moscow, and position of being opposed by powerful political and economic interests. To men like Dulles, however, such weaknesses did not make the communists any less dangerous. As he warned, "it must be borne in mind that the Communists always operate in terms of small minorities who gain positions of power. In Soviet Russia itself only about 3 per cent of the people are Communists."[40]

The Counterrevolution

The appointment of Ambassador Peurifoy to Guatemala in October, 1953, was apparently the first step in the Eisenhower Administration's plan to get rid of Arbenz. Although subsequently Dulles and other officials would cite a shipment of Czech arms to Guatemala and Guatemala's refusal to endorse a U.S.-sponsored anticommunism resolution in the OAS, both in 1954, as the bases of action against Arbenz, the mobilization of a counterrevolutionary team was by then well under way.[41] Peurifoy in effect was diplomatic coordinator and State's on-the-spot liaison with the CIA.[42] The Agency supplied and trained the "liberation" forces. And Carlos Castillo Armas, an army colonel trained in the United States, who had gone into exile in Honduras after an unsuccessful coup attempt in 1950, was chosen to lead the attack.

As the Guatemalan Government would charge in January, 1954, Castillo Armas entered into a "gentlemen's agreement" with another exile, Miguel Ydigoras Fuentes, that provided for free elections in Guatemala after the coup. At that time, Ydigoras recalled later, Castillo Armas

> told me that he had the promise of assistance from official United States agencies, an offer from the Government of Honduras to give him asylum and allow the common border with Guatemala to be used for the attack, that the Government of Nicaragua had also offered him arms and bases for training troops, and that Generalissimo Rafael Leonidas Trujillo of Santo Domingo [Dominican Republic] was generously supplying him with substantial economic assistance and large quantities of arms.[43]

These facts too were publicized by Arbenz's government, along with a formal indictment of U.S. involvement. There was a clearcut threat to Guatemala of a U.S.-sponsored attack supported by Guatemala's neighbors in violation of the OAS Charter.

The immediacy of the threat was dramatized by Washington's conclusion of mutual defense assistance agreements with Nicaragua and Honduras in April and May, 1954. By that time, Guatemala's relations with these and the other Central American governments, already tense in 1953 over the issues of communism and Guatemala's withdrawal from the Organization of Central American States, had deteriorated sharply. These governments, backed by U.S. officials, accused Guatemalan embassies and local communists of fomenting an eight-week strike in Honduras and infiltrating agents, spreading propaganda, and giving refuge to revolutionaries throughout the area. The Czech arms shipment to Guatemala, which arrived on May 15 by a circuitous route, was consequently interpreted (or rationalized) as giving the Guatemalan armed forces the capability to pose a direct threat to neighboring countries. Again, however, the anticommunist fervor surrounding Arbenz led to gross distortions of Guatemalan actions and intentions. To the extent the strike and other disruptions were inspired or supported by Guatemalans, they may well have been in response to the fact that Nicaragua and Honduras were known by Arbenz to be conspiring with the CIA against his government. The U.S. Ambassador to Honduras would later testify he had "to keep the Honduran Government—which was scared to death about the possibilities of themselves being overthrown—keep them in line so they would allow this revolutionary activity [by Castillo Armas] to continue, based in Honduras."[44]

Moreover, there is no evidence that the Czech arms were intended for anything but defensive purposes. In emphasizing the surreptitious nature of the shipment, Dulles and his colleagues neglected to report: that Guatemala had previously tried to obtain arms from the West; that *Swiss* arms destined for Guatemala were not shipped at Washington's request; and that the Czech arms were evidently intended to equip a civilian militia and upgrade the regular Guatemalan Army in preparation for a CIA-backed invasion. Having thus closed off all but communist sources of arms, and having converted Guatemala's neighbors into bases for aggressive activities, Washington gave Arbenz little choice except to act in self-defense.

A further step in the isolation of Guatemala came at the Tenth Inter-American Conference in Caracas, Venezuela, in March, 1954. Inclusion of discussion of communist penetration of the Americas had been requested by Washington the previous October, so that it was no surprise that the U.S. delegation, led by Dulles, proposed passage of a "Declaration of Solidarity for the Preservation of the Political Integrity of the American States Against International Communist Intervention." Guatemala was the obvious target of the declaration's key point, which was:

> That the domination or control of the political institutions of any American State by the international communist movement . . . would constitute a threat to the sovereignty and political independence of the American States, endangering the peace of America, and would call for a meeting of consultation to consider the adoption of appropriate action in accordance with existing treaties [that is, the Rio Treaty and the OAS Charter].[45]

The final vote on the declaration was 17 in favor, one (Guatemala) opposed, and two abstentions (Mexico and Argentina). There is little doubt that Latin American need of U.S. economic aid, which was the main reason for convening the conference, prompted several of the votes in favor of the declaration.[46]

The Caracas declaration was clearly intended by Washington to lend support to its ongoing plans to oust Arbenz. But at the urging of several Latin delegations, the declaration also reaffirmed the doctrine of nonintervention. Dulles had told the delegates that "the slogan of 'nonintervention' can plausibly be invoked and twisted to give immunity to what is, in fact, flagrant [communist] intervention."[47] Yet the conferees inserted in the declaration reference to the "inalienable right of each American State freely to choose its own form of government and economic system," and to do so "naturally without intervention in its internal or external affairs." In terms of positive action against "threatened" Latin governments, nothing was endorsed beyond disclosure and exchange of information and consultation to "consider" additional steps. The kinds of subversive acts against Guatemala being committed by the United States, Nicaragua, Honduras, and the Dominican Republic were by no means supported.

But the administration evidently did not believe that U.S. intervention in Latin America required specific endorsement from the Latin community. On returning home, Dulles hailed the Caracas declaration as a logical extension of the Monroe Doctrine "if it is properly backed up."[48] The United States assumed that responsibility in June. The CIA gave the 150-man "army" of Castillo Armas the green light to cross the border with Honduras on the 18th. In the United Nations, the administration sought to prevent Guatemala from presenting its case as a victim of aggression to the Security Council.

The small force under Castillo Armas, whose victory would be hailed by Dulles and Peurifoy as the result of an anticommunist uprising by Guatemalans alone, actually advanced no more than a few miles into Guatemala. It relied on three vintage bombers, supplied by the CIA and piloted by Americans, to frighten Arbenz and the army into submission. But on June 22 Eisenhower received word from Allen Dulles, the CIA director, that two of the bombers had been destroyed. The President was concerned as always that U.S. involvement achieve a military success; and he was convinced that a failure in Guatemala would be more harmful to the United States than Latin outrage at another intervention in blatant violation of the treaty clauses on nonintervention.* Eisenhower heeded Allen Dulles's advice to provide additional bombers, knowing "from experience the important psychological impact of even a small amount of air support."[49] The fact that Dulles put the chances of success for Castillo Armas at only "20 percent" did not dissuade the President in the least, perhaps partly because he could count on congressional support for further action.[50]

Eisenhower's calculation proved correct, though not entirely for the reason he expected. The Guatemalan Army refused to support Arbenz at the critical moment, and he turned power over to his loyal armed forces chief on June 27. Another CIA air raid on the capital the next day brought a second change of government that led shortly—and on the intervention of Ambassador Peurifoy—to a deal between Castillo Armas and the new junta leader. On July 8, Castillo Armas became the new president of Guatemala.[51] The army had stood aside, despite having received many benefits from Arbenz to assure its loyalty. It probably *had* been reluctant to counterattack Castillo Armas in view of his American support. But of at least equal importance was that Arbenz's plan, backed by the PGT, to arm the people was regarded by many in the army leadership as detrimental to the army's power position.[52] It was not the army's anticommunism but its self-interest that defeated Arbenz.

On a second front, the U.N. Security Council, a meeting was convened June 20 to consider Guatemala's complaint and its request for an immediate U.N. investigation.[53] But a resolution

* A few days before the invasion began, Eisenhower is quoted as having told colleagues that "if it [the operation] succeeds, it's the people of Guatemala throwing off the yoke of Communism. If it fails, the flag of the United States has failed." (David Wise and Thomas B. Ross, *The Invisible Government* [New York: Bantam, 1964], p. 189.) See also Eisenhower's account (*Mandate for Change, 1953–1956* [Garden City, N.Y.: Doubleday, 1963], pp. 425–26), in which the chief proponent of discontinuing U.S. intervention, Assistant Secretary of State Henry F. Holland, is portrayed as having carried little weight because he rested his case on legal grounds. Allen Dulles is quoted: "Mr. President, when I saw Henry walking into your office with three large law books under his arm, I knew he had lost his case already."

offered by Brazil and Colombia, obviously inspired by Washington, squelched debate by proposing reference of the entire matter to the OAS. Though defeated by a Soviet veto, the resolution reflected U.S. insistence that Guatemala only brought the matter before the U.N. because its Soviet friends were there and because it hoped to win propaganda points. The chief U.S. delegate, Henry Cabot Lodge, made light of the Guatemalan complaint and took the intriguing position that "the situation in Guatemala is clearly a civil—and not an international—war," thus making Security Council action inappropriate.[54] The Guatemalan Government was left with little choice. On June 26, it agreed to an OAS investigation to begin two days later; and on the 28th, the United States pushed through the OAS Council a request that the members meet in early July to consider the communist threat to Guatemala. Neither event occurred: The investigation team got as far as Mexico City, and the OAS Council subsequently approved a U.S.-Honduras request that the July meeting be adjourned *sine die*. As the Americans had evidently hoped, the overthrow of Arbenz made further discussion irrelevant.

Analysis of U.S. Objectives

In Guatemala, a radical nationalist leader had embarked his nation on the path of social revolution—a revolution that, because it had the support of communists as well as other Guatemalan nationalists, was conceived in Washington as threatening U.S. strategic and economic interests throughout the hemisphere. Viewed through the ideological lenses of the Eisenhower Administration, Arbenz was best judged by the company he was keeping. Since any distinction between local and international communism was deemed artificial, Arbenz's revolution was equated with the Bolshevik threat.

In this sinister light, Guatemala appeared as a potential military, political, and economic domino. Referring to Arbenz's government, Dulles said on June 30, 1954: "The master plan of international communism is to gain a solid political base in this hemisphere, a base that can be used to extend Communist penetration to the other peoples of the other American Governments." Because of governmental and PGT relations with the U.S.S.R.,

Guatemala had acquired extraordinary power—so much that, in the words of the State Department desk officer for Central American affairs, "the odds were heavily against the continued independence of Central America, whose governments might sooner or later have been toppled over, one by one, like a row of dominoes."[55] U.S. intervention was thus portrayed as pre-empting a dangerous Soviet-backed takeover. Eisenhower proved that the Roosevelt Corollary, stipulating that U.S. intervention may be necessary to prevent the intrusion of another major power, was very much alive and would be applied with little regard for the complexities and local peculiarities of Latin politics.

Also in keeping with traditional U.S. policy in Latin America, the Guatemala intervention seems to have been intended as a demonstration of U.S. willingness to act against unpalatable governments. The expected communist takeover, said a senior State Department official, posed a unique challenge because it "could be achieved by internal political infiltration, far from the Soviet fatherland, without armed force." Other nationalist revolutionary movements in the region might be similarly subverted, creating a string of Soviet satellites.[56] Thus, he seemed to be arguing for the administration, U.S. intervention would not be constrained by the lack of an overt Soviet presence, a communist army, or a card-carrying communist as head of government. The burden of proof of communist "control and domination" was at one stroke greatly lightened; all that now seemed required of U.S. governments was an *anxiety* that communists were active in the revolutionary movement or government.

A specific concern of at least some high U.S. officials at the time was that the communization of Guatemala would directly jeopardize U.S. security and strategic assets such as the Panama Canal. In this regard, the intervention decision reflected classic "worst case" hypothesizing. Since, projected to its logical limit, a Soviet-dominated Guatemala might accept jets within a few hours' flying time of the canal or continental U.S. targets, the obvious solution was to get rid of Arbenz. Arguments about Guatemala's lack of facilities for Soviet jets, or about U.S. capability to detect a military buildup in Guatemala, or about the implausibility of an attack from Guatemala on a government allied with the United

States, would be to no avail, since strategic projections must take account of the worst possible, even unimaginable, situations.

The Administration surely also addressed the larger economic questions raised by the expropriations of United Fruit Company lands. Dulles avoided the issue when he dismissed the United Fruit compensation claim as central to the government's concern about Guatemala.[57] He, his brother, and Henry Cabot Lodge at one time or another had ties with the company[58] that may explain why it was able to recover most of its expropriated land after Castillo Armas became president. Yet U.S. policy was possibly more deeply influenced by the $5 billion in American investments throughout Latin America than by United Fruit's $50 million in Guatemala. Although specific evidence is lacking, it would be consistent with the Eisenhower Administration's Latin America policy that Arbenz's overthrow should be engineered to protect U.S. business interests regionwide. Other governments would be expected to draw the appropriate conclusions and not attempt to break the grip of U.S. corporations on local economies.

As has usually happened, the intervention was successful only in its negative aim; it did not help create better government. Castillo Armas set up a National Committee for the Defense Against Communism that put extensive powers in the hands of the police. Thousands of arrests, summary executions of former officials, and other measures typical of a dictatorship followed. The agrarian revolution was substantially reversed. Labor unions lost most of their power, in line with U.S. corporate and union sentiment.

In July, 1957, Castillo Armas was assassinated, and Ydigoras Fuentes, with whom the "gentlemen's agreement" on elections had been concluded but never honored, became president the following year. It was during his term, in 1960, that the CIA was permitted to establish a training base for anti-Castro Cuban exiles.[59] Ydigoras's approval lengthened his tenure: The CIA helped put down a coup attempt that same year.[60] But the CIA stood aside in March, 1963, when military officers deposed Ydigoras and thus prevented the holding of new elections, scheduled for November, that might have turned power over to former president Arevalo. A military coup was evidently preferable in Washington to a civilian suspected of being soft on communism.[61] Thus the 1954 counterrevolution spawned reactionary rule, military government, and dependence on U.S. power, postponing in the meantime social and economic progress for the Guatemalan lower classes.

THE INVASION OF CUBA

The April, 1961, landing of Cuban exiles at the Bay of Pigs was one of the worst concealed of the American interventions in the Third World, and one of the few that failed to achieve its objectives. Many assessments of the event, especially those by former Kennedy aides, have treated it as a tactical and bureaucratic problem. Their concern about the Bay of Pigs "tragedy" or "fiasco" has been over the reasons a bad decision was made—the intelligence gap, poor planning and coordination, domestic political considerations, and bureaucratic momentum. Such a focus, however, divorces the intervention from its political and ideological contexts, and hence distorts its broader significance. It implies that the intervention is to be criticized only because it was imperfectly executed. Yet the Bay of Pigs operation was no mere decision-making failure; it was a direct outgrowth of American antinationalism, expressed in a profound distrust of, and contempt for, Castro's revolution.

Kennedy's thinking about Cuba showed a remarkable transformation between 1958 and 1961. As senator, he called Fidel Castro "part of the legacy of Bolivar," a "fiery young rebel" whose overthrow of the Fulgencio Batista dictatorship on New Year's Day, 1959, was a just revolution.[62] Critical of American paternalism and mindless anticommunism in dealing with Latin America, the senator spoke forcefully in behalf of nonintervention. He seemed more concerned with U.S. support of rightist dictatorships than with the threat that might be posed by governments of the Castro type, whose anti-Americanism, he believed, was influenced by that support.[63] During the 1960 Presidential campaign against Vice-President Nixon, however, anti-Castroism and anticommunism were among Kennedy's major weapons.

The dominant theme of candidate Kennedy's assault on the Eisenhower Administration's Cuba policy was that it was not doing enough to reverse Castro's revolution, which the senator considered illegitimate. Eisenhower was criticized on two counts— for having helped Batista to consolidate his regime, and for failing to encourage resistance to Castro by "liberty-loving Cubans" in exile. (Both charges were only partially accurate.) * "Castro betrayed the revolution," said Kennedy on several occasions; its worthy beginnings had ended in communist dictatorship and the creation of "a hostile and militant Communist satellite" only 90 miles from American shores. Kennedy accepted Eisenhower's economic containment of Cuba during 1960, saying, "For the present, Cuba is gone."[64] But the senator, without much attention to consistency, kept demanding that Eisenhower do something to break the back of the Cuban revolution. At one point, he urged that the United States "attempt to strengthen the non-Batista democratic anti-Castro forces in exile, and in Cuba itself, who offer eventual hope of overthrowing Castro." But at another, Kennedy disavowed any suggestion of American intervention contrary to U.S. treaty obligations or international law.[65]

What Kennedy did not know, or purported not to know, was that the Eisenhower Administration, dating from an Executive Order of March 17, 1960,[66] had authorized the CIA to establish a base in Guatemala for the arming and training of anti-Castro Cubans. It was a decision that candidate Nixon "had been advo-

---

* In March, 1958, the administration, while maintaining military training missions in Cuba, halted arms shipments to Batista and discouraged other governments from selling to him, acts that, according to Ambassador Earl E. T. Smith, dealt a severe blow to Batista's armed forces. (See his testimony in U.S. Senate, Committee on the Judiciary, Subcommittee to Investigate the Administration of the Internal Security Act and other Internal Security Laws, *Communist Threat to the United States Through the Caribbean*, pt. 9, 86th Cong., 2d Sess., August 27, 30, 1960 [Washington, D.C.: Government Printing Office, 1960], p. 687.) And lax enforcement of U.S. neutrality laws allegedly enabled Castro to receive arms and men from Florida. (*Ibid.*, p. 689.)

Once Castro took power and, almost predictably, began expropriating U.S. corporate landholdings and businesses, the administration did more than simply protest and demand just compensation. Several bombing "incidents" by aircraft that crossed the Florida Straits indicated that the administration could be as tolerant of illegal acts against Castro as it had been of the same against Batista. The U.S. Ambassador, Philip Bonsal, could dismiss the raids as "trivial," but to Castro they clearly signaled American hostility. (On the raids, see Bonsal, *Cuba, Castro, and the United States* [Pittsburgh, Pa.: University of Pittsburgh Press, 1971], pp. 98, 104–5.)

cating for nine months," but about which he could say nothing publicly to counter Kennedy's accusations of a do-nothing policy.[67] Nor could Eisenhower, although, at press conferences, he warned that the United States would not "permit the establishment of a regime dominated by international Communism in the Western Hemisphere."[68] And he said, in response to a question on Cuba, that while the United States would not intervene to overthrow a "freely" established but objectionable government, "I don't believe there is any case in the whole world when any group of people have freely voted to . . . regiment themselves."[69]

Prior to the break in diplomatic relations between Cuba and the United States on January 3, 1961, after Castro ordered a reduction in the American Embassy staff, further efforts were made on behalf of the exile force. CIA plans for a guerrilla operation were replaced with plans for an invasion by a few hundred men. Eisenhower suggested that a rebel front organization be established and that the exiles select a leader whom the United States could recognize as "head of government." Only because such a leader could not be found, Eisenhower related, was U.S. recognition and implementation of the invasion plans before Kennedy's inauguration impossible.[70]

Thus, when Kennedy took office, he found plans already well under way to overthrow Castro, with the CIA largely running the show. Like Eisenhower, Kennedy became aware that Latin governmental opinion was far more inclined to support the overthrow of Trujillo in the Dominican Republic than of Fidel Castro.[71] Unlike Eisenhower, Kennedy was neither impressed by that opinion nor deterred by the lack of a united Cuban exile leadership, which was held together only by the CIA's machinations.[72] The driving force behind Kennedy's subsequent authorization of the CIA's plans and behind his willingness to believe the CIA's assurances that an invasion by 1,400 men would lead to an uprising of the Cuban people against socialism was his conviction that such a political system was intolerable to the Cuban people. True to his campaign rhetoric, Kennedy said privately: "Our objection isn't to the Cuban Revolution, it is to the fact that Castro has turned it over to the communists."[73] Presumably, it would not be intervention if the United States supported the efforts of "free" Cubans to recover their "lost" country. Indeed, Kennedy is reported to have believed that to have done *nothing* about Castro while many Cubans were clamoring to fight him would have been immoral because it would have amounted to *protecting* Castro from his enemies.[74] "Cubanizing" the operation and minimizing overt American participation were considered ways of enhancing the invasion's legitimacy.

As had occurred under Eisenhower on the eve of Castro's take-over,[75] Kennedy looked for an alternative to the leftist Castro and the extreme-right Batistists. CIA support swung to those émigrés newly arrived in Guatemala who had fought and served with Castro but then fled the island. They fit well Kennedy's definition of a legitimate revolutionary alternative, one that could credibly redeem the revolution. For as the State Department's White Paper on Cuba would reiterate, Castro's illegitimate regime posed a challenge to the United States:

> The challenge results from the fact that the leaders of the revolutionary regime betrayed their own revolution, delivered that revolution into the hands of powers alien to the hemisphere, and transformed it into an instrument employed with calculated effect to suppress the rekindled hopes of the Cuban people for democracy . . . We call once again on the Castro regime to sever its links with the international Communist movement, to return to the original purposes which brought so many gallant men together in the Sierra Maestra, and to restore the integrity of the Cuban Revolution.[76]

Believing that overthrowing Castro would be just as pure an act as the revolution he led contributed mightily to the administration's obliviousness to arguments against the invasion. The assumption of Castro's unpopularity, hence the likelihood of an uprising against him, ran contrary to public opinion polls and reports by Western correspondents that showed popular sentiment running strongly in Castro's favor. Nor were the arguments put before Kennedy and his advisers by Senator J. William Fulbright persuasive, namely, that even a successful invasion "would be denounced from the Rio Grande to Patagonia as an example of imperialism," might force the United States to assume responsibility for administering the island, might require the direct commitment of U.S. military resources to ensure complete victory, and would be a direct "violation of the spirit, and probably the letter as well, of treaties to which the United States is a party and of U.S. domestic legislation."[77] Even Arthur Schlesinger, who opposed the invasion on practical political and military grounds, acknowledged that "if we could achieve this by a swift, surgical stroke, I would be for it."[78] That kind of opposition played into the hands of the CIA and the military, both of which were deeply committed to making the invasion work.

The invasion of Cuba, far from having been simply a case of contingency plans generating their own momentum, as Schlesinger argues,[79] was a classic instance of "liberal" intervention. "Good" ends were worth achieving by illegal means. In keeping with what Schlesinger describes as "a proud tradition of supporting refugees against tyranny,"[80] the U.S. Government used a diverse group of anti-Castro Cubans in a vain attempt to eradicate a socialist revolution. It was never asked, apparently, why these exiles, who without CIA management were incapable of organizing, uniting, or fighting, should have been able to sustain Castro's revolutionary program without Castroism or Batistism. Nor was it considered that if Castro had truly betrayed the revolution, the place for rebellion to begin would have to be within, not outside, Cuba, in the same manner that Castro himself seized power. But these were not relevant questions to an administration dominated by anti-communist and specifically anti-Castro sentiment.

It is hardly surprising that, for Kennedy, the lessons of the Bay of Pigs did not entail a new respect for the nonintervention principle or a new appreciation of self-determination in Latin America. Instead, he was concerned principally with bureaucratic lessons—never again trusting the CIA's or the military's judgment so facilely, suspecting the State Department's utility in foreign policy decisions—and with the importance of subverting Castro's Cuba by other means. In his speech of April 20, 1961, cited earlier, Kennedy linked the Cuba problem to other areas of communist threat.

> Power is the hallmark of this offensive—power and discipline and deceit. The legitimate discontent of yearning peoples is exploited. The legitimate trappings of self-determination are employed. But once in power, all talk of discontent is repressed—all self-determination disappears—and the promise of a revolution of hope is betrayed, as in Cuba, into a reign of terror. . . . We dare not fail to see the

insidious nature of this new and deeper struggle. We dare not fail to grasp the new concepts, the new tools, the new sense of urgency we will need to combat it—whether in Cuba or south Viet-Nam. . . . The message of Cuba, of Laos, of the rising din of Communist voices in Asia and Latin America—these messages are all the same. . . . Now it should be clear . . . that our security may be lost piece by piece, country by country, without the firing of a single missile or the crossing of a single border.[81]

The Bay of Pigs meant for Kennedy the need to develop better means of counterrevolution and intervention. His call would be answered in Vietnam, Laos, and the Congo.

Kennedy's Cuba policy provided the backdrop to Castro's closeness with the U.S.S.R., culminating in the 1962 missile crisis. The administration's hostile statements about Castro's "betrayal" continued after the Bay of Pigs debacle. In support of this charge, references were made to speeches by Castro—one on April 16, another on December 2, 1961—in which he proclaimed his socialist leanings and then aligned himself with the U.S.S.R., claiming he had all along been a Marxist-Leninist. Ignored were the timing and politics of these speeches: They occurred after the Bay of Pigs invasion had begun, they facilitated Castro's acquisition of Soviet aid and protection, and they helped to legitimize his social revolution. Containment of Cuba was an easier course for Washington than trying to understand Castro's anxieties. The administration obtained OAS condemnation of Cuba, an arms embargo, the removal of Cuba from the Inter-American Defense Board, and Cuba's exclusion from the Latin America Free Trade Association. And the Congress, alarmed by Castro's welcoming of Soviet military deliveries, which the Premier said were necessary for Cuba's self-defense, passed resolutions during 1962 to reinforce Kennedy's warnings that a Soviet buildup of offensive weapons on Cuba would be regarded as a threat to U.S. security.[82] In the ensuing missile crisis, it is worth speculating that Kennedy's interpretation of the Soviet weapons as a political and psychological threat to American global interests was nurtured by his failure to get rid of Castro the year before, and by Castro's subsequent alignment with Moscow in open defiance of U.S. "imperialism."

The abortive invasion, crowning an intense period of American hostility toward Castro's Cuba, also assured a prolonged estrangement between the two countries. The reason is not simply that the memory will linger among Cubans of another North American intervention in their affairs. It is more basically that, as Lester D. Langley has written, Castro's communism is an "open denial of the Jacksonian credos of democracy, capitalism, and progress" that Americans have wished to see adopted by Cuban governments since 1898.[83] Castro was tolerable only so long as he was a moderate reformer, a social democrat. Acceptance of Castro's legitimacy hence will require a major transformation of official American thinking; and the fact that, by 1973, the United States had established relations with Mao's China and signed peace agreements with North Vietnam but still was hostile to Castro indicates the depth of feeling about a socialist revolutionary in America's backyard.

The final and perhaps the most enduring legacy of the Bay of Pigs experience was the American determination that there not be "another Cuba" in Latin America. If Castro could not be removed, he could at least serve as an example to the rest of the hemisphere of the consequences of irresolution and lack of alertness. In a speech of November 18, 1963, Kennedy sounded the "never again" theme:

> The American states must be ready to come to the aid of any government requesting aid to prevent a takeover aligned to the policies of foreign communism rather than to an internal desire for change. My own country is prepared to do this. We in this hemisphere must also use every resource at our command to prevent the establishment of another Cuba in this hemisphere.[84]

In a typical denial that socialist revolutionaries can have popular support, Kennedy said "a small band of conspirators has stripped the Cuban people of their freedom and handed over the independence and sovereignty of the Cuban nation to forces beyond the hemisphere." He offered the Cuban people America's traditional hand of friendship "once Cuban sovereignty has been restored." To the end, the President could not understand or accept the legitimacy of the revolution he himself had once enthusiastically endorsed.

Thus, avoidance of "another Cuba" was Kennedy's contribution to the elastic U.S. conception of the nonintervention doctrine. In pursuit of that objective, Kennedy, in October, 1963, ordered a high priority Defense Department study of U.S. preparedness for "active . . . military intervention" in the Caribbean and Central America. One of his specific concerns was the American capability for rapidly dispatching troops to the Dominican Republic.[85] During April, 1965, Lyndon Johnson would feel challenged to support Kennedy's doctrine using the improved capability by then at his disposal.

PREVENTING ANOTHER CUBA: THE DOMINICAN INTERVENTION

Several aspects of U.S. relations with Santo Domingo have their parallel in the over-all history of U.S. involvement in Latin America. Economic penetration and military occupation into the 1930's, unabashed support of a Latin dictator friendly to U.S. political and economic interests, insensitivity to local politics and sources of popular unrest, and willingness to intervene in support of preferred factions—all these elements characterized U.S. policy in the Dominican Republic prior to April, 1965, and contributed to the massive intervention that month. In explaining the intervention this pattern of U.S. policy needs to be kept in mind, all the more so as the motives, methods, and objectives of U.S. policy-makers responsible for the Dominican intervention were strikingly similar to those that dictated the Guatemalan and Bay of Pigs adventures.

U.S. Objectives in the Dominican Republic

From the first and second U.S. military interventions in 1905 and 1916 to the third in 1965, American policy toward the Dominican Republic seemed to have two closely related objectives. First, U.S. governments acted to ensure that the country was politically stable, which meant amenable to American influence and advice on the structure of the country's politics and international relations. Political stability also was desired in order to facilitate economic access and the maintenance of the Dominican economy's dependence on U.S. capital and the U.S. market.[86] U.S. private investments, mainly in sugar but also in fruits, bauxite, communications, and banking, comprised the overwhelming share of total foreign investments of about $200 million in the early 1960's. Washington was the only foreign creditor on a bilateral basis; and most multilateral credit was extended to the Dominican Republic by U.S.-dominated lending institutions (the Inter-American Development Bank and the International Monetary Fund) and by U.S. banks. In her external trade, the Dominican Republic (in 1963) imported 48 per cent of all goods, by value, from the United States and exported 76 per cent of all its products to the United States. Sugar and sugar products, the main Dominican export, which is always at the mercy of world price fluctuations, required constant support from the U.S. quota system. These price supports were critical to the Dominican capacity to import (primarily U.S.) consumer and capital goods. But this and other forms of aid had major political implications and contributed to the popular resentment and political intrigue of the prerevolution period.

U.S. governments also seemed anxious to make the Dominican Republic a model of democracy and orderly, constitutional administration. Dictators and military juntas were generally unpalatable to Washington; but they were tolerated because—as was most clearly demonstrated in U.S. relations with Rafael Trujillo's regime (1930–61)—in the Americans' scale of values, law and order had higher priority than political liberalism. Even in the Kennedy period, when the "democratic left" became the preferred form of Latin government, a Dominican dictatorship was not ruled out because the likely alternative was believed to be a Castroite regime.[87]

A third U.S. objective emerged in the 1960's: the prevention of "another Cuba," both for domestic political and foreign-policy reasons. Whether "another Cuba" was understood in Washington as a security threat or as a political threat is a critical question when explaining the 1965 intervention. One writer asserts that "the fundamental U.S. aim in the Dominican Republic and the entire Caribbean has always been the same: to assure that no situation actually or even potentially damaging to U.S. security has a chance to develop."[88] The Dominican revolution was perceived in threatening terms, in this view, because it was linked in the minds of U.S. decision-makers to the likelihood of foreign (Soviet) influence and eventual control. I will argue, along with some other writers, that the principal purpose of the 1965 intervention was to abort a *mass revolution* that would decrease and might even eliminate U.S. influence in, and access to, a country whose politics and economy, like Cuba's before Castro, had long been American-dominated. Security from revolution preceded concern over security from international communism.

Background to Revolution and Intervention

The methods used in pursuit of U.S. objectives in the early 1960's reflect the pervasiveness of U.S. intervention in Dominican affairs and hence form the essential backdrop to the events of April, 1965. The Eisenhower Administration's interest, by 1960, in unseating Trujillo was a direct function of its primary concern about Castro. Since, wrote Eisenhower, "most of [Castro's] Latin American neighbors considered him less of a threat than" Trujillo, the obvious solution was to work toward Trujillo's removal in order to mobilize resistance to Castro. Eisenhower continued: ". . . we knew that until the American nations made some effective move together against Trujillo, they would do nothing against Castro. . . . It was certain that public opinion in the Americas would not condemn Castro until we had moved against Trujillo who, in July, was accused of attempting the assassination of President Betancourt [of Venezuela]."[89]

A number of steps were therefore taken by Washington to weaken Trujillo's rule. The CIA constructed a radio station off the Honduran coast to make anti-Trujillo broadcasts. Lobbying in the OAS produced a declaration in June, 1960, condemning the Trujillo regime's violation of human rights. In August, the OAS foreign ministers called on member governments to break relations with the Dominican Republic and institute an arms and economic embargo. The Dominican sugar quota was severely cut by the Congress and diplomatic relations were terminated. The President was quite prepared, moreover, to intervene directly once Trujillo was overthrown and a provisional government established. He said to his Secretary of State: "If such a government takes over, we should recognize it quickly. Then, if necessary, we could move in troops at its request."[90]

The anticipated blowup in Santo Domingo, which U.S. officials certainly encouraged and may even have materially assisted,[91] came with the assassination of Trujillo and the investiture of a new government under Joaquin Balaguer. Kennedy viewed Balaguer as a useful, and usable, point of departure: " 'Balaguer is our only tool,' he said. 'The anti-communist liberals aren't strong enough. We must use our influence to take Balaguer along the road to democracy.' "[92] One immediate way was the pressure put on Balaguer to deport twelve "Moscow-trained Communists" the CIA had identified.[93] Another occurred when Trujillo's son, still the armed forces chief, appeared to be preparing a coup. Kennedy mobilized U.S. military power to prevent it. Twelve American warships with 1,800 Marines on board were deployed just outside Dominican waters in November, 1961, "ready to go in if the Balaguer government asked for them."[94] Balaguer survived, and Latin opinion reportedly supported Kennedy's move. But once again, an intervention was justified on the basis of its "liberal," stabilizing motives.

In the unsteady interim before Juan Bosch's election in December, 1962, Washington sustained its intervention in Dominican affairs by other measures short of direct military involvement. It used political, economic, and military pressures to influence the composition of a new Council of State and to thwart another coup attempt. It provided the Council with the critical tools of authority, not only through the U.S. aid program but also through police and counterinsurgency training to deal with dissenters. And the American Embassy became directly involved in the electoral process to ensure that it would work smoothly and that the results would be respected.[95]

The victory of Bosch and his Partido Revolucionario Dominicano (PRD) in the country's first free elections in thirty years seemed to fit well the Kennedy Administration's model of progressive, left-of-center government. But the welcome accorded Bosch soon wore thin, especially at the U.S. Embassy. Preoccupied with the "Castro-Communist threat," Ambassador John Bartlow Martin did not look kindly on Bosch's efforts to cut into the influence of Dominican oligarchies, his economic reforms, and his refusal to engage in communist headhunting. Bosch's nationalism, the ambassador believed, made him vulnerable to the communists; hence the necessity of intensifying CIA surveillance, of keeping Americans involved in a wide range of Dominican government and labor activities, and of increasing U.S. military aid.[96] Such "assistance" ultimately worked against Bosch: It put him under pressure to prove his anticommunist credentials when he was anxious to avoid using *trujillista* tactics;[97] and it may have encouraged the military to overthrow Bosch on September 25, 1963, using the communism issue and the Pentagon's equipment.[98]

Kennedy's disturbance over the coup, manifested in the suspension of all aid and diplomatic relations, was quickly reversed by Lyndon Johnson. The Dominican military triumvirate was recognized by Washington on December 14, 1963, and it was not long before the aid programs resumed and the embassy, now headed by W. Tapley Bennett, Jr., was deeply involved again in Dominican politics, the economy, and military affairs.[99]

As Jerome Slater has commented, however, the policy change that occurred under Johnson flowed from the perspective of Kennedy and his appointees.[100] For one thing, rule by a military junta was clearly preferable to either the communist threat so feared by Martin or to another round of Trujilloism. Under Johnson and his Assistant Secretary of State for Inter-American Affairs, Thomas C. Mann, this perspective was put more positively: "The Latin American military contain in their ranks many able and dedicated men who do not deserve to be smeared with the brush that ought to be reserved for the few."[101] So long as the military gave token acknowledgment to constitutional procedures—such as the Dominican military did in 1963, when it promised elections in 1965—it was acceptable.

A second concern shared by the two administrations was Bosch's alleged susceptibility to manipulation by leftists. For all his personal charm and idealism, Bosch was considered ill-suited for dynamic leadership in the American style. "He could inspire men with his words," wrote Johnson, "but actions rarely followed the rhetoric. He lacked the capacity to unite under his leadership the various elements that wanted progress and constitutional government—elements of the non-Communist left and center."[102] In other words, Bosch was "soft" on communism because he was willing to work with the radical parties, as Thomas Mann would later say.[103]

Greater tolerance for military government and lack of confidence in Bosch and the PRD would help frame Johnson's reaction to the events of April, 1965. Another critical element was the President's conviction that Cuba was an increasing threat to the hemisphere. In two Caribbean "crises" early in 1964—one in January over the Panama Canal, another in February, when the Cuban Government cut off the water supply to the Guantanamo naval base—Johnson believed Castro was testing his mettle.[104] Characteristically, in the first days of the Dominican uprising, the President's thoughts turned to Castro: "He was promoting subversion in many countries in the Western Hemisphere, and we knew he had his eye on the Dominican Republic."[105]

In light of these administration perspectives, it is understandable that Washington was concerned about the broad political movement favorable to Bosch's return to power that gained momentum between late 1963 and early 1965. This "constitutionalist" movement included military officers, a large number of professionals and intellectuals, labor and student groups, and, in alliance with the PRD, the Christian Democratic Partido Revolucionario Social Cristiano (PRSC). As an economic depression set in and the government of Donald Reid Cabral began to totter, workers, farmers, and even business and commercial leaders also saw their interests in terms of getting rid of the military and restoring constitutional government.[106] The U.S. Embassy's response to these developments was, typically, to advise sharply increased economic aid to bail out Reid and improve his popular image. The political implications of failing to do so were narrowly construed as avoiding a leftist resurgence: "Little foxes, some of them red, are nibbling at the grapes," Ambassador Bennett warned Washington.[107]

The ambassador's concern was misplaced. He assumed that the PRD was cooperating with the Dominican communists, who were organized in three parties frequently at odds on doctrinal and tactical questions. One of these parties, the Partido Socialista Popular (PSP), issued a manifesto on March 16, 1965, supporting Bosch's return without elections. But, as Theodore Draper has argued,[108] the purpose of the manifesto was a belated effort to attach the communists to the Boschist bandwagon. Recognizing the developing mass movement for Bosch, and having been excluded from both the PRD-PRSC alliance and the pro-Bosch movement within the armed forces, the PSP needed Bosch far more than he needed it. Moreover, the party did not see Bosch as its potential instrument but, to the contrary, expressed concern in the manifesto about U.S. support of him contrary to the interests of the Dominican masses. In short, the "communists" hoped to gain from a constitutionalist victory; but they were wary of Bosch and were in the back seat of his movement—a circumstance the PSP lamented in self-criticism after the revolution failed.[109]

The Intervention

In a nationwide address on May 2, 1965, President Johnson explained why he had ordered approximately 23,000 U.S. troops to the Dominican Republic. As in statements of previous days, he referred to the threat to American lives—hardly the real issue, since no American life was lost until after the first landing of Marines on April 28. Johnson on this occasion emphasized a new element—a communist takeover of a popular revolution that threatened to turn the Dominican Republic into another Cuba. He said:

> The revolutionary movement took a tragic turn. Communist leaders, many of them trained in Cuba, seeing a chance to increase disorder, to gain a foothold, joined the revolution. They took increasing control. And what began as a popular democratic revolution, committed to democracy and social justice, very shortly moved and was taken over and really seized and placed into the hands of a band of Communist conspirators. . . . The American nations cannot, must not, and will not permit the establishment of another Communist government in the Western Hemisphere. . . . We believe that change comes, and we are glad it does, and it should come through peaceful process. But revolution in any country is a matter for that country to deal with. It becomes a matter calling for hemispheric action only—repeat, only—when the object is the establishment of a Communist dictatorship.[110]

The President's account raised a number of questions about the events of April 24–30. Did U.S. decision-makers regard the Dominican revolution at its outset as a "popular democratic revolution"? Did Dominican communists seize control of the revolution? Was the intervention designed to prevent a communist takeover or a Boschist victory? Did the intervention have the wider objectives sometimes claimed for it of securing "democracy and social justice" through free elections and reform of the Dominican military? And finally, in the absence of U.S. involvement, was there a legitimate danger of another Cuba, so that intervention was Washington's only recourse? It is these questions that the analysis will address after briefly describing the April uprising.

Beginning at mid-day on April 24 and extending into the early morning of the 25th, members of the PRD and pro-Bosch military officers and units staged a coup in Santo Domingo against the Reid Cabral regime. Soon the coup became a mass uprising as constitutionalist officers distributed arms to urban dwellers, perhaps as many as 10,000. Reid, failing to get support from the army and air force chiefs, resigned, and José Molina Ureña, who was committed to the return of Bosch, became provisional President. American officials had refused Reid's request to intervene on his behalf; but were they equally committed not to intervene against Bosch?

The available evidence indicates that in these first critical moments of a successful revolution, U.S. officials decided to keep Bosch from power, *even before the issue of a communist threat or an imminent communist takeover became prominent.* The possibility of acceding to Bosch's return was not considered. Rather, the principal question for decision was *how directly* to become involved in order to *prevent* his return. And *that* question involved another: What alternative was there to the ineffective Reid and the unacceptable Bosch?[111]

The choices were all made on April 25. Early that morning, the wheels of intervention were set in motion when Johnson "ordered the Atlantic Fleet to move ships toward Santo Domingo. The ships were to remain out of sight of land but to stand by in case of need."[112] The U.S. Embassy's chargé was authorized to support formation of a military junta; supporting Bosch's return was thus excluded at the outset.[113] But the embassy found that only one armed forces commander, General Wessin y Wessin, with no more than 250 men at his command, was willing to fight the revolution.[114] Other military leaders evidently joined Wessin, however, in charging that there were communists among the rebels. This was enough for the State Department, which is said to have cabled the chargé that "the embassy should contact the leaders of the Dominican armed forces and urge them to form a provisional government that could restore order, prevent a Communist takeover, and prepare the country for free elections."[115] As the chargé reported later in the day, contact was successfully made. Now, with Washington behind them, the navy and air force chiefs joined with Wessin; and the embassy team unanimously urged that "Bosch's return and resumption of control of the government is against U.S. interests in view of extremists in the coup and Communist advocacy of Bosch return."[116] The Dominican armed forces would thus become U.S. proxies. Their first act of counterrevolution was to strafe the presidential palace, probably causing more civilians to join the rebels.

It is important to note that the objective of preventing a communist takeover was secondary during April 24–25 to that of defeating the pro-Bosch movement. Only in later days—specifically, according to Lyndon Johnson's address of May 2, beginning April 27—were communists said to have "taken over" the revolution. Indeed, neither the State Department's version nor Johnson's memoirs sought to establish communist control in the first days of the revolution. Both sources focused on communist *participation* in the army's distribution of arms and characterized the situation in Santo Domingo as a mob action.[117] The landing of U.S. troops on April 28 was purportedly to forestall a communist takeover; but the motive for backing the Dominican military leadership on April 25 was to thwart a Bosch-PRD victory at the head of a mass-based revolution.

In keeping with previous U.S. interventions in Latin America, officials in Washington and the Dominican Republic sought to accomplish their objective with the minimum direct application of force. The President reportedly emphasized to Ambassador Bennett, who on April 26 was preparing to return to his post from home leave, that "another Cuba in this Hemisphere" would be unacceptable.[118] Instructions to the ambassador that he work toward a cease-fire and the formation of a military junta were accordingly interpreted by him to mean presiding over a rebel surrender. When, on the 27th, the military situation turned temporarily in favor of Wessin's forces, Bennett, in the name of "nonintervention," refused to mediate between the opposing sides. He evidently anticipated the revolution would soon be crushed without having to bargain with the PRD and rebel officers—and without having to bring in the Marines. Mistrust of Bosch and an exaggerated view of the communist role in his movement thus undermined a major opportunity to avoid direct U.S. intervention.[119]

As rebel forces again gained the upper hand on April 28, the ambassador threw caution to the winds. Two days before he had turned down the generals' request for U.S. forces. Now, he cabled Washington that "a military solution" might be necessary because "the issue is really between those who want a Castro-type solution and those who oppose it."[120] Initially, he urged equipping the Wessin forces with walkie-talkies; later on, he asserted the "time has come to land the Marines"; and still later, when the first Marine contingents had landed, he recommended authorizing intervention that would "go beyond the mere protection of Americans and seek to establish order in this strife-ridden country."[121] The rapid U.S. buildup to nearly 23,000 men thus began.

As in the other cases studied, the U.S. Government sought to cloak the Dominican intervention with approval from several sources. In this case, however, Johnson's determination, shared unanimously by his advisers, to act quickly and decisively outpaced considerations of legitimacy. U.S. troops had already landed when Johnson received Dominican, congressional, and OAS sanction.[122] The go-ahead from the Dominican generals came after Washington insisted they produce a written request for intervention to save American lives, without mention of the communist threat.[123] With congressional leaders, the script was altered: Three Dominican communists were identified as spearheading a Moscow-Havana takeover bid, which was enough to convince the congressmen of the need for action.[124]

The OAS, which LBJ viewed with disdain,[125] but whose sanction he valued, was simply notified of the intervention. "The [OAS] Council moved too slowly to permit a collective decision in the time available," Johnson alleged.[126] More likely, Washington could not have obtained two-thirds approval from OAS members.[127] Its role was limited to calling for a cease-fire, which was achieved on April 30, and to contributing to an Inter-American Peace Force, which was predominately American and which lent legitimacy to a U.S. military occupation. While it has been argued that OAS involvement restrained U.S. military actions after the intervention, the record also reveals how much the

United States manipulated the organization to strengthen the Dominican military's hand at the rebels' expense.[128] The OAS thus supported an intervention it never voted on—one that, as Senator Fulbright would say, was doubly illegal because it violated Articles 15 and 17 of the OAS Charter and circumvented Article 6, which requires advance consultation and agreement to any "measures . . . for the maintenance of the peace and security of the continent."[129]

Why Intervention?

In explaining the Dominican intervention, I proposed at the outset that fear of "another Cuba"—that is, of an internal mass upheaval antithetical to U.S. influence—was the overriding consideration affecting American officials' decisions. Before developing that thesis further, the explanations of other commentators need to be examined, both for what they contribute and for what they seem to neglect.

One explanation is that Presidential actions in April, 1965, were dictated largely by the accidental and deliberate choices of lower-echelon officials in Washington and Santo Domingo.[130] Bureaucratic politics, which at key points involved the supplying of inaccurate or distorted information to decision-makers, thus led to a Marine landing, even though "none of [these lesser officials] seems to have expected or wished his decisions to lead to military intervention."[131] The major difficulty of this assessment is that while accident or mistake may be the correct interpretation of U.S. officials' behavior at certain times in the crisis, it ignores the structure imposed on their behavior by Presidential perspective and prior American policy, in theory and practice, when dealing with Latin America generally and the Dominican Republic in particular. Of course no U.S. official at any level wanted direct intervention; as in Guatemala and the Bay of Pigs, officials hoped to achieve U.S. objectives through local proxies. But those objectives—to ensure stability, preserve access and predominant influence, and prevent "another Cuba"—had the President's endorsement and were widely shared in the government bureaucracy from top to bottom. U.S. officials' distorted reporting on the Bosch movement and Dominican communism was therefore very likely to find a receptive audience in Lyndon Johnson, and to lead him toward a military response.

What has been labeled the "liberal" view sees the intervention as an aberrant episode in U.S. policy characterized by sound motives and poor execution.[132] According to Jerome Slater, the United States sought "the reestablishment of democratic government through genuinely free elections in the near future" and "the opportunity to begin gradually to reform and restructure the Dominican military establishment, the main bulwark of the status quo." After the intervention, writes Slater, "the most serious criticism" of U.S. policy is that it failed to bring about reform of the military.[133] But, as Theodore Draper has commented,[134] neither of these alleged motives can be accepted as explanations of the intervention. "Free elections" presupposed Bosch's defeat (by Balaguer) and prevention of a communist victory—conditions made possible by the U.S. military occupation. Reforming the military "was an afterthought"; the U.S. intervention aimed above all at *preserving* the Dominican military, precisely because it stood for the status quo.

The intervention has also been explained in terms of the U.S. economic stake in the Dominican Republic. It has been pointed out that several persons closely associated with President Johnson's Latin American policy had personal interests in Dominican sugar.[135] Two writers have dismissed the economic argument by contending, rather persuasively, that the persons cited were not part of the decision-making group on intervention, that the United States was not dependent on Dominican sugar exports, and that the U.S. business community was never a major or effective source of pressure on U.S. policy toward the Dominican Republic.[136] But their retort does not consider wider economic motives that might have stimulated the intervention. As in the Guatemala case, U.S. officials may have decided to reaffirm by example that American business in Latin America will be protected by force if necessary. In addition, or alternatively, these same officials, without necessarily wishing to protect specific business interests in Santo Domingo, may have been determined to preserve the longstanding dependency relationship between the two countries. One reason that Bosch was generally opposed by Dominican businessmen, while Reid and later General Wessin received their support, may be that business had become reliant on the U.S. market and American investment. U.S. officials, always interested in maintaining that dependency as a lever on Dominican politics, likewise viewed Bosch as a threat to Dominican "stability."

Once a mass movement developed in conjunction with the pro-Bosch coup that began April 24—once the civilian population was armed and Wessin's forces proved unable to crush the revolution—the initial U.S. efforts to keep Bosch from power moved inexorably toward direct military intervention.[137] The "popular democratic revolution" that President Johnson said was welcome in fact was opposed from its inception—*not* because of fear that the Dominican Republic would become a Soviet base, and *not* because a communist takeover was believed imminent. What U.S. officials most feared in those first hours was that, as in Cuba, "extremists" would gain the ascendancy, channeling the revolution in an anti-capitalist, anti-imperialist direction. The assertion of Dominican nationalism, not communism, was Washington's first concern.

But to the American leadership, communism was not a phoney issue. While it was not the issue that initiated the intervention against Bosch, it was responsible for the escalation of U.S. involvement. Once communists were identified as being among Bosch's supporters, it mattered little that there were so few—the CIA director initially reported three, but subsequent government lists gave between 53 and 58[138]—or that the communists were hopelessly divided. As Johnson would later write: "Unless one understands how a few purposeful men can seize power in the midst of chaos, it may be difficult to accept the idea that 4,000 members of three Communist factions in the Dominican Republic could have been victorious before the end of April."[139] Difficult indeed; yet Ambassador Bennett, Secretary of State Rusk, and probably others held the same opinion.[140] For these men, a government under Bosch and the PRD had, by April 28, become unacceptable because it was liable to be subverted by communists as well as because it was infiltrated by radical nationalists.

Some writers have argued that an appropriate U.S. alternative would have been to support the return of Bosch and the moderate PRD leadership—a choice that, as has been seen, was ruled out from the start of the revolution. Several opportunities were available between April 24 and 27 for U.S. representatives to have sided with the constitutionalists against the military leaders. So doing, the fighting could have been reduced or avoided, the constitutional government of 1963 would have been restored, and the chance of a communist takeover would have been made negligible.[141]

The difficulty of this alternative, so attractive on its face, is that it would have represented only another form of intervention—the exertion of a "liberalizing" U.S. influence on Dominican politics in order to assure the accession of a moderate and compliant government. Like Johnson's policy, it would have sought to cut short the mass revolution, but for the benefit of Bosch rather than the military, and with the hope that adroit diplomacy would contain the fighting and remove the need of a U.S. military commitment. It is one thing, however, for the United States to have refused to encourage the Dominican military's resistance; it is quite another for the United States to have worked actively in the PRD's (or any other group's) behalf. Only a policy that allowed the Dominican revolution to play itself out, accepting whatever result—a government under Bosch, Balaguer, or some more radical leader—would have been genuinely noninterventionist. Any policy that went beyond nonaction, for whatever motive, would simply have repeated the historical pattern of U.S. interference in Dominican affairs.

Lessons Learned?

With regard to the future of U.S. policy in Latin America, the "success" of the Dominican intervention is as discouraging as the motives that prompted it. For while it has been persuasively argued that the intervention increased the strength of the Dominican communists, deepened the island's political crisis, undermined the OAS, and further eroded confidence in the Alliance for Progress,[142] it is equally undeniable that the intervention achieved its political objectives at minimal immediate cost. A strong-arm junta took power the first week of May, 1965. U.S. forces were able to move in and out of the Dominican Republic with relative ease, incurring few casualties and—sensibly—facing almost no resistance. Bosch's support was seriously weakened during the occupation, and he was defeated by Joaquin Balaguer in elections held June 1, 1966. During and after the intervention, the administration had the support of public opinion and Congress.

The Dominican intervention thus stands in sharp contrast with Vietnam, and for that reason it may become the kind of model to which other administrations will turn should new "Cubas" arise in Latin America. As the Dominican experience recedes from memory, it is likely to be recalled in official circles as a quick and decisive surgical operation rather than as a gross intrusion in the affairs of another country based on a distorted sense of threat. Indeed, Lyndon Johnson offered precisely this latter reading of the intervention. Paying lip service to self-determination, he proposed that henceforth the American republics would have to act boldly and quickly against "the forces of slavery and subversion." And he offered what has sometimes been called the Johnson Doctrine —which he later correctly insisted represented nothing new in U.S. policy—to rationalize interventionism:

> The first reality is that old concepts and old labels are largely obsolete. In today's world, with the enemies of freedom talking about "wars of national liberation," the old distinction between "civil war" and "international war" has already lost much of its meaning.[143]

In the same spirit as Kennedy's post–Bay of Pigs assessment, then, Johnson understood the Dominican experience to mean: that the United States should continue efforts to block Castro's influence in Latin America and stifle popular movements of the left; that the United States should be able to commit enough power to do an effective job if active containment became necessary; that the military in Latin America, for all its faults, may be a safer bet to support than the democratic left; and that a communist presence in Latin America, however small, fragmented, and unpopular, should always be regarded as a threat to "free institutions," especially in times of political chaos. It was precisely this understanding that dictated the Nixon Administration's intervention in Chilean politics between 1970 and 1973—cooperation between the CIA and International Telephone & Telegraph Corporation, first to prevent the election of Salvador Allende, then to block his confirmation, and finally to subvert his government.[144] There is no sign, consequently, that the motives behind the Guatemala, Cuba, and Dominican interventions have changed significantly enough to warrant optimism about future U.S. policy in Latin America.

5

Nixon and Asia

Introduction

Nowhere in the Third World has there been a greater gap between American ambitions and accomplishments, or between the price America has paid (in blood, treasure, and domestic division) and the return on its "investment," than in Asia. In China, toward the end of World War II and for four years thereafter, the Roosevelt and Truman administrations looked to Chiang Kai-shek as the leader of a revitalized democratic power and supported him against the communist forces with all means short of direct intervention. Mao's victory in 1949 engendered recriminations in the United States whose effects on China policy and American politics are still evident. In Korea, which American military leaders had considered undesirable to defend, President Truman committed U.S. forces because the war was seen as another in a series of Soviet tests of American will to defend "Free World interests." The successful containment of the conflict at the 38th parallel was overshadowed, however, by Chinese intervention, which thwarted U.S. plans to reunify Korea by force; by the dismissal of General MacArthur and the rejection of his recommendations for carrying the war into China; and over 150,000 American casualties sustained in a "limited" war that Republicans called "no-win" strategic nonsense.

And finally Vietnam, in which five Presidents, influenced by the disappointments and debates over China and Korea, created an ever expanding personal and national stake in victory, accepted the costs of it—the frightening military and civilian casualties, the political disruption at home, the expenditure of perhaps $150 billion—and very probably will not be able to show, any more than in China or Korea, that containment and intervention will have been worth the effort.

In this chapter on American intervention and subversion in Asia, the main study is the Bangladesh war for independence in 1971. What relationship does Bangladesh have to China and Vietnam, and why include Bangladesh at all, since the United States was not directly involved in the hostilities? I shall argue that U.S. policy in the conflict over Bangladesh is rooted in China and Vietnam, not in the sense of historical or geographical linkage, but conceptually in the American approach to Asian revolutions. The American perception of conflict in China and Vietnam was to treat these revolutions as, respectively, a civil war and a foreign aggression, and the revolutionaries as rebels and insurgents. Similar perceptions guided the American response to the revolution that created Bangladesh. All three cases, and others that also will be discussed at lesser length, reflect the consistent inability of Americans in high places to accept the historical and social legitimacy of *revolutionary nationalism*.

THE LEGACIES OF CHINA

The victory of the Chinese communist movement in October, 1949, ended a little more than a century of American involvement in China, and began a period of hostile confrontation between the governments of the two countries that has only recently abated. An event of such magnitude and consequences as the Chinese communist revolution inevitably spawns a number of myths about American policy, the most pervasive of which, in the months preceding Mao Tse-tung's triumph, was that the United States had "lost" China. To counter the myth, the Truman Administration issued a White Paper (August, 1949) to show how senseless all-out support would have been to a government as corrupt, militarily incompetent, financially chaotic, and politically bankrupt as Chiang Kai-shek's. In the process, however, the administration created myths of its own.

Five myths about the motives and objectives of American policy emerge from the White Paper and other official documents of the wartime and civil war periods in China (1943–49). The first myth is that, historically, the United States had been a consistent supporter and protector of Chinese territorial integrity and independence. In keeping with that role, according to the second myth, the U.S. Government tried to persuade Chiang to reconstitute a broadly representative coalition government, the only real alternative to continued disorder and economic ruin. Such a government, headed by Chiang Kai-shek, could make China the cornerstone of Asian stability—myth three. To implement the second and third myths required a fourth: that the United States, in line with a tradition of nonintervention and respect for self-determination, sought to mediate differences between Mao's Chinese Communist Party (CCP) and Chiang's Kuomintang (KMT) without taking sides. When mediation failed and the Nationalist forces began the steep decline to defeat, the final myth emerged: The Chinese communists and the United States had no interests in common; the CCP was a Soviet tool; the communist movement, and then the communist government, of China "is not Chinese."

Myth 1: America Is China's Dependable Friend

In presenting the China White Paper to the President, Secretary of State Dean Acheson summarized the history of American friendship for China by writing:

> . . . our friendship for that country has . . . been attested by many acts of good will over a period of many years, including the use of the Boxer indemnity for the education of Chinese students, the abolition of extraterritoriality during the Second World War, and our extensive aid to China during and since the close of the war. The record shows that the United States has consistently maintained and still maintains those fundamental principles of our foreign policy toward China which include the doctrine of the Open Door, respect for the administrative and territorial integrity of China, and opposition to any foreign domination of China.[1]

In contrast, an eminent historian of Sino-American relations has concluded: "Our policies toward China have not been so high-minded, so oblivious of the pragmatic issues of trade and power politics. . . . Although the United States has often shown an appreciation of what might also be in the interests of China, this by no means has invariably been the case, but occurred only when those interests conformed to our own."[2] An examination of the historical record bears out the historian's, not the Secretary's, assessment.

American contact with China from the first treaty in 1844 to the Yalta Conference in February, 1945, did show U.S. policy to be consistent, but not in China's behalf. Secretary of State Hay's insistence at the turn of the century on "fair field and no favor" for all powers in China adequately summarized policy both before and after. The primary American objectives were an equitable *share* of the potentially vast China trade (which never materialized) and *partnership* in a balance of (foreign) powers capable of imparting stability to Chinese politics and assuring equal American access and influence in China. To the extent that those objectives could be accomplished by American support of China's "administrative and territorial integrity," the United States was China's friend. But with equal constancy of purpose, no American government ever placed sufficiently high value on China's integrity to warrant its protection from other powers by force or pressure. Mao Tse-tung would remind Acheson in 1949 of this important limit on American friendship.

A brief review of some key developments in U.S. policy on the road to Yalta may be useful.[3] Beginning in the 1840's, the United States joined with the major Western imperial powers in their successful efforts to "open up" China to trade and diplomacy. Taking a dim view of Chinese governmental efficiency and the possibilities of Chinese nationalism, American administrations did not seek an end to the scramble for foreign concessions and did not stand in the way of Japanese expansionism during and after the war with China of 1894–95. The Open Door notes of Secretary Hay emphasized China's territorial integrity in the hope of gaining consent to the proposition that no one power should acquire a dominant position in China. America demanded a fair share of the spoils, no more— a goal best understood by recalling that, by 1900, the United States was well on the way to becoming a Pacific power, having acquired Hawaii, Samoa, Guam, and the Philippines, Accordingly, the American Government also hoped that instability and disorder within China could be prevented. The participation of American Marines in suppressing the Boxer uprising was an exceptional direct U.S. intervention to help stabilize China and thus protect U.S. "interests" against other imperialists.

In the early 1900's, American policy vacillated in the face of the expansion of Japanese power in Korea, Mongolia, and eventually Chinese Manchuria. Unable and unwilling to contest Japanese inroads, Washington meekly protested when Tokyo presented the Chinese Government with the infamous Twenty-one Demands. Japan's "special relations" with the areas it had seized or in which it was acquiring influence were acknowledged by the United States. Woodrow Wilson's inspiring talk of "self-determination" as World War I ended did not reverse Japanese gains at the Versailles Peace Conference.

Faced with the choice of confronting Japan, and thereby becoming China's sole protector, or accommodating itself to Japanese power in the hope of moderating its outward thrusts, Washington chose the latter course. At the Washington Naval Conference of 1922, the United States failed to use the opportunity of big-power arms limitations and renewed agreement on the principle of Chinese integrity to renounce extraterritoriality, press for the restoration of China's tariff autonomy, or propose an end to spheres of influence in China. When Japanese aggression occurred in Manchuria in 1931, Washington refused to recognize the puppet state of Manchukuo, but otherwise took no steps to prevent China's dismemberment. Lend-Lease aid to American allies in Europe was not matched by aid to China until May, 1941, well after Japan had become an Axis power.

During the world war, China and Chiang Kai-shek were relegated to the position of second-class ally with respect both to the amount of military assistance provided and China's diplomatic status as a member of the Grand Alliance. China was represented at only one of the wartime heads-of-state conferences (at Cairo in 1943). The critical one at Yalta, where Soviet "pre-eminent interests" in Manchuria were recognized and Soviet rights in Chinese railways and ports were granted, did not find China represented. The Yalta decisions were afterward presented to Chiang, sweetened by Soviet agreement to conclude a treaty of friendship and alliance (which was agreed upon in August, 1945); he had little choice but to accept.

Regardless of their leanings, politically involved Chinese with an awareness of history probably well understood that the wartime Sino-American alliance was based on traditional American self-interest. Certainly Chiang, Mao, and their respective senior subordinates understood. For Chiang, the critical postwar challenge was to retain American interest in a KMT-run China by persuading Washington that his leadership was essential to the goal of a united, stable, ideologically compatible government. For Mao, the task was to convince the Americans of the KMT's irreversible weaknesses, of the desirability of military and political contacts between his party and American officials, and of the long-term strategic and economic interests that the Chinese communists shared with the United States.

Myth 2: Reform and Coalition

The consistent announced goal of American policy after the defeat of Japan was, in President Truman's words, "a strong, united and democratic China." The goal required that a cease-fire be arranged among the contending Chinese armies, that a national political conference be convened to decide the makeup of a "broadly representative government," and that all "autonomous armies" such as those under the CCP be integrated into the Chinese National Army.[4] But it was also explicit in Truman's pronouncements that the Nationalist regime, as the sole recognized government, would be the core of a unified China; and his ambassador, General Patrick Hurley, conceived of his mission as safeguarding Chiang Kai-shek as China's unrivaled leader.[5]

The mission to China of General (and later Secretary of State) George C. Marshall, from December, 1945, to January, 1947, was for the purpose of implementing American objectives and preferences by mediating Nationalist-Communist differences. He failed; and on his return home he offered the opinion that because of the two parties' irreconcilable philosophies and mutual suspicions, the only path to China's unity lay in "the assumption of leadership by the liberals in the Government and in the minority parties . . . under the leadership of Generalissimo Chiang

Kai-shek."[6] The communists, whom Marshall labeled uncompromising, might be allowed representation in the government, but only if they saw "fit to assume their share of responsibility for the future of China."[7] Over a year later, however, the President said it had *never* been American policy to include communists in a broadened government, "in China, or anywhere else, if we can help it." What Marshall and he intended was that Chinese "liberals" join with KMT elements to form a coalition.[8]

Chiang chose civil war rather than risk depreciating his authority in a coalition government of any kind. The consequence, portrayed by Secretary Acheson, was that the incompetence and unpopularity of Chiang's administration proved more powerful than U.S. assistance, foreign recognition, and KMT numerical superiority over the communist forces. According to Acheson, Chiang was not defeated by the CCP; the CCP took over a government that had already disintegrated:

> What has happened in my judgment is that the almost in[ex]haustible patience of the Chinese people in their misery ended. They did not bother to overthrow this government. There was really nothing to overthrow. They simply ignored it throughout the country. They took the solution of their immediate village problems into their own hands. . . . The Communists did not create this condition. They did not create a great force which moved out from under Chiang Kai-shek. But they were shrewd and cunning to mount it, to ride this thing into victory and into power.[9]

Acheson repeated this theme on another occasion, saying "the Communists won by default, not by what they offered."[10]

What Marshall's opinion, Truman's decision, and Acheson's explanation had in common was an unwillingness or inability on the part of senior American officials to comprehend the revolutionary nature of the Chinese communist movement. The cure for China's ills was reform around Chiang; the backbone of his "coalition" would be non-Communist "liberals"; the Chinese communists would have to be absorbed into his government, they were a rebel movement, an "autonomous army" as Truman put it, not a legitimate alternative to Chiang and the bankrupt system he represented. As Truman later wrote, he and Marshall well understood that Mao's forces were no mere "agrarian reformers" but were real communists, out to get power. "What I hoped to achieve was to see China made into a country in which Communism would lose its appeal to the masses because the needs of the people and the voice of the people would have been answered."[11] If Chiang was unwilling to revitalize his government by replacing reactionaries with liberals, or if—as General Stilwell finally decided[12]—Chiang would never streamline his army and put it under effective leadership, the only American alternative was to get out.

The fruitless American effort to liberalize the political and military machinery under Chiang reflected two serious misjudgments. One, to which we will turn momentarily, was that the Chinese communists were essentially a military threat rather than a popular political movement. The other was that Chiang could be moved toward reform by consistent American displays of confidence in him—in particular, by referring to and treating his regime as the sole legitimate government, and by channeling all aid through it. Yet, as U.S. Foreign Service officers with firsthand experience in China were warning Washington as early as 1943, such support was not only eroding American opportunities to pressure Chiang to reform, it was also hastening the day of KMT-CCP civil war and alienating precisely those "liberals" in whom administration leaders placed high hopes. These officers proposed that the United States keep open the option of giving the communist forces arms and supplies to fight the Japanese, making clear to Chiang "that he has forfeited any claim to exclusive support."[13] The expectation was that Chiang would have no choice but to negotiate seriously with the CCP and reach agreement on a genuinely coalition government.

Thus challenged, Chiang might have attempted to entrap the Americans into a long-term, increasingly direct commitment by "reforming" just enough to make abandonment of him politically risky back home. Had Chiang been less protective of his personalist system of authority and less convinced of his ultimate victory, he might have turned reformism against its advocates. It was far more likely, however, that he would not be moved toward compromise unless faced with the reality of American cooperation with the communists. Some Foreign Service memoranda suggested, therefore, giving the CCP *equivalent status* with Chiang in recognition of the communists' revolutionary achievements and their potential to become China's dominant political and military power. Without withdrawing support from the national government or abandoning the objective of Chinese political unity and military integration, the United States might have established permanent contact with the CCP at its Yenan headquarters,[14] provided the Chinese communist forces with a reasonable share of American military and economic assistance (during the world war), refrained from giving further military aid to either side once civil war resumed in 1946 (instead of intervening on Chiang's side, as discussed below), and avoided the kind of partisan politicking for a negotiated settlement that characterized Ambassador Hurley's mediation efforts. As Mao fervently argued in a lengthy interview with an American Embassy official in August, 1944, the United States should be prepared for the likelihood that Chiang would try to exterminate the CCP rather than compromise or reform. Rather than engage in meaningful cooperation with the CCP looking toward future good relations, Mao asked, "Will the United States continue to give recognition and support to a government that in ineffectiveness and lack of popular support can only be compared to the old Peking government?"[15]

American policy amounted to a positive reply to Mao's question. The recommendations of the State Department's China specialists were ignored; Washington, with Hurley's strong endorsement, abided by Chiang's insistence that no U.S. arms go to the communists. When, in January, 1945, Mao and Chou En-lai proposed making an unofficial visit to Washington to discuss military cooperation against the Japanese, Hurley intervened to scuttle the trip.[16] In view of suspicions among top U.S. officials about the Chinese communists' relationship with Moscow, the postwar intensification of Soviet-American conflict in Europe, and the traditional U.S. concern for "stability,"[17] the refusal to cooperate with, or accept a visit by, Mao is not surprising. The administration much preferred dealing with a known quantity such as Chiang, who professed agreement with American hopes for a "strong, united China," to taking a chance on a minority party whose leaders preached Marxism-Leninism. Mao returned American indifference with hostility, writing caustically of U.S. policy for the first time in 1945.[18]

Here again, administration leaders failed to learn from Foreign

Service reports from China that, without discounting the communism of Mao Tse-tung, repeatedly stressed the CCP's thoroughgoing social and economic revolution in the countryside, its widespread popular support, and its bestowal of democracy and dignity where there had been neither.[19] Contrasting the contending Chinese forces from the vantage point of having traveled and conducted interviews throughout China, and not merely in KMT-held territory, these officers independently came to the same conclusion: The United States should not turn aside the Chinese communists' offer of friendship and assistance by putting its entire stake in China's future with the forces of reaction, the KMT.

Quite possibly, assessments of this kind could not be accepted because, even had Mao's movement been noncommunist and even had the American Government not then been gripped by cold war anxieties, the ideology of American foreign policy compelled alignment with reformism and moderation rather than revolution. The Chinese communist movement represented something so sweeping, so dramatic, so violent a departure from the China America had been used to and hoped still to see that perhaps no American administration would have dared attempt to cope with it.

Myth 3: China in the Balance

A further reason why the United States stuck with Chiang Kai-shek to the exclusion of establishing a cooperative relationship with the Chinese communists is that American officials were convinced postwar China would be pivotal in the Asian balance of power. The assessment originated with President Roosevelt. As described by Barbara Tuchman:

> Roosevelt's governing idea was that China should be one of the great powers after the war to fill the vacuum left by Japan. He was not unaware of shortcomings for he once acknowledged to his son that China "was still in the eighteenth century." Nevertheless that great and ancient country with its 500 million enduring people, however frustrated by endless misgovernment, was a geopolitical fact. Roosevelt wanted it on America's side in the future.[20]

To Churchill's dismay, Roosevelt insisted that the China theater was vital to the anti-Japanese war effort and that Chiang should be treated (as at Cairo) as one of the great allied powers. Even when Roosevelt came to recognize the Chiang regime's "corruption and inefficiency" and its lack of concern for the people, he retained his faith in the Generalissimo. "With all their shortcomings," he said, "we've got to depend on the Chiangs."[21]

When Truman became President, he was advised to continue Roosevelt's policy. The State Department informed him that Chiang's government "thus far offers the best hope for unification and for avoidance of chaos in China's war effort."[22] A few months later, as the war against Japan was coming to a close, General Alfred Wedemeyer, reporting critically about the motives and capabilities of all the Chinese political leaders, still had "the impression that the Generalissimo's leadership offers best opportunity at this time for stabilization in the area, political and economic."[23] Both sources naturally enough urged flexibility when dealing with Chiang; but, as Truman's speech of December 15, 1945, indicated, the future American effort in China would seek to build stability around Chiang and the KMT.

Like Roosevelt's, Truman's policy, too, stressed the strategic value of supporting Chiang, even before tensions with the Soviet Union in Europe had crystallized into cold war. Four days before his speech on China, at a meeting with his chief advisers, Truman was informed by Marshall that in the event the General's impending mission failed because of Chiang's intransigence, "and the U.S. abandoned continued support of the Generalissimo, there would follow the tragic consequences of a divided China and a probable Russian resumption of power in Manchuria, the combined effect of this resulting in the defeat or loss of the major purpose of our war in the Pacific." Marshall was instructed, accordingly, that he should still authorize U.S. assistance to enable Chiang's forces to move into northern China, the area in which they would have to contend with communist forces for the surrender of Japanese men and equipment.[24] The Americans, in other words, were prepared to throw away whatever leverage their aid gave them with Chiang for fear that part of China would move into the Soviet camp, replacing Japan as a threat to U.S. interests in Asia.

This dire projection of events proved to be largely self-fulfilling. Believing that Chiang was, for all his faults, America's only salvation, the administration forfeited opportunities for cooperating with the CCP, confirmed the division of China, contributed to the likelihood of civil war, gave Mao no recourse but to rely entirely on Soviet aid and later to become the U.S.S.R.'s ally, and by the fall of 1949 faced the hostile China it had set out to avoid. Mao had tried to convince American visitors to Yenan that of necessity American friendship and economic help would be greatly desired, first because only the United States among the great powers would be able to provide capital and technical assistance to China after the war, and second (by implication) because in the absence of America's competitive influence, Sino-Soviet relations would quickly evolve in Stalin's favor.[25] But in Washington, Roosevelt's premise that only Chiang's China could be "on America's side" gained in acceptance as the cold war developed in Europe. General Wedemeyer's report of September, 1947, after a month-long visit to China at Truman's direction, affirmed and expanded the strategic importance of China:

> The National Government has consistently, since 1927, opposed Communism. Today the same political leader and same civil and military officials are determined to prevent their country from becoming a Communist-dominated State or Soviet statellite. . . .
>   To advise at this time a policy of "no assistance" to China . . . would be equivalent to cutting the ground from under the feet of the Chinese Government. Removal of American assistance, without removal of Soviet assistance [to the CCP], would certainly lay the country open to eventual Communist domination. It would have repercussions in other parts of Asia, would lower American prestige in the Far East and would make easier the spread of Soviet influence and Soviet political expansion not only in Asia but in other areas of the world.[26]

By that time, the Chinese communists had lost hope of gaining American support and had begun a vigorous propaganda campaign against "U.S. imperialism."

Myth 4: Nonintervention

American avowals of interest in compromising KMT-CCP differences in actuality meant furtherance of Chiang's position at the CCP's expense. In his December, 1945, speech on China, Truman insisted that U.S. policy would be guided by respect for the internal affairs of other countries and by the principle of self-determination. Only the Chinese parties could work out matters of political unity, he said; "intervention by any foreign government would be inappropriate."[27] Not until publication of the White Paper did Secretary Acheson elaborate that the administration's choice "to assist in working out a *modus vivendi* which would avert civil war" included the aim to "preserve and even increase the influence of [Chiang's] National Government."[28] To Acheson, assisting the KMT while acting as a mediator was a consistent and responsible alternative to a complete pull-out or direct U.S. intervention on the KMT's side—the only choices he listed. But to the CCP, there was a flagrant contradiction between posing as a disinterested mediator and actively supporting one side to the dispute.

Nor were the communists alone in their assessment. General Wedemeyer, for instance, wrote to Washington on two occasions in 1945 to point out the impossibility of strictly adhering to instructions that he, on one hand, avoid involving his military mission in the civil war but, on the other, assist Chiang's forces to move into northern China. As Wedemeyer stated, "Chinese Central Government forces are now being diverted to the task of opposing Chinese Communist forces" and were employing Japanese troops "to protect lines of communication and installations against depredation and attack by Chinese Communists."[29] U.S. assistance, in other words, was being used and would continue to be used by the KMT armies to weaken the communists' grip in the north, at precisely the same time that Washington was talking about avoiding civil war.

Wedemeyer's orders were not changed. Truman was well aware that without American logistical and manpower support, and use of Japanese troops as garrison forces, "the entire country would be taken over by the Communists."

> So the Japanese were instructed to hold their places and maintain order. In due course Chinese troops under Chiang Kai-shek would appear, the Japanese would surrender to them, march to the seaports, and we would send them back to Japan. This operation of using the Japanese to hold off the Communists was a joint decision of the State and Defense Departments which I approved.[30]

Moreover, approximately 50,000 U.S. Marines were landed to secure the north China ports and other facilities, while the Air

Force ferried between 400,000 and 500,000 Nationalist troops into the major cities.[31] This strategy, which went into effect soon after V-J Day, was not formally unveiled until over a year later, in Truman's December, 1946, policy statement.[32]

Somehow, Truman did not consider these activities incompatible with either his stricture against U.S. intervention or his expressed concern for Chinese self-determination. Yet it is difficult to interpret them as other than intervention. American military personnel in China—a peak of 113,000 at the end of 1945, roughly 12,000 at the end of 1946,[33] 6,200 in 1947 and 1,500 in 1948[34]— almost inevitably had to become "involved" in Chinese politics, especially when their mission in the north brought them face to face with the communist forces.[35] And U.S. manpower was only part of the story. After V-J Day, about $2 billion in American aid, half economic and half military, was given to the Nationalists. As the White Paper notes, this "extensive" program included "sufficient matériel [under Lend-Lease] to complete the remaining 50 percent of the wartime program designed to equip 39 Chinese divisions, 101 million dollars of surplus military equipment including over 300 aircraft and very large quantities of ammunition, and 125 million dollars under the China Aid Act of 1948, expended largely for military equipment during 1948 and 1949."[36] When the Marines left north China in 1947, while there was a temporary ban on U.S. arms and ammunition exports to China, large quantities of small arms and ammunition (about 6,500 tons) were "abandoned" to Chiang's forces without charge.[37]

The CCP leadership sharply criticized the American aid program, rightly insisting it not only was incompatible with U.S. mediation but also was bound to lead to a resumption of civil war. "The Kuomintang couldn't fight us if they didn't get gasoline for their airplanes and ships for their troops," Marshall Chu Teh told an American journalist. "I cannot understand why America should want to support a dictatorial government."[38] "There are some people abroad who are giving aid to the Kuomintang," said Chairman Mao. "These supplies should be stopped, and the democratic peoples of other countries should oppose the sending of ammunition to the Kuomintang. There are people abroad who do not want or approve of democracy in this country: these people are acting in consonance with the reactionaries in China. Let them know that whatever happens, if we are faced with mechanized war, we shall fight on, if necessary with our hands and feet."[39] When Chou En-lai protested to General Marshall about an August, 1946, surplus property sale to Chiang's regime that included machinery, trucks, and communications equipment, Marshall retorted that these were noncombat items and dismissed the communists' persistent criticism as predictable propaganda.[40]

Myth 5: The Chinese Communists Are "Not Chinese"

Behind the Washington-Nanking alliance lay the American dread of a communist takeover of China. And when Mao announced a foreign policy of "leaning to one side" (June 30, 1949), when Chiang's legions were overwhelmed by the communist forces, and when a People's Republic was established in Peking, the Truman Administration's response was that it had all along been correct in its evaluation of Mao's ultimate loyalty. To its credit, it did not then use the assumed Sino-Soviet conspiracy as a pretext to aid and protect Chiang's regime on Taiwan; that second intervention in China's affairs would await the Korean conflict.* But the administration did go to some lengths to perpetuate the myth of the CCP's "un-Chineseness" and to establish American hostility toward China as a cornerstone of U.S. policy in Asia.

Formalization of this myth began with Acheson's forwarding letter to the White Paper, in which he declared:

> The Communist leaders [of China] have foresworn their Chinese heritage and have publicly announced their subservience to a foreign power, Russia . . . the foreign domination has been masked behind the façade of a vast crusading movement which apparently has seemed to many Chinese to be wholly indigenous and national. [American policy] will necessarily be influenced by the degree to which the Chinese people come to recognize that the Communist regime serves not their interests but those of Soviet Russia and the

* See Truman's statement on Formosa of January 5, 1950, in *Department of State Bulletin*, January 16, 1950, p. 79. In that statement, Truman announced an American policy of noninterference in the matter of Taiwan, including no further deliveries of military aid to Chiang's forces and no deployment of American power to influence Taiwan's future. When the Korean war broke out in June, 1950, however, Truman ordered the Seventh Fleet into the Taiwan Strait, thus again interposing the United States in the Chinese civil war.

manner in which, having become aware of the facts, they react to this foreign domination.[41]

Acheson neglected to mention that Mao had announced his "leaning" toward Russia only after he had waited over a month for Washington to approve an invitation to Ambassador John Leighton Stuart to visit Peking. The visit was to be personal, not official, but it was proposed at a time when Mao and other CCP leaders were publicly discussing the desirability of foreign aid from all nations.[42]

When the next logical steps in Sino-Soviet relations occurred in February and March, 1950—the signing of a Treaty of Friendship, Alliance and Mutual Assistance, followed by economic agreements —Acheson had new evidence of Mao's previously hidden intentions. "For while neighboring peoples . . . are at last achieving true national independence," the Secretary said, "China, with its long proud history, is being forced into the Soviet orbit as a dependency of the Soviet political system and the Soviet economy." As China's "old friends," Americans could only hope that one day soon its people would be able to exercise their real preferences and would react against the Chinese leadership that was permitting the Soviets to become an "empire builder at China's expense."[43]

Acheson's assault on the integrity and legitimacy of the Chinese People's Republic was joined by two colleagues and eventual successors, John Foster Dulles and Dean Rusk. Dulles, contending that "there is little patriotism in China," wrote in 1950 that the Chinese "armies" might be able to impose discipline on the country. "But it would be a miracle" if they could overcome Chinese separateness, individualism, chronic disorder, and food distribution problems, particularly since China's "ally and backer is a country—the Soviet Union—which *takes from* its associates rather than a country like the United States which *gives to* its associates."[44] Assistant Secretary Rusk, pointing to the Soviet-sponsored Chinese "aggression" in Korea, told a New York City audience on May 18, 1951:

> We do not recognize the authorities in Peiping for what they pretend to be. The Peiping regime may be a colonial Russian government—a Slavic Manchukuo on a larger scale. It is not the govern-

ment of China. It does not pass the first test. It is not Chinese. It is not entitled to speak for China in the Community of Nations. It is entitled only to the fruits of its own conduct—the fruits of aggression upon which it is now willfully, openly and senselessly embarked.

The concern amply reflected in official American statements such as these that China had become an instrument of Soviet foreign policy overlooked evidence of dissension and divergent interests in Chinese communist relations with the Soviet party. Mao's opposition to the Comintern line on party strategy between 1927 and 1935; the funneling of all Soviet wartime aid to China to the KMT while maintaining minimal contact with Yenan; Stalin's recognition of Chiang's postwar leadership at the Teheran and Yalta conferences; the conclusion of a friendship treaty between Stalin and Chiang in August, 1945; Stalin's doubts about the capacity of the CCP to defeat Chiang, and his admission that Mao was acting on his own by engaging in civil war;[45] and statements from Chinese communist sources in 1949 that Mao and the party had creatively developed Marxist-Leninist ideology and revolutionary strategy—these and other circumstances outbalanced the CCP's adherence to the Soviet international line in the prewar years and put Chinese Marxism in a different light.

Acheson and others were correct in citing the inequalities of the 1950 Sino-Soviet arrangements, for they enabled the Russians to maintain a privileged position in northern China for five more years (after having looted Manchuria of industrial equipment at the close of the war) and enforced Chinese dependency on Soviet assistance (not grants but loans given at interest). But these officials missed the vital implication, namely, that the United States had had an opportunity, repeatedly suggested by its specialists in China, to be the new Chinese Government's principal foreign assistant, to prevent Russia from exploiting its aid to keep Peking weak, noncompetitive, and politically loyal, and even to influence the character of Chinese socialism.[46]

The Heritage

Appropriate though it was, the American determination not to bail out Chiang by intervening directly in his behalf stemmed from purely practical considerations, not from a belief that the

Chinese communist revolution might bring China closer to the strength, unity, and democracy Truman sought. As Secretary Acheson would explain, no amount of American aid could compensate for the deficiencies of the KMT. An American takeover of China's economy and administration would have deeply offended all Chinese, the American public and a majority in the Congress would not have tolerated the massive and unending U.S. troop intervention required, the United States was in any event in the midst of postwar demobilization, and direct intervention in China might have escalated into an international conflict.[47] That further U.S. involvement in China would have been counterrevolutionary and antinationalist was never mentioned.

Nonintervention in 1949 helped sustain the myths of nonintervention after V-J Day and of historic American friendship for the Chinese people. It also facilitated the attack on the communists' "Chineseness," their subservience to Moscow, hence their ingrained hostility to the United States. The image of a Sino-Soviet monolith, prepared to expand international communism wherever "Free World" strength was limited or absent, became a fixture in the American foreign-policy establishment. America's subsequent involvement in Korea and protracted engagement in Indochina were based squarely on acceptance of that image as representing reality.

Reinforcement of the monolith image was not the only legacy of the China experience that contributed to the Korea and Indochina ventures. There was, after all, the indisputable fact that American policy in China from 1945 to 1949 had failed to achieve its stated objectives. As much as the Truman Administration sought to quash the myth of the "loss" of China, it *did* apparently feel a deep sense of having failed, a sense undoubtedly reinforced by the criticisms and accusations of Republican congressmen and the sweeping indictment of the Foreign Service by General Hurley on his resignation. Perhaps for domestic political reasons no less than on strategic grounds, the administration could not allow "Soviet-Communist imperialism" (Acheson's phrase) to gain additional territory. To be sure, after the fall of China Acheson distinctly said it was a "misrepresentation" that the American interest in Asia was "merely to stop the spread of communism," because America's real interest was to help people help themselves retain their dignity and independence. But self-reliance, as he further stated, was only a more reliable, healthier way to the same end—"about the best way that anyone knows of stopping this spread of communism."[48] It followed that, where the ideal of self-reliance could not be realized, the United States would have to step directly into the breach—as in Korea, where full-scale American military involvement was authorized, and in Indochina, under both Truman and Eisenhower, where the United States financed and equipped French colonialism to fight the Vietnamese communist revolution.

As important, indeed decisive, as the China experience was for American policy elsewhere in Asia, it had no greater impact than on the subsequent formulation of policy toward China itself. Hurley's charges of procommunism in the ranks of the Foreign Service struck a responsive chord among many Americans in need of scapegoats for the China disaster. The reassignment and purge of the State Department's China specialists who had so accurately reported conditions there bereft the government's ranks for years to come of persons qualified by experience, temperament, and proven intellectual integrity to comprehend the Chinese revolution. Ambassador Hurley had started a cultural revolution of his own that led directly to the McCarthyite terror of the early 1950's.

More than that, the purge solidified the hold on China policy of those men who, having lived through the dark postwar days in senior policy-making positions, were least likely to accept the legitimacy and permanency of communism in China: Dean Acheson, John Foster Dulles, and Dean Rusk, among others. The legacy of hostility toward China would become all the harder to discard, particularly after Korea and the reinvolvement of America in the Chinese civil war (by Truman's order placing the Seventh Fleet between Taiwan and the mainland). Despite the resumption of Sino-American diplomacy and trade in 1971, intervention in China continues on Taiwan—through military assistance programs, military use of the island for U.S. logistics and intelligence operations, a military presence, and political, economic, and defense ties. Over twenty years after the victory of the Chinese communist revolution, Chiang Kai-shek's regime is still treated as an alternative China.

Vietnam: Revolution and Escalation[49]

How could it happen in Vietnam that a "small" commitment in the mid-1950's became a massive one in the mid-1960's? Several former administration "insiders" have provided answers. Beginning in the Eisenhower years, we are told by George Ball, a series of "small steps" were taken "almost absentmindedly" until the United States became "absorbed" into Vietnam.[50] It was the "politics of inadvertence," Arthur M. Schlesinger, Jr., has written in evident agreement with Ball.[51] Yet the basic policies and concepts were right, implies Roger Hilsman;[52] the American failure was a failure of implementation, a case of inept execution. Quite the contrary, Leslie H. Gelb has argued: The decision-making system worked as its participants intended it to work, on the basis of a misguided consensus about the international and domestic political dangers of failing in Vietnam.[53] Daniel Ellsberg, while supporting much of Gelb's analysis, has added that Presidential concern about future elections and the threat of a right-wing reaction to withdrawal short of victory was the first "rule" of policy-making on Vietnam.[54]

The Pentagon Papers are a vital source for reassessing not only the key decisions on Vietnam in the 1960's, but also the explanations of them by the "insiders." Some of these explanations now appear to be misleading, while others give only a partial, unidimensional accounting. Choices to escalate rather than de-escalate or disengage were made deliberately, not haphazardly; policies were not merely implemented poorly, they were ill-conceived; concern over elections explains why changes in policy may have been postponed rather than why they resulted in increased involvement. If the "system" as a whole worked so perversely well, it is because of a disposition among American decision-makers to respond to failure in ways that perpetuate the "success" of America's mission abroad. The decisions that were taken on Vietnam—always to press ahead with the war, usually to expand it—reflected much more than calculations about the domestic and international repercussions. They were manifestations of deeper drives to preserve and expand personal, institutional, and national power while denying the legitimacy of the revolution that stood in America's way.

The most fateful decisions on Vietnam occurred in the 1960's. While the origins of American involvement can be traced on a direct line to and beyond Mao's victory in China, it was in the 1960's that U.S. officials embraced the goal of an "independent, non-communist South Vietnam" and enlarged the perceived stakes of the war to include the stability of the American-led "Free World" alliance. In retrospect, six decision points seem to have been crucial. At each of them, the level of involvement was maintained or raised while opportunities for disengagement were ignored or rejected.

The Decisions

1. In the fall of 1961, President Kennedy, having secretly approved (in April and May) sending 500 Special Forces and advisory personnel to South Vietnam and continuing covert warfare operations against the Democratic Republic of Vietnam (DRV), authorized a further buildup of advisers, along with additional financial and military assistance. By the end of the year, there were approximately 2,600 U.S. servicemen in South Vietnam, a figure that would more than double (to about 5,500) during the first six months of 1962. Kennedy's decision was made against the background of a deterioration of President Ngo Dinh Diem's position (he had defeated a coup attempt in November, 1960), significant gains in communist territorial control, and perhaps most significantly, a belief in the administration that the United States was on the defensive internationally. Soviet Premier Khrushchev had issued a statement in January, 1961, that was widely (and mistakenly) interpreted to signal increased support for "wars of national liberation"; crises in Berlin and Laos had been eased, but not under circumstances favorable to any long-term settlement; and the disastrous Bay of Pigs landing left Castro in firmer control of Cuba than before.

Like other escalatory decisions that would follow, Kennedy's was made in the conviction it represented a small quantitative rather than a qualitative change in the American role in Vietnam. But this was true only in comparison with the decision some of his key advisers would have liked him to make. General Maxwell Taylor and Walt W. Rostow had returned from Vietnam with the recommendation that the country could be "saved" *only* if the President were willing to commit up to 8,000 combat troops.[55] The President was also advised that Hanoi would match any such American escalation rather than be deterred from supporting communist forces in the South; that a commitment beyond the 8,000 men would almost certainly be required later, and even then without any assurance that the fall of South Vietnam could be prevented; and that—in Secretary of Defense Robert McNamara's words of November 8, 1961—a warning of "punitive retaliation against North Vietnam" would be indispensable to showing that the United States "mean[s] business."[56] Kennedy's step-up of U.S. ground and air support was thus an extraordinary decision, because it entailed a "small" escalation of involvement when his experts were saying that major changes in U.S. policy (to a direct combat role and the start of bombing of the North) were "essential," urgent, and even then uncertain of attaining American objectives.

2. In the fall of 1963, President Kennedy decided to encourage and support a coup against Diem by a group of South Vietnamese army generals. The decision, prompted by Diem's repression of Buddhist demonstrations and, in October, by increasing success for the National Liberation Front (NLF, or Viet Cong) forces, marked another threshold in American involvement. It meant that the United States would henceforth exercise the option of intervening directly in South Vietnam's national politics rather than simply urge reforms from afar.*

To Saigon's new leaders, and those who would follow in rapid

---

* Not that the U.S. Government had never before considered intervening in Saigon politics. In the spring of 1955, Diem appeared on the verge of removal when he accepted conflict with various sects (notably, the Binh Xuyen) and quickly found his forces unable even to control Saigon. President Eisenhower and Secretary Dulles had already sent a cable to the American Embassy withdrawing support from Diem and making him a figurehead in a new government when Diem unexpectedly overcame the sects' resistance. The cable was rapidly replaced by another. The Pentagon Papers do not touch at all on these events: see *The Senator Gravel Edition, The Pentagon Papers: The Defense Department History of United States Decisionmaking on Vietnam*, 5 vols. (Boston, Mass.: Beacon Press, 1972), vol. I, pp. 303–4. But see the account in Robert Shaplen, *The Lost Revolution: The U.S. in Vietnam, 1946–1966*, rev. ed. (New York: Harper & Row, 1966), pp. 121–24.

succession, the American action also indicated that the United States would support any government willing to make the anticommunist struggle its first priority and capable of maintaining some semblance of political order. Neither in Washington nor in Saigon was there any firm notion about the quality of the men the United States had chosen to back against Diem. The cabal of the generals was the "lesser evil," promising "a high probability of political instability," according to Roger Hilsman's recollections.[57] Ambassador Henry Cabot Lodge was not very encouraging when he speculated: "It seems at least an even bet that the next government [in Saigon] would not bungle and stumble as much as the present one has."[58] Kennedy's actions offered the first evidence that the composition and effectiveness of the government being helped were largely irrelevant to American decisions on the war; the United States wanted only a regime that would permit the Americans to get on with the job with minimal inconvenience.

3. In August, 1964, President Johnson ordered retaliatory air raids against the DRV after two clashes between American destroyers and Vietnamese torpedo boats reportedly occurred in the Tonkin Gulf. He strengthened U.S. air power in and around South Vietnam, and obtained congressional authority "to take all necessary measures" in dealing with Hanoi's "aggression." It is now known that these actions came after the administration had made extensive preparations for obtaining congressional assent to "reprisals" against the DRV; after Operation Plan 34A for covert warfare against the North, begun under Kennedy, had intensified; after renewed fighting in Laos had put royal government forces on the defensive and led to air attacks (using Thai and American pilots and U.S. planes) against targets in Laos and on *both* sides of the Laos–North Vietnam border; and after growing weakness and ineffectiveness had again become pronounced in Saigon, leading Premier Nguyen Khanh to favor "going North."

The retaliatory strikes took the wraps off a new strategy—graduated escalation. Under the circumstances in which the strategy gained acceptance—calls for rallying behind the flag and showing American resolve—there was a high probability that "tit-for-tat" bombing would evolve into a full-scale aerial campaign, which several Presidential advisers were already advocating.

4. On February 13, 1965, Johnson ordered the start of "Rolling

Thunder," the continuous air bombardment of strategic targets in the DRV. It was again a time of political chaos in Saigon, the failure of existing strategies to deflect Hanoi's support of the NLF or buttress Saigon, and uncertainty about how much closer escalation would bring the United States to the goal of a noncommunist South Vietnam. The air war was apparently undertaken because, among other reasons, there seemed to be no other decisive action left to take.

5. Less than two months later, on April 1, the President authorized a change of mission for American ground forces in South Vietnam—to offensive combat—and increased the U.S. presence by almost 20,000 men. Contrary to the expectations of Johnson's advisers—notably McGeorge Bundy, the Special Assistant for National Security Affairs, in his influential memorandum urging a "sustained reprisal" policy[59]—"Rolling Thunder" had not had a long-term uplifting effect on Saigon's morale, had not increased U.S. leverage to develop a more stable and effective Vietnamese government, had not eroded the confidence of NLF cadres in the ultimate success of their revolution, and had not diminished—in fact, had increased—the resolve and capacity of DRV leaders to continue supporting the war in the South. Johnson's April 1 decision was not publicized; neither was its sequel, in mid-July, which approved General William Westmoreland's request for an additional 200,000 troops.

6. In his speech of March 31, 1968, removing himself from electoral politics, President Johnson announced a cutback of the bombing of the DRV to (in effect) the 19th parallel and expressed the hope Hanoi's leaders would agree to begin "serious" negotiations. Johnson thus rejected General Westmoreland's request for over 206,000 more men, plus an even larger reserve call-up. He also did not take up the recommendations of a special task force, chaired by the newly appointed Defense Secretary, Clark Clifford, for a 22,000-man increase, no new peace proposal, and (reflecting division in the group) either a major extension of bombing or a "seasonal step-up through the spring."[60]

The conventional interpretation of Johnson's decision is that it was a long-awaited de-escalation in response to pressures from various quarters. Johnson, it is said,[61] could not resist the combined effects of the unprecedented January (Tet) NLF offensive, which at the least showed how ineffective the bombing campaign had been; Westmoreland's extraordinary troop request; Senator Eugene McCarthy's Presidential primary victory in New Hampshire, followed by Senator Robert Kennedy's entry into the campaign; the private recommendations in March by Clifford and Secretary Rusk of a bombing suspension; and the urgings of the President's so-called Senior Informal Advisory Group, a nine-man bipartisan panel of former high-ranking government officials, which for the first time told the President his wisest course was to move toward peace talks rather than invest further in bombing and troop increases.[62]

The March, 1968, decision should be seen, however, in terms of its *intention* as much as its results. For one thing, the decision did entail more troops, specifically 13,500 in supporting roles and a call-up of 48,500 reserves. Of greater significance—there is evidence from the Pentagon Papers that Johnson expected his offer to be rejected and, in keeping with the strategy of previous peace "initiatives," could then neutralize his critics and clear the decks for renewed bombing. A State Department cable of March 31 outlining Johnson's decision urged U.S. ambassadors to "make clear that Hanoi is most likely to denounce the project and thus free our hand after a short period." A complete U.S. bombing halt in return for North Vietnamese restraint "we regard . . . as unlikely."[63] Rusk had testified only a few weeks earlier that a bombing halt would not be productive, a view shared by CIA analysts.[64] The State Department cable thus went on to explain, in line with Rusk's suggestions to the President on March 5,[65] that limiting the bombing could work to American advantage: "We are not giving up anything really serious" because there were weather limitations on bombing the northern part of the DRV anyway; the planes taken off that assignment could be used in Laos and South Vietnam, where no bombing restrictions would apply; and Hanoi's expected rejection would "put the monkey firmly on Hanoi's back for whatever follows." DRV leaders may have accepted Johnson's invitation on April 3 because they suspected that a President who had just removed himself from the campaign would be especially dangerous if spurned. If so, they were probably right.

The Motives

What motivated these decisions and the critical if less dramatic steps in between? In search of explanations, three kinds of policy rationales emerge: those based on national interest calculations, on Presidential power, and on bureaucratic behavior.

Interests, Commitments, and Will. All administrations concerned with Vietnam have shared several bedrock assumptions about American responsibility for dealing with communist-supported revolutions, about the critical nature of the war for the United States and the "Free World," and about the psycho-political importance of being firm in the face of the adversary's provocations. These assumptions, clearly articulated in public and repeated in private, were: (1) that the DRV was committing aggression against South Vietnam that, unless checked by U.S. military power, would as surely encourage further aggression as had allied reluctance to confront the Japanese in 1931 and the Nazis in 1938; (2) that America's fulfillment of its obligations to South Vietnam would have an important, even decisive, bearing on the credibility of U.S. commitments to allies world-wide; (3) that the war in South Vietnam was a test of America's ability to cope with "wars of national liberation"; (4) that the war was also a test of American will and determination to continue to be the champion of "Free World" interests.

The first assumption—the essence of the "domino principle"—was stated by President Kennedy when asked whether he believed it.

> I believe it. I think that the struggle is close enough. China is so large, looms so high just beyond the frontiers, that if South Viet-Nam went, it would not only give them an improved geographic position for a guerrilla assault on Malaya but would also give the impression that the wave of the future in Southeast Asia was China and the Communists. So I believe it.[66]

As senator in June, 1956, Kennedy had spoken of Vietnam as "the cornerstone of the Free World in Southeast Asia, the Keystone to the arch, the finger in the dike."[67] Seven years later he was no less certain: "We are not going to withdraw from that effort. In my opinion, for us to withdraw from that effort would mean a collapse not only of South Viet-Nam, but Southeast Asia. So we are going to stay there."[68] Those who cite in contrast Kennedy's televised remarks of September 2, 1963—"In the final analysis it is their war" and "they have to win it"—ignore the essential point that Kennedy, as he demonstrated in throwing support to the anti-Diem generals, wanted this war won and believed it "would be a great mistake" for the United States, having successfully defended Europe, to turn its back on Asia.[69] And in that conviction, he had firm support from all his senior advisers and his Vice-President, Lyndon Johnson.

Closely linked to the concern about encouraging new aggressions was the belief that America's global commitments were on the firing line. President Johnson said in 1965:

> We are also there to strengthen world order. Around the globe, from Berlin to Thailand, are people whose well-being rests in part on the belief that they can count on us if they are attacked. To leave Viet-Nam to its fate would shake the confidence of all these people in the value of an American commitment and in the value of America's word. The result would be an increased unrest and instability, and even wider war.[70]

In Dean Rusk's view, "the integrity of the American commitment is at the heart" of the Vietnam issue, and "if our adversaries should discover that the American commitment is not worth anything, then the world would face dangers of which we have not yet dreamed."[71] The fact that that commitment had begun under Eisenhower and been expanded by Kennedy gave it greater legitimacy in the Johnson Administration, and indeed was one of the President's most frequent arguments for maintaining it.

The third assumption, the now-familiar "test case" hypothesis, likewise became stronger as American involvement dragged on. National Security Action Memorandum 288 (March 17, 1964) states that, even in the absence of U.S. involvement in Vietnam, a communist victory would produce falling dominoes and widespread accommodation to Asian communist forces. The fact of heavy U.S. involvement "accentuates the impact of a Communist South Vietnam not only in Asia but in the rest of the world, where the South Vietnam conflict is regarded as a test case of U.S.

capacity to help a nation to meet the Communist 'war of liberation.' "[72] This classified conclusion was in accord with what had been publicly stated—for instance, by President Kennedy before the United Nations in September, 1961, and in his 1962 State of the Union message, by Secretary Rusk in several speeches,[73] and by Assistant Secretary of State William P. Bundy in a review of the major reasons for U.S. involvement.[74]

Since the necessity of involvement was widely accepted, all that remained to be determined was how much will, resourcefulness, and perseverance the American leadership could muster in pursuit of its objectives. As phrased by Walt Rostow in a memorandum to Dean Rusk (November 23, 1964), victory in Vietnam was assured "if we enter the exercise with the same determination and staying power that we entered the long test on Berlin and the short test on the Cuba missiles. But it will take that kind of Presidential commitment and staying power."[75] For Rostow as for others, Vietnam represented yet another probe of American power by the communist bloc; to blunt the probe meant acceptance of "the simple fact that at this stage of history we are the greatest power in the world—if we behave like it."[76] In the midst of such a test—this "struggle of will and determination,"[77] this challenge only for those with "very steady nerves"[78]—disengagement was not only undesirable, it was unthinkable.

In the early 1960's, according to Arthur Schlesinger, decision-makers "became every succeeding year more imprisoned" by the war.[79] There was a sense of no turning back; and as commitments and rhetoric expanded, especially in 1965, the main concern of some officials shifted to the "humiliating defeat"[80] the United States would suffer if it continued to present a weak posture in Vietnam. The war had become a matter of America's face. "It is essential . . . that U.S. emerge as a 'good doctor,' " wrote John T. McNaughton, McNamara's principal aide. "We must have kept promises, been tough, taken risks, gotten bloodied, and hurt the enemy very badly."[81] In the same memorandum McNaughton, said by some writers to have been trying to convince his superiors of Vietnam's declining importance, asserted that "70%" of American objectives was to avoid "a humiliating U.S. defeat," while only "20%" involved South Vietnam's independence and "10%" letting the South Vietnamese people "enjoy a better, freer way of life."[82] But McNaughton misread the temper of these men, most of whom believed avoiding defeat *was* an objective worth paying a substantial price for. Whether they based their belief on ideological and strategic grounds or, like Under Secretary of State George Ball, on the practical ground that too much American prestige, "authority," and resources had been committed to warrant rapid disengagement,[83] they were all hostages to a policy of escalation.

Presidential Power. Policy on Vietnam suffered from pride of authorship as each President approved courses of action that made the war peculiarly his own. Success or failure became identified with his personal credibility, authority, and place in history as much as with his chances for re-election. Those in his inner circle either learned to share in the burden or, as Chester Cooper has commented, were excluded from the "team" and kept in the dark about sensitive information.[84]

For President Kennedy, the fall of 1963 seems to have been the beginning of his personal identification with winning in Vietnam, as indicated by statements quoted above. If the Bay of Pigs disaster had encouraged him to compensate with strong action in Vietnam in 1961, as many writers claim, the Cuban missile crisis in 1962 may have emboldened him to support Diem's overthrow and thus fully restore his credentials as a decisive President. "Strongly in our mind," Kennedy declared at the height of the Buddhist crisis, "is what happened in the case of China at the end of World War II, where China was lost—a weak government became increasingly unable to control events. We don't want that."[85]

Johnson adopted Kennedy's belief that Southeast Asia should not be "lost" the way China had been. "I am not going to be the President who saw Southeast Asia go the way China went," he is quoted as having told Ambassador Lodge.[86] Like Kennedy, Johnson could not see himself shrinking from Rostow's challenge to show "Presidential commitment and staying power." Neither President could see *himself*, not to mention the nation, losing a war. All the more so as Vietnam could become their political albatross just as China had been Truman's. The fear of sparking a new wave of McCarthyism,[87] and the determination not to let charges of "softness" on (Vietnamese) communism impede re-election chances,[88] combined with the psychological need to emerge a winner to keep Presidents on course toward deeper involvement.

Opting In: The Bureaucratic Dimension. A number of bureaucratic pressures and circumstances contributed significantly to the decisions that kept the United States entrapped in a spiraling war. Their effects were to create demands for action, to put a premium on the exploitation of U.S. power and military potential, to bias the choices available to the President, to instill an urge to act tough, and to coopt policy dissidents on the inside. Some former officials have explained these effects in terms of executive fatigue, bureaucratic secrecy on Vietnam, poor staffing, and duplication of effort. These, however, were only surface manifestations of much deeper institutional problems; they were symptoms of a "disease" indigenous to the decision-making process.

In the face of failing policies, bureaucratic leaders make constant demands upon their staffs to come up with "something new." That is their job, and it is performed zealously when personal and bureaucratic reputations are on the line. The demands multiply by the time they reach the President, and the pressure on him to respond with new action directives can be intense. In the case of Vietnam, the President's response had to take account of conflicting interests. On the one hand, Kennedy and Johnson, no less than some of their advisers, were anxious to avoid precipitate moves that would arouse public opinion, offend allies, and stimulate countermoves by the DRV and its allies. On the other, since Vietnam was believed to be a case of naked communist aggression, both Presidents felt justified in selecting policies that would increase the use of military power.

The bureaucracy, as evidenced by the elaborate scenarios in the Pentagon Papers, was run by men well versed in the art of manipulating power. They facilitated Presidential decisions by coming up with "modest" escalatory steps that would enable the President to tell the public he was responding with "restraint" to the other side's provocations. Presidents also found these suggestions appealing as tactical accommodations to their bureaucracy: Such "small" steps would buy them time (though time for what was never clearly articulated), get critics off their back, and warn the opponent of harsher measures unless he desisted in South Vietnam. "Restrained" escalation became bureaucratic appeasement.[89]

The 1965 bombing decision is a case in point. In the several months preceding the decision, the bureaucracy had run ahead of Johnson. Believing that air attacks on the DRV were essential and inevitable, the President's advisers laid out for him all the appropriate scenarios, including the proper way to sell the air war to the American public. When the President, in February, finally decided to run with the ball, he was persuaded that he had no other course. *He* evidently believed that the North Vietnamese had forced him into the bombing decision; the *bureaucracy*, especially the military and the State Department, could be satisfied that it had put all the high cards in the President's hand and persuaded him to raise the ante.

One reason why, when the ante was raised, it was raised only a step at a time is that, in addition to the constraining effects of domestic politics and European allies' opinion, bureaucratic leaders and Presidents alike never lost confidence in their ability to "orchestrate" power. They consistently believed that the ambitious national objectives they had defined could be achieved through the adroit handling of limited force, that is, force sufficient to bring the DRV to accept negotiations on American terms, but not so great as to provoke an escalation in response by one or both of the major communist powers. Kennedy's decision in 1961 to increase U.S. ground and air strength in South Vietnam is a perfect illustration of this behavior. So, too, is the whole range of options drawn up for Johnson during 1964 and 1965 to exploit American air power against the DRV. Both the policy planners and the policy-makers shared the belief they could control the pace and boundaries of the war—a major objective that was never realized.

A significant point in common about policy planning on Vietnam is that it always involved a consensus to move policy in the same direction. The bureaucracy consistently limited the President's alternatives to different kinds of escalation and rarely included strategies of disengagement. Where disengagement was included —and the Pentagon Papers contain no scenarios for pulling out or working toward a settlement—it was not a "live" option but rather a throwaway to give the appearance of balance. Options become genuine, in the bureaucratic game, only when there are officials who believe in them and are willing to fight for them. In the 1960's the option of disengaging had neither strong institutional support nor unflagging personal endorsement, which explains why no serious reassessment of American national interests in Vietnam was ever undertaken at the highest level.

To illustrate, the National Security Council met on August 31, 1963, to consider U.S. policy toward Diem after plans for a coup had temporarily fizzled. Rusk, McNamara, and Vice-President Johnson quickly stacked the options. When Paul Kattenburg of the State Department suggested the time had arrived to disengage (a possibility also raised, though less strongly, by Attorney General Robert Kennedy), Rusk reportedly dismissed it out of hand. Further discussion of alternatives, he declared with the endorsement of his colleagues, would *assume* no withdrawal of forces "until the war is won."[90] Later in the year, when General Taylor was sent to Vietnam, he was instructed to consider only three strategies: a high-level troop commitment, a low-level troop commitment, and additional military aid.

Similarly, in late 1964, the only "realistic" options that survived the planning process were alternative means of bombing the DRV to the conference table—reprisal raids, massive and uninterrupted attacks, and graduated escalation. William Bundy later wrote that moving "toward withdrawal" was one choice Johnson's key advisers considered as late as January, 1965.[91] But withdrawal by then was merely a token option; it was quickly discarded as being inconsistent with U.S. purposes (as was any negotiating position that Hanoi might conceivably have found attractive). An insight into why withdrawal alternatives could not see the light of day is provided by McGeorge Bundy's proposal of "sustained reprisals" in February, 1965. One of his basic arguments was that even the failure of air strikes, which he rated a good possibility, would be better than doing nothing or beginning to do less, since such attacks would at least show that the United States had done all it could do for the Saigon regime.

The fact that option-building was almost always done by committees and task forces also helps explain the biased results. The task force under Clark Clifford in early 1968, for example, had a mandate to undertake a complete ("A to Z") policy review. But the four options that were considered all related to General Westmoreland's massive troop request. Clifford may personally have communicated his support of a bombing cutback to the

President; he had no other choice, since his task force was compromised from the outset by the presence of the major proponents of large-scale bombing. It is hence not surprising that, as already mentioned, the Clifford group's recommendations included a modest troop increase and disagreement over *how much* the bombing should be stepped up.

In those few cases in which part of the bureaucracy sought to challenge the leadership's basic assumptions—such as CIA studies that destroyed the domino thesis, cogently criticized the bombing strategy, and closely questioned the feasibility of "rooting out" the Viet Cong "infrastructure"—it was ignored. The men around the President would not accept contrary opinion as evidence. Once the framework of policy had been established, bureaucratic leaders would "absorb" only those fragments of information that fit with the established line. It was as if to say, "there is no point telling us that what we've been doing is based on wrong assumptions; if you want to have impact, tell us how we can improve on what we're determined to do."

Prestigious individual dissenters were treated differently. They were exploited. They became "institutionalized," as James C. Thomson has written—house doves whom the leadership could point to in evidence of its openness to dissent.[92] Conceivably, the arguments of men like Ball softened or delayed escalatory decisions. But the price of these concessions was agreement to "stand by the President" and make nationwide appearances in behalf of his policies. And this was only one of several ways in which the "team" image was preserved at a time when important defections and a breakup of the policy consensus might have had immensely constructive consequences.

American Strategy and the Vietnamese

A reader of the Pentagon Papers might well put the volumes down and wonder what happened to the Vietnamese. In a curious but important sense, American officials do not seem to have been concerned about the Vietnamese, "North" or "South," except insofar as they contributed to or obstructed the attainment of U.S. objectives in Southeast Asia. To these officials, what was important about Vietnam was its strategic and symbolic value, not its people or its historic setting as the milieu of a profound nationalist (as well as communist) revolution that was still unfinished. To be sure, official American rhetoric periodically referred to the need to allow South Vietnamese to determine their own future. In reality, once having decided that on Vietnam's outcome hinged the global balance of power, American administrations could not possibly let the Vietnamese decide the future by themselves. This may be the reason why administration spokesmen would so often declare, after giving their version of the war's origin, that the only relevant fact for policy purposes was that "we're there." Vietnam could not be evaluated in legal, moral, human, or social-historical terms; it was a strategic, bureaucratic, and political *problem.*

A significant consequence of this typically pragmatic or, as officials would say, hard-headed approach to Vietnam is that their planning and choices were not influenced by the nationalism of the Vietnamese communists. Indeed, the Pentagon Papers show clearly the inability of officials to see that the strength and effectiveness of the "enemy," which they freely and often acknowledged, was closely related to his popularity. In the Eisenhower Administration, there had been grudging acceptance by the President and Secretary of State Dulles that the Vietnamese communists would win an election conducted in 1954, a conclusion that accounts for subsequent American support of Diem's refusal to carry out the election provision of the Final Declaration of the Geneva Conference. With the unexpected solidification of Diem's rule in the late 1950's, Washington officials and congressmen reevaluated Diem and found him to be "Free Vietnam's" answer to Ho Chi Minh. By the time Kennedy took over, any lingering doubts in official circles about the respective nationalist credentials of the two Vietnams and their leaders had long since become submerged in cold war politics.

Publicly, Washington's case was that even if the NLF movement had a large southern Vietnamese component, it had become powerful only because of the critical addition of cadres and soldiers from the North. White Papers were published in 1961 and 1965 to document DRV "aggression." Dean Rusk often declared that if only the DRV would "stop doing what it is doing" in the South, there would be no security problem there, hence no need of American troops. Walt Rostow proposed that the NLF based its operations "more on murder than on political or psychological appeal."[93] In a far more sophisticated analysis, a U.S. Information Agency official with extensive experience in Vietnam concluded, on the basis of captured documents and interviews, that most Vietnamese "were recruited [into the NLF] under circumstances where there was no alternative"; that Viet Cong units "were highly effective because they were composed of professionals," not because they were highly motivated; and that the key to the NLF's success was its "careful organization building, not . . . some unique spirit or élan."[94]

In private, American officials puzzled over the NLF's continuing growth and effectiveness. Ambassador Taylor, returning to Washington in November, 1964, to brief officials, attributed the NLF's success to aid from the North and Saigon's inadequacies, but he admitted there was a missing element he could not explain:

> The ability of the Vietcong continuously to rebuild their units and to make good their losses is one of the mysteries of this guerrilla war. We are aware of the recruiting methods by which local boys are induced or compelled to join the Viet Cong ranks and have some general appreciation of the amount of infiltration of personnel from the outside. Yet taking both of these sources into account, we still find no plausible explanation of the continued strength of the Vietcong if our data on Viet Cong losses are even approximately correct. Not only do the Viet Cong units have the recuperative powers of the phoenix, but they have an amazing ability to maintain morale. Only in rare cases have we found evidences of bad morale among Viet Cong prisoners or recorded in captured Viet Cong documents.[95]

Three months later, McGeorge Bundy, discussing the "grim" prospects in South Vietnam, also commented on the enemy's extraordinary resiliency but concluded: "Yet the weary country does not want them to win."[96]

Assessments such as these refused to credit the communist forces in the South with a political appeal attractive to Vietnamese peasants. Yet there were a number of classified studies available to U.S. officials from the RAND Corporation that contradicted these assessments on the basis of extensive interviews of NLF and North Vietnamese army personnel captured or surrendered in the South. While focusing on different aspects of the communist forces, several of these studies came to similar conclusions.[97] They reported that the NLF was no mere creature of the North but had its origins in reaction against Diem's repressions of the late 1950's, his alliance with the United States, and his refusal to hold national elections in 1956; that while *initial* NLF strength could be accounted for by southern former Viet Minh who had either buried their weapons and remained behind in 1954 or returned to the South from regroupment in the DRV, from the late 1950's until early 1965 the vast majority of NLF soldiers were recruited in South Vietnam on the basis of the movement's attractive land reform and political programs; that the NLF's cohesion and high morale were not only the result of tight organization, but were due also to its members' belief they were fighting for a just cause, their hatred of the United States as France's "neocolonialist" successor, the bond of friendship and respect between NLF soldiers and villagers, and the trust and dependence built up between cadres and rank-and-file soldiers. These were the reasons American military power could neither undermine the morale of communist forces in the South nor break the will of the DRV leadership to keep supporting them. These were the explanations Ambassador Taylor and others overlooked for the communists' constant ability to replenish their forces and for the extremely low number of cadre defections to the Saigon government. The Vietnamese communist units *did* have a feeling of mission that sustained them: to drive the Americans from their country, get rid of the *My-Viet* (American-Vietnamese) leadership in Saigon, and reunite Vietnam.

Unable or unwilling to accept the phenomenon unfolding before them, American officials were attracted to stratagems that were almost bound to fail. Some urged bombing the North in the expectation Hanoi would "call off" its organization in the South. Others, like McGeorge Bundy (in his previously cited "sustained reprisal" memorandum), believed one of the effects of bombing the DRV would be its "substantial depressing effect upon the morale of Viet Cong cadres." "Carrot and stick" combinations were tried to bring DRV leaders to accept negotiations—by threatening to bomb the DRV if American proposals were rejected; offering Vietnamese leaders fringe benefits (such as Lodge's proposed economic aid in 1964 in return for stopping the war and

Johnson's 1965 offer to include the DRV in a $1 billion program of aid for Mekong River Valley development); and then employing force when, predictably, American blackmail was denounced. Finally, in South Vietnam, several futile projects were initiated to untrack the NLF express. Psychological warfare leaflets were dropped over the DRV and South Vietnam to undermine communist morale; *Chieu-Hoi* (Open Arms) centers were established for defectors; money was offered to defecting communist cadres; and Operation Phoenix was launched to destroy the communist organizational apparatus in the villages, using counterterror and propaganda.

The essential antinationalism that was reflected in these programs and perceptions of the DRV and the NLF also characterized American dealings with Saigon. Throughout the Kennedy Administration and into the first years of Johnson's Administration, the hope persisted that Saigon could be motivated, by American aid and later by bombing the North, to reform itself. The beginning of the end of that hope was the 1963 Buddhist crisis, when officials came to share Ambassador Lodge's view that finding a way to pressure Diem into broadening his government and carrying out other reforms "would be one of the greatest discoveries since the enactment of the Marshall Plan in 1947 because, so far as I know, the U.S. had never yet been able to control any of the very unsatisfactory governments through which we have had to work."[98] Direct intervention took the place of reform, and would thereafter remain the dominant motif of U.S. policy. As Kennedy strongly implied in a news conference of September 12, 1963, the war had become too important to the United States to make further intervention dependent on the Vietnamese:

> What helps to win the war, we support; what interferes with the war effort, we oppose. . . . In some ways I think the Vietnamese people and ourselves agree; we want the war to be won, the Communists to be contained, and the Americans to go home. . . . But we are not there to see a war lost, and we will follow the policy which I have indicated today of advancing those causes and issues which help win the war.[99]

Reforming Saigon thereafter is seen less and less in internal government documents; instead, the arguments are that the Saigon government could hardly be expected to be democratic in wartime and that the United States is in Vietnam to protect its own interests and not merely those of the Vietnamese and their government.

Any comprehensive explanation of U.S. escalation in Vietnam must therefore take account of this antinationalist dimension—the determination to win the war despite the Vietnamese, if necessary, and the over-all American failure to comprehend the background and implications of Vietnamese nationalism. U.S. international concerns and domestic politics had led the Truman Administration to cast aside opportunities to identify with Ho Chi Minh's movement in the late 1940's, just as in China; and similar considerations, with different elements, accounted for the American takeover from the French of responsibility for Vietnam's security in the mid-1950's. Even so, opportunities still remained in the 1960's to recognize that the NLF-DRV alliance indeed represented the dynamic force of Vietnamese nationalism, and accordingly not to oppose it. But to have retreated from rather than perpetuated intervention, as was decided on in the case of China, would probably have required a radical alteration of setting and actors. The background of China's "loss," the impact of a protracted war on the Presidency and the decision-making apparatus, the persistent belief in the validity and necessity of intervention to capture the high stakes seen on the table, and the refusal to see the communist opponents as representing a movement of revolutionary scope and nationalist origins all propelled a response quite opposite from the one in 1949. One can only wonder what the response would have been had the Chinese communist challenge to Chiang's authority occurred after the "loss" of Vietnam to Ho Chi Minh.

STABILIZING ASIA: NIXON AND BANGLADESH

The Nixon Doctrine

Any President entering office in 1969 would have felt compelled, because of the Vietnam war's divisive effects on American society, the heavy toll it exacted on American manpower and the budget, and America's failure to achieve the lofty objectives set by previous administrations, to offer the public and Congress "something new" in foreign policy. The Nixon Doctrine, first spelled out during a Presidential stopover on Guam in July, 1969, was designed to meet that expectation. More particularly, the Doctrine seemed to promise the removal of U.S. forces from Vietnam while working for a negotiated settlement and upgrading the caliber of the South Vietnamese Army; the avoidance of new foreign commitments; and the elimination of excesses in defense spending.

Yet President Nixon, seeing himself standing "in the middle of the crossfire" between neo-isolationist "superdoves" and Fortress America "superhawks," also believed most Americans still wanted the nation to play a "responsible" role in Asian and world affairs.[100] Whether or not this was true, it is evident that Nixon himself was determined that the United States remain an active participant in Asia's politics and security problems. "We are a Pacific power," he stated on Guam and many times thereafter, and only by having a significant presence in the region could the United States avoid unwanted involvements.[101] The underlying message of the Doctrine was not that America's traditional mission in Asia would change, but rather that there would be alterations in the manner in which the mission would be carried out.

A second reason why there would be only tactical adjustments in America's Asia policies was Nixon's belief that although Russia and China had become more responsible powers, their leaders still clung to an expansionist philosophy. The old politics of containment and intervention, he seemed to conclude, had to be replaced by the politics of balance of power; and "only the United States has sufficient strength to be able to help maintain a balance in Europe and other areas."[102] In Asia, such an equilibrium among the major powers required a "stable" environment in which bigpower negotiations, economic development problems, and the resolution of regional tensions and conflicts could be satisfactorily resolved. "Stability" became one of the Doctrine's watchwords: "The challenge for the future," Nixon reported in 1971, "is to ensure that it [the new Pacific international structure] is a structure of stability." American "economic interest in a prosperous Asia" was linked with "our political interest in the stability of the area."[103] And in his view, as he wrote less than two years before becoming President, stability was legitimate only if achieved "by evolutionary rather than revolutionary means."[104]

Did an interest in stability and balance of power mean a revision downward of U.S. national interests in Asia? The Nixon Administration sought to reassure allies that the Doctrine did not mean an abandonment of American commitments to their protection. "We must above all tend to our national obligations," Nixon told an interviewer. "We must not forget our alliances or our interests."[105] Thus, although the Doctrine spoke about making commitments conform to national interests, rather than the other way around, past commitments would continue to preoccupy U.S. foreign policy. Two potential drawbacks could be anticipated: The United States might become tied to policies or practices of allies that it should not approve; or, as in Cambodia in the spring of 1970, sudden events could enlarge existing commitments and create new national interests.

To meet existing commitments, fulfill interests, and yet accommodate domestic demands for greater stringency overseas, the Nixon Doctrine emphasized Asian self-reliance. The expectation was that through regional cooperation in economic development and defense, the buildup of the armed forces of friendly Asian nations using increased U.S. military assistance, and the maintenance of an imposing but reduced U.S. strategic capability in the area, both undue dependence on American protection and the danger of becoming enmeshed in another Vietnam could be avoided. Noncommunist Asians would do their own fighting against communist Asians; the United States would be a "low-profile" partner, involved but not necessarily committed. In a sense, Nixon was returning American policy in Asia to the hopeful days of Eisenhower's New Look defense program, when it was likewise expected that U.S. military aid and deterrent strength would combine with "Free Asian" ground forces to keep local revolutionaries and their communist supporters at bay.

The Nixon Doctrine represented a reworking of standard postwar American containment strategy to fit changed international and domestic circumstances. It showed no evidence of a basic reappraisal of American interests, least of all in Indochina, where the "Vietnamization" program entailed trading ground force reductions for increased air and naval power, widening the air war over Laos and the DRV, and committing the United States to the survival of a noncommunist government in Cambodia. The stress in the Doctrine on stability, power balance, maintaining treaty commitments, and containment by proxy suggested that the new administration agreed with its predecessors that revolutionary nationalist movements were threats. They were destabilizing, raised the prospect of a superpower confrontation, were invariably directed against friendly or allied governments, and challenged the self-reliance concept. The Bangladesh movement was interpreted in precisely this way.

Revolution in Bangladesh

Between March and December, 1971, while thousands of Bengalis in what was then East Pakistan were being slaughtered, and while a guerrilla movement was seeking to win independence as Bangladesh, the Nixon Administration pursued power politics in the Indian subcontinent. The responsibility of the West Pakistani leadership for the war and the issue of self-determination for the Bengalis were peripheral in administration policy-making. Nor did administration officials show concern that American arms and economic assistance were enabling West Pakistan to prosecute the war. Classified government records now published, congressional testimony, and other sources reveal that the President's principal interest, shared by his top advisers, was to keep the subcontinent "stable" and thwart India's supposed ambition, with Soviet support, to destroy the delicate power balance that was said to prevail.

Was the administration well advised to give "stability" and the balance of power priority over the struggle to create an independent Bangladesh? What were American interests in the war? What kind of war was it—merely "civil strife" and "disorder," as administration spokesmen characterized it, or a genuine revolution for national liberation, as the leaders of Bangladesh and India saw it? Was U.S. policy, as the administration maintained, evenhanded in its search for a settlement? The answers to these questions shed light on American motivations and objectives in Asia and throughout the Third World.

Background to Revolt. In large part because of the structure of the American decision-making machinery and the shifts in personnel occasioned by changes in administration, sudden upheavals abroad, such as occurred in East Pakistan in 1971, are treated as international crises rather than as the product of often prolonged tension and conflict within societies that have deep historical and socio-economic roots. American policy might have evolved differently in 1971, as it might also in the late 1940's in China and thereafter in Vietnam, had the origins of revolution been appreciated. An examination of the relationship between the two parts of Pakistan, separated by 1,000 miles of Indian territory, might have led to two basic conclusions: first, politically, that the army's suppression of the Bengali revolt was undertaken in order that the will of the Bengali majority in the East, expressed in free elections, be prevented from vesting control of the Pakistani Government in Bengali hands and giving the East the substantially greater autonomy to which it was entitled; second, economically, that East Pakistan was more a colony than an integral part of the nation, so that secession represented a threat to vested economic (and political) interests in the dominant Western provinces.

The movement for secession and independence by East Pakistanis may now be seen as having originated in tensions that developed a year after Pakistan became a separate state in 1947. The issues were language, military rule, provincial autonomy, and economic benefits. From the outset, one of the principal agitators for the East's interests was Sheikh Mujibur Rahman, who would lead the Bangladesh movement and become the new nation's first Prime Minister. Sheikh Mujib's activities earned him jail terms in 1948, 1949–51, 1958–59, 1962, 1966–68, and 1971, the last of which showed the ultimate futility of national reconciliation.[106]

The events that seem to have been critical in moving the East toward open rebellion all concerned the military's domination of politics beginning in 1958. General Mohammad Ayub Khan's takeover intensified provincial frictions and "foreclosed what might truly have been a revolution, the national elections scheduled for early 1959 that would probably have seen H. S. Suhrawardy (a Bengali politician) Prime Minister and a much more representative legislature supporting the cabinet."[107] In 1966, in the wake of the Indo-Pakistani war, Sheikh Mujib's Awami League concluded that the West Pakistan leadership was only interested in protecting its own provinces, not the equally exposed East. The League issued a six-point program for autonomy that would be demanded anew in 1971. Then, in 1968, uprisings occurred in both sectors of the country against repressive military rule; but the Eastern leadership's hope for expanded local authority was met only by a change of military leaders, from Ayub Khan to General Mohammad Yahya Khan. To the Sheikh and his supporters, the prospects seemed remote that military rule by an army and civil service in which Bengalis were grossly underrepresented could integrate the country on an equitable basis.[108]

The East's poverty and its neglect and exploitation by the Western sector gave the autonomy movement its momentum. For the East's differentness was not simply a matter of geography, language, and culture. More basically, it rested on a 60 per cent lower per capita income; an increasing gap between East and West in national income, with higher population growth cutting into the East's lower share; only about one-third of public and private investment going to the East (despite having about 60 per cent of Pakistan's total population); a declining percentage of total student enrollment at all levels; the necessity of relying for manufactured goods on the West, on terms less favorable than could have been obtained on the world market; and the duty to transfer to the West a disproportionate share of Bengali resources for processing, as well as tax revenues from foreign exchange earnings (most of which were earned in the East, where the major export, jute, originates).[109] With the West thus progressing at the East's expense, it is not surprising to find that:

> By 1968, when the army had been ruling for less than ten years, twenty West Pakistani families controlled 97 per cent of the country's insurance, 80 per cent of the banking and 66 per cent of the industry. Thus, not only was Bengal reduced to semicolonial status but West Pakistan itself was gripped by a small, cohesive, incredibly powerful group of exploiters. And the army was consuming 60 per cent of the national budget.[110]

In November, 1970, a devastating cyclone ripped through East Pakistan, killing perhaps a half million people and ruining the chronically weak economy. The West's response was indicative of the low priority that had long been assigned the Bengalis, and undoubtedly was remembered when the Assembly elections were held soon afterward. With famine threatening the approximately 2 million people living in the cyclone area, the principal relief work was done by international voluntary agencies. Pakistani authorities, as U.S. Government sources testified, were shockingly lax about coordinating a relief effort, seemed to supply the absolute minimum of food over the next six months, and actually spent, in that period, only $4.7 million of a special congressional relief appropriation of $7.5 million.[111]

In 1970, however, it was still possible to salvage Pakistani unity. President Yahya promised elections for a Constituent Assembly that would enable formation of a civilian government. But Yahya hedged his bet by issuing a Legal Framework Order (LFO) that, in effect, gave the Punjabis in the West a veto power over the constitution the Constituent Assembly would draw up. Yahya was correct to be concerned, for in the elections, which were generally accepted as quite fairly run, Sheikh Mujib's Awami League won overwhelmingly. In keeping with the provincial basis of party politics in Pakistan, the League won 167 of 169 Bengali seats, while former Foreign Minister Zulfikar Ali Bhutto's People's Party garnered 82 of 138 seats in the West. As matters developed, neither Yahya nor Bhutto was about to let the Sheikh become Prime Minister or the Awami League determine the constitution.

The first step in the scuttling of the elections mandate was Bhutto's announcement in mid-February, 1971, that his party would not attend the Assembly's meeting in Dacca (East Pakistan) scheduled for March 3. Yahya was then persuaded by Bhutto, who probably threatened an army revolt, to postpone the Assembly—and then, on second thought, as Bengali unrest began, called for the Assembly to meet March 25. Yahya was too late. Sheikh Mujib, under great pressure to declare for Bangladesh, insisted (among other demands) that martial law be ended, which would have entailed Yahya's abandonment of the LFO veto. While also insisting he wanted autonomy, not secession, the Sheikh authorized a civil disobedience movement; and he responded to another offer by Yahya—that he form a central coalition government, but with Bhutto included—by saying any new government would have to be his alone to form. Negotiations continued in this manner, and it remains unclear how serious either party was about compromise, given the excited state of each leader's constituents. The combination of mutual mistrust, secessionist rallies, and Bhutto's behind-the-scenes machinations to heighten suspicions of the Sheikh's intentions certainly made compromise improbable.

Two days after the Bangladesh flag was unfurled for the first time in Dacca, on March 25, West Pakistani troops moved in to decide the issue by force. Sheikh Mujib was arrested on the charge of high treason and removed to the West. The Awami League was outlawed. East Pakistan became a killing ground, with all Bengalis, Muslim and Hindu, acceptable targets. Within a few months, roughly 80,000 soldiers were stationed in the East; a Bengali Liberation Army (Mukti Bahini) was formed that eventually numbered anywhere from 50,000 to 100,000 fighters and supporters; and Indian border forces were training, supplying, and providing sanctuary for the guerrillas.

Formative Factors in the American Response. American policy toward the Bangladesh movement was conditioned not only by the operating principles of the Nixon Doctrine, but also by over fifteen years of fairly close defense association with, and economic support of, the Pakistani Government in Islamabad. When the President decided to "tilt" toward (West) Pakistan in the 1971 conflict, he was acting in accordance with both traditional balance-of-power thinking and a preference in American South Asia policy for Pakistan over India.

American arms for Pakistan were first delivered in 1954, after the Eisenhower Administration decided that Pakistan was ideally situated to be a keystone of the so-called Northern Tier defense against the Soviet Union. As a Muslim Asian state with anticommunist leaders, Pakistan was believed to be a useful ally of the United States in the containment strategy for both Southeast Asia and the Middle East. Pakistan joined SEATO (Southeast Asia Treaty Organization) in 1954 and the Baghdad Pact (later, the Central Treaty Organization) in 1955. The arms buildup that evolved from 1954 to 1965—over $1 billion worth, it is generally figured[112]—bought little so far as American defense interests were concerned, however. Except for intelligence facilities, such as the one at Peshawar from which U-2 spy flights took off, the arms aid was not primarily used (nor did it have much need to be used) for Northern Tier defense. As one writer has pointed out,[113] the main significance of the arms was threefold: They enabled the army to become the central political force in the country; they enabled

Pakistan to adopt a tougher policy toward India; and they ensured West Pakistan's dominance of the East.

The fruits of this policy were reaped in the 1965 Indo-Pakistani war, which convinced the Johnson Administration that a lot of good military hardware and millions of dollars in economic aid were being wasted in conflict between neighbors. All U.S. foreign assistance was cut off to both countries in 1965; and although economic aid was resumed in 1966, the embargo remained on military aid, with an exception for spare parts ("nonlethal" equipment) in April, 1967. A great deal of damage had, however, occurred in the meantime, mainly in American-Indian relations. The Indian leadership, while grateful for U.S. economic aid of about $9 billion since independence, never could accept the rationale for U.S. arming of the Pakistanis, who were considered bound to use their military power against India rather than against communism. When the opportunity arose in 1965 to counter U.S. arms shipments to Pakistan with Soviet and East European weapons, Delhi took it.

The Nixon Administration entered office to find that the Indian Government, while moralizing about nonalignment, had "decisively" shifted the arms balance on the subcontinent in its favor. Over $730 million in equipment had been delivered since the 1965 war from the U.S.S.R. and East Europe,[114] less than a fourth what Pakistan had obtained, mainly from China. To an administration with a "deep interest in ensuring that the subcontinent does not become a focus of great power conflict," and with an announced objective "to bring our activity into a stable balance with that of the other major powers with interests in the area,"[115] Indian foreign policy was out of step with the Nixon Doctrine.[116]

But what of American arms policy? Was it as disinterested and insignificant as the 1965 embargo and the 1967 spare-parts exception made it appear? The answer is that while U.S. military assistance to Pakistan from 1967 on was small in dollar value, it contributed importantly to the upkeep and readiness of the West's armed forces that swept across and over East Pakistan in 1971. Although most military sales figures were classified to hide the extent of the assistance and avoid questions about its composition, it was revealed *after* the fighting began that: (1) the "nonlethal" equipment included "trainer and transport aircraft; transport equipment such as trucks and jeeps; and communications, medical and engineering equipment," all delivered since 1967 at a yearly value of about $7.5 million; (2) annual deliveries beginning in 1967 of $2.5 million in ammunition; and (3) a $200,000 per year military training program.[117] Even these admissions, totaling $40.8 million for 1967–70, may not tell the full story. One official testified that fiscal year 1970 military sales to Pakistan were about $20 million;[118] a reporter, Tad Szulc of the *New York Times*, found that "the flow of military equipment to Pakistan from Air Force sales alone had reached $47,944,781 between 1967 and April 30, 1970";[119] and the President himself said that when nearly all arms deliveries to Pakistan were shut off in April, 1971, about $35 million worth was in the aid pipeline.[120]

In short, "lethal" as well as "nonlethal" equipment was shipped despite the embargo—and all of it went to the Pakistani forces in the West, which then transferred a good deal of it and equipment obtained from the United States before 1965 to the East. Had the war not broken out, Washington was also prepared to begin delivery of F-104 fighter planes, B-57 bombers, and other equipment under a "one-time exception" announced in October, 1970.[121] Although no deliveries were actually made on these items, the government of India was unlikely to consider that the sale was any less destabilizing than its purchases from Moscow. More important, in terms of the next year's events, the end runs around the embargo begun under Johnson set a pattern that the Nixon Administration followed to assist West Pakistan's repression of Bangladesh.

For all the military assistance provided West Pakistan since 1954, American economic aid may have been even more critical to the West's ability to prosecute a war in the East. Between 1947 and 1970, Washington committed about $4 billion in loans and grants—roughly $250 million annually and between 50 and 60 per cent of foreign economic aid to Pakistan from all sources.[122] As one specialist with long experience in Pakistan's development programs testified, "West Pakistan received a disproportionate share" of American and all other aid simply because most of the development projects were located there.

We rarely asked [he continued] whose economic development the projects contributed to. But that is a critical question in a bifurcated country such as Pakistan since projects in one part of the country make virtually no contribution to the advancement of the other part. By following this normally sound principle, we have contributed to the economic deprivation of East Pakistan. We can see now that that policy was a grievous mistake and bears some of the responsibility for the current crisis [in 1971].[123]

American banks in Pakistan followed the same investment pattern.[124]

When the war against Bangladesh broke out, the West's dependence on foreign, but particularly American, economic assistance naturally increased. By then reportedly $4.6 billion in debt to foreign creditors, and with foreign reserves under $200 million, Pakistan could not for long afford a war that was estimated to cost $70 million a month.[125] This was especially so inasmuch as the East had been providing most of the trade revenue, with American aid covering "about half of Pakistan's adverse balance of trade."[126] In June, 1971, all the World Bank members of the Pakistan aid consortium decided not to extend additional credit; the United States was the sole exception.

U.S. Policy: The Official Case. American military and economic aid to the Pakistani Government provides the background against which to assess both the official and unofficial versions of U.S. policy in 1971. That policy may be considered in two stages: The first, from the end of March through November, found the administration undertaking a humanitarian relief effort for Bengalis in East Pakistan and in India, seeking to influence a settlement between East and West Pakistan, and coping with the increased danger of war between Pakistan and India; the second, in December, involved the American response to Indo-Pakistani fighting.

In making decisions with respect to the first stage of hostilities, administration officials began with several key assumptions about the nature of, and responsibility for, them. Pakistan's repression of the Bangladesh movement, using U.S.-made tanks, jets, and other equipment, was an "internal matter" of "concern" to Washington.[127] This characterization was considered necessary, it was later asserted,[128] because a public condemnation of Pakistan would reduce U.S. influence in bringing about the desired outcome, which was—as Nixon wrote President Yahya on May 28, 1971— "to restore conditions in East Pakistan conducive to the return of refugees from Indian territory as quickly as possible."[129] Bengali refugees were pouring into India at an initial rate of 100,000 a day —they later would number about 9 million—and it was the administration's view that, through "quiet diplomacy," Islamabad might agree to put "an end to the civil strife," enable the refugees to return, and thus end the extraordinary strain they were placing on the Indian Government's resources.[130]

A chief concern of the administration was that as the refugee flow reached intolerable proportions, Indian support of the Mukti Bahini guerrillas might dramatically increase. To prevent India's full-fledged entry into the war, the administration urged upon Prime Minister Gandhi patience and prudence. It committed $249 million for relief operations in India and East Pakistan, and promised $250 million more. And it claimed to have informed the government of India that Washington favored "political autonomy for East Bengal" and was prepared "even to discuss with them [West Pakistani officials and Awami League members] a political timetable, a precise timetable" for autonomy.[131] It was only because, in the administration's view, Mme. Gandhi's government proved truculent that, in August, Secretary of State Rogers had to resort to a threat, telling the Indian Ambassador "that the Administration could not continue economic assistance to a nation that started a war."[132]

The administration's case contends further that as part of the strategy of keeping the lid on a potentially explosive situation, it virtually cut off all economic and military aid to West Pakistan. On the economic side, Henry A. Kissinger, the President's chief foreign-policy adviser as head of the National Security Council, declared "the United States has made no new development loans to Pakistan since March 1971."[133] The cutoff of military aid was less categorically asserted. In late March, the State Department stated that no U.S. arms or ammunition was being sent to Pakistan. During the next two months, it insisted that only "limited quantities" of "nonlethal" spare parts and ammunition had been sold before the war began to keep previously supplied U.S. equipment operating and because "the suspension of U.S. military sales will not shut off a flow of supplies from other sources."[134] But the Department also maintained that, since March 25, "no military sales items including spare parts and ammunition have been provided" to Pakistan "and the question of deliveries is under review." Not until June did a Department official admit, under questioning, that licenses granted before early April for the export of munitions to Pakistan were being honored[135]—and even that exception, assertedly amounting in value to about $5 million, was not the entire accounting.

Escalation of the "civil strife" in Bangladesh to involve India should never have happened, in the administration's view. "Quiet diplomacy" was having its intended effects in West Pakistan, where Yahya Khan was said to have become flexible on a number of issues. President Nixon's 1972 foreign-policy report cites several agreements obtained from the Pakistani leader before December: Sheikh Mujib would not be executed; amnesty would be granted to all returning refugees (June 10); civilian rule would be restored by the end of December (June 28); an internationalized relief mission would be permitted in East Pakistan (August); East Pakistan's military governor (who had presided over the massacres) would be replaced by a civilian (September); and (November) Yahya would be ready to begin negotiations "with any representative of this group [of Bengali separatists in Calcutta] not charged with high crimes in Pakistan, or with Awami League leaders still in East Pakistan."

But the "practical progress toward a political accommodation" in Pakistan anticipated by Secretary Rogers on November 12 never developed. Full-scale hostilities between Pakistan and India began December 3; and not until December 7, by which time "the capture of East Pakistan [by Indian forces] was a *fait accompli*," did the U.N. General Assembly pass a cease-fire resolution backed by the United States.[136] The President contends that during the week of December 6 a greater danger had developed:

> We received convincing evidence that India was seriously contemplating the seizure of Pakistan-held portions of Kashmir and the destruction of Pakistan's military forces in the West. We could not ignore this evidence. Nor could we ignore the fact that when we repeatedly asked India and its supporters for clear assurances to the contrary, we did not receive them. We had to take action to prevent a wider war.[137]

In Kissinger's words at the time, "what started as a tragedy in East Bengal is now becoming an attempt to dismember a sovereign state and a member of the United Nations."[138]

To the administration, there were only two choices to consider as war raged and the cease-fire resolution was debated: "We could take a stand against the war and try to stop it," said the President, "or we could maintain a 'neutral' position and acquiesce in it."[139] Although there was the "risk of failure" in the first alternative, the second "ran even greater risks" that were "unacceptable." These risks were that a prolonged war would lead to an attack on West Pakistan; that the "restraints" against war elsewhere in the world, especially the Middle East, would be weakened, and U.N. efforts for peace undermined, by a military solution in East Pakistan; that war might be encouraged to resolve ethnic tensions in other Third World countries; and that détente with Russia and China's healthier foreign-policy orientation would be adversely influenced.[140]

The fact that Indian-Pakistani clashes in the western sector did not lead to full-scale war there, and that a cease-fire finally was reached on December 17, was attributed by the administration to its coupling of firm diplomacy with a show of military power. About $80 million in bilateral economic aid to India was cut off. Delhi and Moscow were made aware that the United States would not tolerate an Indian attempt to "dismember" West Pakistan. And the nuclear aircraft carrier *Enterprise* headed a naval task force carrying 2,000 Marines into the Indian Ocean, ostensibly to help evacuate Americans from East Pakistan.[141] These actions are said to have convinced the Soviets, who in turn convinced the Indians, that Washington meant business. The United States had "failed," in the President's year-end assessment, to prevent escalation or help reconcile East and West Pakistan; but it had succeeded at short-circuiting a major war and possibly preventing a superpower clash in the subcontinent.

U.S. Policy: A Second Look. The public explanation that West Pakistan's effort to crush resistance in the East was purely an "internal matter" cannot be accepted. A majority of the people of Pakistan had democratically registered their support of Sheikh Mujibur and the Awami League, and found instead that constitutional processes were suspended, their leader imprisoned, and their lives and property under assault. To Yahya Khan's question on Pakistani television, "How can a government repress its own people?" the answer is clear: When such a government ceases to represent the majority and must rule by force and illegality. More-over, the use of American military equipment in the suppression; the reports of atrocities and genocide in violation of the Geneva Convention;[142] and the mass exodus of refugees to India, creating monumental relief problems and the danger of communal (Muslim-Hindu) strife,[143] all gave international dimensions to the assertedly civil war. Yet, at the United Nations, the American delegation chose to categorize only Indian involvement in Bangladesh as a "threat to the peace," not the Pakistani invasion that had precipitated it. The parallel with American policy in the Congo, when Soviet involvement received U.S. attention while the mercenaries were forgotten, is striking.

It is now quite clear that the administration went no farther than to express "concern" about developments in East Pakistan because, until the war escalated in December, it expected (and hoped?) that the Bangladesh resistance would be quashed with minimal upset to the subcontinent's "stability" and balance of power. This expectation could be seen, for instance, in Nixon's letter of May 28 to Yahya, in which the first priority was stated as putting "an end to the civil strife." It could be seen in the refusal of U.S. officials to meet with members of the Bangladesh Government, after it had announced its independence. It could be seen in the administration's constant talk about a "political accommodation" and "settlement" in Pakistan, at a time when—as will be seen in a moment—such an accommodation was not only virtually inconceivable, except in terms of Bengali subjugation, but also was far shorter of attainment than administration spokesmen claimed. And the expectation could be seen, finally, in the surreptitious deliveries of military and economic aid to Pakistan simultaneous with administration assertions that nearly all assistance had ceased.

Rather than acknowledge, even to themselves, the justifiability and legitimacy of the Bangladesh independence movement, administration officials banked on Yahya Khan's granting the East "some form of autonomy" within the Pakistani nation.[144] The secret deliberations of the NSC Washington Special Action Group (WSAG) released by columnist Jack Anderson[145] reveal not a trace of comprehension of the roots of Bengali resistance, much less the necessity of it. The documents further show that the American view on autonomy was registered only in conversations with *Indian* officials; Ambassador Keating's cable to Secretary Rogers of December 8 disputes Washington's claim that U.S. officials discussed with Islamabad a precise timetable for East Pakistan's autonomy, or even that the U.S. Government was on record in favor of autonomy. Contrary to President Nixon's assertion, cited earlier, of substantial concessions from Yahya as a result of U.S. pressure, Keating's cable also noted: that, contrary to a USIA news story then being circulated, Washington never obtained Yahya's authorization to contact Mujibur and begin arrangements for negotiations between the Awami League and the government;[146] and that Yahya's offer of amnesty to all refugees did not apply to those "charged with specific criminal acts." (In fact, 48 members of the Awami League and 17 other persons, many of whom had fled the country, were ordered to trial by a military court in September on sedition and other charges.)[147] Nor, Keating might have added, did Yahya's "flexibility" extend to acceptance of Mujibur's authority, the assurance that a successor to Yahya (Bhutto) would keep the President's promises, or satisfaction of Bengali demands before independence was proclaimed concerning the end of martial law and the granting of broad political powers to the East.

American willingness to accept Yahya's promises at face value was accompanied by unwillingness, for fear of losing "influence," to criticize Pakistan's Government for using American equipment in the East. Although, as a State Department official commented, U.S. military aid was not prohibited from being used for internal security, or transferred from West to East Pakistan,[148] the clear and admitted purpose of the aid was for defense against the presumed Soviet threat to the north. Yet, neither publicly nor privately did Washington officials express "concern" that U.S.-supplied weapons were being used by the "largely U.S.-equipped" Pakistani Army[149] to suppress a popular uprising. Indeed, the same State Department official noted in May, by way of explaining away the use of U.S. arms, that "the conflict in East Pakistan in terms of an active resistance movement appears already to have largely subsided."[150] The only "bloodbath" that the Anderson documents record as having concerned U.S. officials was one that *might* occur against the Bihari (non-Bengali Muslim) minority in the East; the bloodbath then being perpetrated against the Bengalis went unmentioned.[151]

In fact, the administration did not cut off all military aid to Pakistan. Hearings before a Senate subcommittee disclosed that despite the Defense Department's March 25 directive holding up all arms shipments, licenses issued before that date to ships carrying arms to Pakistan were honored. Though admitting the power to revoke the licenses without having to declare an embargo, the administration, arguing anew the need to maintain a "constructive dialogue" with Islamabad, permitted at least ten ships to sail with cargoes of $5 million or more in military hardware.[152] The subcommittee also uncovered the fact that U.S. military officers were drawing up sales contracts with Pakistani officials for jet aircraft and other military equipment. Twenty-four contracts worth over $10 million were concluded after March 25.[153] The government contended no deliveries of weapons were made under these contracts; but it could not answer why, if the administration was so concerned about keeping U.S. weapons out of the conflict, it was allowing arms sales to continue.

Were the shipments after March 25, or for that matter the arms sales, simply the result of a bureaucratic mixup between the Defense Department's lower echelons and higher authority? Some reporters adopted this explanation, but the available evidence indicates that the shipments and sales were part of administration policy. In his foreign-policy report of 1971, Secretary Rogers noted that licenses for arms shipments to Pakistan were not finally canceled until *November 8, 1971*, months after the State Department admitted it knew of valid licenses.[154] Kissinger, at a meeting of the WSAG on December 8, "suggested that if we had not cut the sale of arms to Pakistan, the current problem would not exist." He said the President should have time to consider the suggestion of Jordan's King Hussein that F-104 jet fighters be sold to Pakistan through Jordan.[155] According to Jack Anderson, this alternative was not implemented but was kept alive to let the Indian Government ponder the implications.[156] But a later news story reported that during the conflict Jordan had sent F-104's and Libya had provided Northrup F-5's.[157]

The apparent American intention to benefit Pakistan at the expense of the resistance forces extended to the refugee relief program. In announcing a $158 million contribution in East Pakistan, Washington allegedly hoped "to gain the needed time for a political process to work" between East and West Pakistan;[158] and it pointed to Yahya's agreement that a U.N. mission could be stationed in the East. But there were some major difficulties with the logic and practice of this planning. The President put ending the "civil strife" before launching a major relief program; Mme. Gandhi evidently believed that only if the Americans were prepared to use economic aid to *pressure* Islamabad into granting full autonomy would a relief program make sense. Otherwise, Pakistani authorities would use the relief for their armed forces while making it extremely difficult for the U.N. Relief Mission to perform its work.

If that was Indian thinking, it was precisely on the mark. Ambassador Keating reported to Rogers that the relief program "was always in Pakistani Government hands." Its agreement to U.N. distribution of the supplies "obscures the fact that the UN never had nor intended to have sufficient personnel in East Pakistan to handle actual distribution."[159] Senator Edward Kennedy's on-the-spot survey of relief conditions in Bangladesh confirmed Keating's assessment.[160] The relief program had the effect, instead, of enhancing the Pakistani Army's mobility and communications, to the detriment of the Mukti Bahini guerrillas. This was why, Keating explained, India opposed U.S. relief prior to a settlement. Journalists reported these developments in the East during the conflict; but not until several months after the end of the war did the State Department admit that it had had to cancel $10 million in aid to Pakistan because of the diversion of Bangladesh relief funds to the army's use.[161]

Even the stated amount of relief—$158 million—may have been exaggerated. Just as the 1970 cyclone relief appropriation was only partially spent in East Pakistan, the $158 million included money programmed for Pakistan before the conflict, food and other aid that never arrived in Bangladesh, and unsigned or canceled contracts. Senator Kennedy's staff, working with AID and Government Accounting Office figures, could only count about $3 *million* that definitely went for relief work in Bangladesh.[162] These apparent misrepresentations can be dismissed as bureaucratic error, like the arms transactions; or they can be seen as part of a deliberate administration effort to reduce the Pakistani Army's difficulties in putting down the Bangladesh movement before India decided to enter the war.

The final element of an American policy to stabilize the subcontinent by preserving the status quo was the continuation of economic assistance. While Henry Kissinger may have been accurate in saying at his December 7, 1971, background news conference that no "new" development loans were being offered to Pakistan, this apparently did not mean that the spigot had been completely turned off. The President, Kissinger privately reported to the WSAG after full-scale war had broken out, wanted economic aid cut off for India alone. Information concerning why Pakistan would continue receiving economic aid, he said, would be "kept for background only."[163] Precisely how much aid Pakistan did receive is not known; but whatever the amount, it had to be of help to Islamabad's war effort, directly or indirectly.

After December 3 and open Indo-Pakistani hostilities, the administration's distaste for Indian foreign policy, which was already considerable because of the Vietnam war and closer Delhi-Moscow relations as well as over Bangladesh, turned to barely disguised anger. Neither the entreaty to Mme. Gandhi in May, nor the many rounds of diplomacy with Indian officials, nor the Prime Minister's visit to Washington in November had prevented escalation of the war and a presumed threat to the balance of South Asian power. President Nixon's possible feeling of betrayal by the government of India cannot be documented. But the private record does give abundant evidence that the cutoff of aid to India, the search for backdoor methods of keeping Pakistan supplied with aircraft, the continuation of economic aid to Pakistan alone, and eventually the show of force in the Bay of Bengal all stemmed in some part from Nixon's belief that "India is the attacker" and that his subordinates would have to be "tougher" on India.[164] Only after Kissinger directed on December 4 that official statements convey the President's attitude did administration spokesmen drop all pretense at evenhandedness and directly accuse India of being responsible for the "crisis."

Presidential pique at India is at best only one explanation of U.S. policy after December 3. Another and, according to Nixon's version previously quoted, more compelling motive was the "evidence" of India's intention to move on from Bangladesh and seize the remainder of Kashmir. As put by Kissinger, India was interested in "turning half of Pakistan into an impotent state and the other half into a vassal."[165] The WSAG documents note only one source for this assessment. Richard Helms, director of the CIA, is recorded as having told the WSAG meeting of December 8:

> Mrs. Gandhi has indicated that before heeding a U.N. call for cease-fire, she intends to straighten out the southern border of Azad Kashmir. It is reported that prior to terminating present hostilities, Mrs. Gandhi intends to attempt to eliminate Pakistan's armor and air force capabilities.

Helms's statement evidently was based on CIA reports that "India now intends not only to liberate East Bengal but also to straighten its borders in Kashmir and to destroy West Pakistan's air and armored forces."[166]

But evidence of this kind was hardly overwhelming, and it was challenged by some officials and contradicted by other CIA reports. At a WSAG meeting of December 8, Joseph Sisco, Assistant Secretary for the Near East and South Asia, "doubted" that India intended to take Pakistani territory in the West, and cited assurances from the Indian Foreign Minister to Ambassador Keating. Generals William Westmoreland and John Ryan, in separate WSAG meetings, also expressed reservations. Both pointed out that it would take a considerable time for Indian forces to shift from East to West Pakistan even if they were so inclined.[167] And the same CIA reports that supported Helms's statement also noted Mme. Gandhi's willingness to accept a cease-fire once Bangladesh was liberated. The Agency additionally cited assurances to Keating and a statement by the Soviet Ambassador to India that, after the fall of Dacca, "It is therefore unnecessary for India to launch an offensive into West Pakistan to crush a military machine that no longer exists."[168]

The President doubtless believed he *had* convincing evidence of Indian ambitions in the West; but what he actually had was contradictory evidence and advice from at least three WSAG members to the effect that a major new Indian offensive was unlikely very soon, if at all. By choosing to make a show of force—the documents make clear Nixon's and Kissinger's total disenchantment with the United Nations—the administration carried its pre-December "tilting" toward Pakistan to its own logical conclusion.

Looking at the decision-making process, what is also important about Nixon's insistence that U.S. policy be more convincingly anti-Indian is that it had the effect of excluding any possibility of supporting Bangladesh as an alternative course. The WSAG discussions after December 3 centered on the tactics of confronting India, in and outside the United Nations. Differences of opinion emerged over the U.S. position in the Organization (the American delegation evidently was reluctant to criticize India too strongly) and, as already mentioned, Indian intentions in Kashmir and the propriety of selling jets to Pakistan through a third country. Only David Packard, the Deputy Secretary of Defense, seemed to suggest a policy of inaction: "Let's not get in if we know we are going to lose" was his recorded position at the December 8 meeting. But neither he nor anyone else challenged the feasibility and desirability of the basic Nixon-Kissinger posture of favoring Pakistan and opposing Bangladesh.

The President, instead, believed there were "unacceptable" risks in American inaction. But were there? An evaluation requires raising these questions: Which of the risks cited by Nixon affected the U.S. interests, under the Nixon Doctrine, of avoiding great power conflict in South Asia and maintaining a "stable balance" with the major powers there? Were there not better ways to achieve those interests? Finally, are there interests besides the two stated that should have been considered during the decision-making on Bangladesh?

Risks, Decisions, and Alternatives. Of the four "risks" cited by the President, only one—the possibility of an Indian attack on West Pakistan—affected U.S. interests as he defined them. The loosening of restraints against war and undermining of the U.N.'s peacekeeping mission were not risks to U.S. interests in South Asia or anywhere else; rather, they were generalized and unsubstantiated *fears* based on the distorted belief that Indian involvement in the Bangladesh revolution, rather than West Pakistan's attempt to crush it, was the primary reason for the crisis. Similarly, the "risk" of encouraging ethnic strife elsewhere in the world was an unpleasant prospect, but not a risk in the sense of a challenge to national interests that the United States might, as in the Congo, decide to meet by intervening. Nor was ethnic tension the real issue in Bangladesh; unlike the Katangans or Biafrans, the Bengalis were in the majority, a fact the administration seemed anxious to keep in the background.

The final one of Nixon's "risks"—the effects of the conflict on Moscow and Peking—also rested on misguided logic. Bangladesh was hardly a case of Soviet "strategic expansion," although clearly a victory for the Bangladesh movement, which had Soviet and Indian support but not American, would stand the Soviet leadership in good stead with the new nation. Nor is it credible that the Chinese leadership's future preference for force or restraint in foreign policy would be critically, or even importantly, influenced by the outcome of the conflict. Nixon and Kissinger underrated the domestic and regional considerations that have long guided Chinese policy toward the subcontinent. Chinese leaders found themselves having to support Pakistan's repression of a "national liberation movement" because of the implications of a successful Bengali separation for Tibet and possibly other minority areas of China, and because unfriendly Sino-Indian relations demanded that Peking maintain good relations with the Islamabad government.

If an attack on Pakistani Kashmir was the only real U.S. interest that might be affected, it is difficult to understand the strategy developed to protect that interest. In the process of trying to divert Indian forces from the West and East, the administration's gunboat diplomacy accepted some possibility of a naval confrontation with a Soviet task force then in the area. A CIA document reported that the Soviet Ambassador to India warned that Moscow "will not allow the Seventh Fleet to intervene."[169] Even if a U.S.-Soviet confrontation was unlikely, it is hard to accept the administration's evident calculation that a show of force was either useful as a deterrent to an Indian attack in the West or warranted in support of an "ally" whose invasion of the East had initiated the crisis in the first place. At best, the U.S. fleet could deflect India's attention; at worst, it would heighten tensions between the combatants and the major powers alike.

Accepting for the moment the administration's narrow definition of U.S. interests, an alternative policy would have been based on the inevitability of Bangladesh independence. Only when Pakistan acknowledged the separation of Bangladesh, removed forces from the East, and thereby paved the way for the return of the refugees from India was the presumed threat of a wider war likely to dissipate—or be tested. By making policy on the basis of Indian guilt and Pakistani grievances, the administration weakened what little influence it may have had in the crisis, aligned the United States closer to the Pakistani dictatorship, and forfeited opportunities for a close working relationship with the Bangladesh Government. This represented not merely a failure of policy; it showed a denigration of the nationalist forces at work and a neglect of vital political, legal, and moral issues for the sake of keeping the contending powers in balance.

Indeed, if stability in South Asia was so valuable to Washington, American officials might have considered that a divided Pakistan—not West and East, but Pakistan and Bangladesh—would have greater prospects for independent survival than a reunited country. Revolutionary nationalism was in train and reconciliation was extremely remote; the old territorial arrangement could be retained only by force, with a strong prospect of continued guerrillaism, covertly supported by India. The creation of a new state would require substantial foreign assistance. But it would remove the tensions and inequities of a semicolonial relationship between East and West; would enable the refugees to return, easing India's burden and anxieties; would replace Indo-Pakistani hostility in the East with Indo-Bangladesh harmony; and would reduce the chance that a protracted war would fragment the Bangladesh movement, possibly eroding its social democratic leadership under pressure from leftist extremists. *In its own self-interest,* independence for Bangladesh should have been preferred in Washington to "autonomy" and "political accommodation."

To have reached that conclusion, however, required that the Nixon Administration refine its list of U.S. interests. A "stable balance" in South Asia depends above all on sound relations between Washington and Delhi. A policy favorable to Bangladesh would have helped to improve those relations and to counterbalance Soviet influence in India. Yet the President, who in 1967 had called India "the most populous representative democracy in the world,"[170] acted as though India were an enemy, provoking its government with military supplies to Pakistan during the conflict, rumors of jet transfers, termination of economic aid, and dispatch of the *Enterprise*. To have ended the conflict with Indo-American relations at their lowest point, and with Pakistan and its new ruler, Bhutto, a long-time critic of the United States, as the only American friend on the subcontinent—even then, a friend closer to Peking than to Washington—was a fitting tribute to the shortsightedness of American diplomacy.

A corollary of American interest in India's friendship is the promotion of the economic and political health of the subcontinent. The administration may have believed it was acting consistently with that interest by urging "an end to the civil strife," but in fact its relief and economic aid programs were contributing to the perpetuation of antinationalist violence in Bangladesh. As the government of India reportedly contended, U.S. assistance would only "bail out Yahya," not solve the refugee problem. On finding that relief aid to Bangladesh was being appropriated by the Pakistani forces, the administration should have suspended further assistance. It should also have suspended all economic aid to Pakistan as well as to India pending an end of hostilities. One of the heights of the decision-makers' misplaced concern during the conflict was reached when Dr. Kissinger, asking whether the United States might have to rescue Bangladesh from famine and told that Bangladesh would be an "international basket case," replied "it will not necessarily be our basket case."[171]

Still another neglected interest was that the United States be faithful to the principle of self-determination, hence in favor of the carrying out of constitutional processes in Bangladesh without the use of U.S. military equipment for domestic repression. The administration acted as though self-determination were in contradiction with stability when, in fact, the two were mutually supportive. To implement that interest required that Washington: (1) terminate all military deliveries, suspend all military sales, and revoke all licenses for military equipment shipments to Pakistan; (2) publicly as well as privately deplore Islamabad's resort to force in the East, criticize the transfer of U.S. equipment for that purpose, and propose that the only alternative to Bangladesh independence—in the earliest stage of the conflict—must be Yahya Khan's acceptance of the election results.

None of these steps was taken because the President wanted to retain some influence; but it has been shown just how little influence Washington was able to exert in Pakistani councils. Influence could come mainly from the threat and actual termination of support of Pakistan, acts that *might* have brought Yahya and Bhutto to their senses. Such pressure, on the other hand, might also have ruptured relations between Washington and Islamabad. This was one "risk" the government had to accept; friendly relations with India and Bangladesh were far more important than friendly relations with Pakistan. And incorporated in that choice would have been a sensitivity to nationalist impulses—a healthy departure from past interventions, one that, in U.S. diplomacy with the Third World, would have stood in marked contrast with China's alignment against Bangladesh.

Some writers have speculated that behind the administration's pro-Pakistan policy was the desire to facilitate the opening of contacts with China. After Kissinger's secret trip to Peking, the President announced on July 15, 1971, that he would be going to China. But the chronology of the U.S. response to the Bangladesh war points to hostility toward India rather than alignment with China as the decisive motive. By the time of the Nixon announcement he had long been convinced that India was in the Soviet camp. This conviction was reflected in the 1970 arms deal with Pakistan and in the fact that U.S. policy "tilted" toward Pakistan from the outset of the fighting in March, 1971. Furthermore, the WSAG documents contain no references whatever to concern about China's friendship. After over twenty years of containment of China, it is difficult to imagine that policy toward the subcontinent, or anywhere else, would be primarily motivated by a need to be "on China's side."

"We shall not forget the role played by the United States against us," the acting president of Bangladesh said as Dacca awaited the release of Sheikh Mujib from his confinement.[172] Practical politics subsequently intervened, and once diplomatic recognition was extended by Washington, after nearly fifty other governments had acted, a major U.S. economic assistance program was accepted. It is doubtful, however, that being the principal donor nation will soon undo the suspicions and anguish of Bangladesh officials over American conduct during their fight for independence.

SOME OTHER INTERVENTIONS

One objective that American opposition to the revolutions in China, Vietnam, and Bangladesh had in common was the promotion or preservation of a balance of power in Asia conducive to the maintenance of the area as, in President Eisenhower's phrase, an "American lake." Revolution has been perceived as threatening that objective, whether conceived in primarily military, diplomatic, or (less often) economic terms. Regardless of party, American postwar administrations have agreed that the objective is sound and the threat is real; to the extent they have disagreed, it has been over the tactics of intervention.

Nor has counterrevolution been the only form of U.S. intervention in Asia. Subversion and outright invasion have also occurred. Three cases that have had lasting effects in Asia will be briefly discussed.

Indonesia, 1958

Soon after President Kennedy took office, he requested Brigadier General Edward G. Lansdale, whose expertise in counterinsurgency had been recognized in the anti-Huk campaign in the Philippines and in service beside Diem in the 1950's, to provide an over-all picture of "unconventional warfare" resources in Southeast Asia. Lansdale's memorandum[173] detailed the operations of the CIA and the Special Forces, including their training, supplying, and advising of Southeast Asian guerrilla forces. Among the CIA's clients he listed Civil Air Transport of Taiwan, which "provides air logistical support under commercial cover to most CIA and other U.S. Government agencies' requirements." One of CAT's "notable achievements" was "complete logistical and tactical air support for the Indonesian operation." Lansdale was referring to unmarked aircraft flown in 1958 by American (and probably other) nationals in support of Indonesians in rebellion against the government of President Sukarno. One such plane was shot down over the Celebes on May 18, and its American pilot captured, three weeks after Eisenhower had described U.S. policy as "one of careful neutrality and proper deportment."[174]

The reason American policy was neither careful nor proper was that Eisenhower and his chief advisers saw the rebellion as an ideological struggle, and decided that a CIA-sponsored bombing program in support of the "anti-communist" rebels might topple Sukarno, just as it had enabled Castillo Armas to overthrow Arbenz in Guatemala. If Americans were implicated in the rebellion, as happened, Washington could profess neutrality and claim the CIA employees were "soldiers of fortune"—as also happened. The American Ambassador to Djakarta could best be protected by not informing him of the CIA operation.[175] The stakes were believed well worth the effort. Sukarno had moved his country to the left and was considered in danger of being overwhelmed by the Communist Party (PKI), transforming Indonesia into a Sino-Soviet dependency.[176] American rubber and oil companies, whose local employees were already PKI supporters, would probably be nationalized, just as Dutch industries had been since the previous December.[177] The immense economic potential of Indonesia would be foreclosed to the West.

What the Eisenhower Administration chose to interpret as Indonesia's drift into the communist orbit should have been understood as postrevolutionary regional and political tension natural enough to a geographically far-flung nation, newly independent (December, 1949), and led by a radical nationalist who had only recently put an end to experimentation with party democracy. Sukarno's substitute program, "Guided Democracy," officially unveiled in February, 1957, called for inclusion of the PKI in a broadly based coalition of political and social forces. To him, the PKI's discipline, organizational strength among peasants and urban workers, and increasing electoral success did not make it a threat but a useful counterbalance to the anticommunist army leadership.[178] To leave the PKI out of the government would ensure its constant criticism and court its active resistance.

John Foster Dulles thought otherwise. His understanding of Guided Democracy was that it "does not entirely satisfy large segments of the population"[179] and "is a nice sounding name for what I fear would end up to be Communist despotism."[180] Sukarno was not to be trusted: His neutralist foreign policy often meant active identification with Chinese criticism of neocolonialism and anti-imperialism; his government, in March, 1958, had concluded a major military and economic aid agreement with the U.S.S.R. (after failing to get assistance from the United States); and he authorized takeovers of the economic interests of the Netherlands, a NATO ally, following another unfavorable vote in the U.N. General Assembly on Dutch-held West Irian (New Guinea). To Washington, these unpleasant political developments and unfriendly acts indicated "a very real possibility of Indonesia's, or at least Java's being lost to the Communists in the immediate future."[181]

An opportunity to undermine Sukarno's rule lay in the control, since late 1956, of Sumatra and other outer islands by regional military commanders. They had seized power from Javanese authorities because of resentment over unfair exchange rates for exports of the outer islands, inequitable returns in social welfare projects from the large share of foreign exchange the islands were annually sending to Java, and centralization of authority in Java and Javanese officials.[182] Sensing, somehow, an anticommunist motivation in this rebellion, Washington, in December, 1957, decided to maintain relations with Djakarta "but adjust U.S. policy so as to emphasize our support for the anti-Communist forces in the outer islands."[183] The "emphasis" was encouragement of the rebel leadership to begin active resistance instead of merely engaging in smuggling their exports. American officials, or agents, apparently promised the rebels military aid and perhaps recognition.* On February 15, 1958, a Revolutionary Government of the Republic of Indonesia was proclaimed from Sumatra; Dulles made comments that appeared to endorse it.[184]

---

* It was reportedly in December, 1957, that the CIA approached Allen Pope, the pilot later shot down, to fly support missions for the rebels. (Wise and Ross, *op. cit.*, p. 147.) As for recognition, it was never granted, although some American operatives apparently preferred it. (See William H. Stevenson, *Birds' Nests in Their Beards* [Boston, Mass.: Houghton Mifflin, 1964], p. 145.) They may have exceeded their authority because, to judge from the account in Howard Palfrey Jones, *Indonesia: The Possible Dream* (New York: Harcourt Brace Jovanovich, 1971), p. 116, Dulles was considering recognition mainly in terms of leverage against Sukarno by letting him know the United States had recognition under active review.

Eisenhower and Dulles were apparently persuaded, no doubt with help from the rebel leaders, that the leftist trend in Java was the key issue in the conflict, despite the American Ambassador's assessment to the contrary.[185] The thinking in official circles was that, at the least, Sumatra—where the major American and Dutch oil fields were located—and some other outer islands could be salvaged if Java "fell" to the "communists." At the most, Sukarno would come under pressure from the army and others to change course politically; he might even be overthrown.[186] Thus, when the ambassador suggested that Indonesia be offered economic and military aid in the hope of influencing a peaceful settlement of the rebellion, the State Department replied that until Sukarno took a firmer stance against the communists, he would get no aid.[187] This brazenly contradictory stance—with one hand intervening in Indonesia's civil dispute, with the other using aid as bait to dictate Indonesia's politics—did not change until after the American bombardier was shot down on May 18. By then, the Indonesian Army had begun a successful drive against rebel positions (although the fighting would not finally end until 1961) and the Indonesian arms deal with Moscow had apparently awakened the State Department leadership to the impracticality of denying assistance to Sukarno.

The attempted subversion of Sukarno's government was not only a flagrant intervention in another nation's affairs; it also showed how a policy built on antinationalism can promote precisely the political trends it is designed to counteract. Encouraging rebellion exacerbated the split between "anticommunist" regional commanders and "anticommunists" in the army leadership. The army as a whole gained in stature and political influence because it put down the rebellion; but probably a number of officers became disillusioned with American intervention and secretly joined the PKI. The party's ranks increased dramatically in the five years after the rebellion, and the proof that "U.S. imperialism" and its Asian allies were conspiring against Indonesia doubtless contributed to that growth. These immediate effects of the intervention had still more adverse long-term consequences. It deepened Sukarno's hostility to the West and his support of Chinese and Soviet international policies; and it helped to polarize Indonesian politics around the army and the PKI at the expense of weaker, noncommunist parties. Sukarno was placed in the position of power balancer between these two forces—a delicate position that collapsed in the abortive coup attempt by leftist forces in the fall of 1965.

Laos, 1958–60

In the abstract, Laos, a nation of fewer than 3 million people, with few natural resources and limited economic potential, administratively and militarily weak, and politically fractionalized, is a most unlikely setting for cold war confrontation. Yet, like Vietnam—indeed, largely because of its proximity to Vietnam—Laos has rarely been at peace since the end of World War II. Larger, more powerful neighbors have attributed strategic value to Laos and have sought to influence its politics—Thailand, because of the country's historic role as a buffer against penetration of the Thai northeast; the DRV, because of its revolutionary partnership with the Pathet Lao movement (officially, since March, 1951), its desire to have a friendly government in Vientiane, and its need of access via eastern Laos to South Vietnam while the revolution continues; China, because only strict Lao neutrality ensures against American (and Thai) conversion of the country into an anticommunist bastion.

Added to these pressures on Lao sovereignty is the interest of the United States in maintaining a stable, noncommunist government in Vientiane. Although the origins of that interest have been obscured by the constant round of fighting, bargaining, and governmental changes over the last fifteen years, they are well worth re-examining. For it was the American estimation of Laos's strategic worth in the mid-1950's, and the ensuing interventions in the country's traditionally fragile politics, that internationalized the competition over Laos and precipitated the highly destructive warfare of the 1960's and early 1970's.

At the 1954 Geneva Conference, where the full sovereignty and independence of Laos were recognized, agreements were reached to bring about political and military unity. Pathet Lao units, which had fought alongside the Viet Minh, were to be regrouped into two provinces bordering on the DRV (Phong Saly and Sam

Neua) pending a political settlement and formation of a single Lao army. Viet Minh forces were to withdraw from Laos. The Royal Lao Government (RLG), in two declarations issued at the close of the conference, guaranteed political rights to all citizens, resolved "never [to] permit the territory of Laos to be used in furtherance of" aggression, and vowed not to join any military alliance or permit the establishment of foreign bases on its soil. The government also pledged that, in the transition to political unification, it would not "request foreign aid, whether in war material, in personnel or in instructors, except for the purpose of its effective territorial defense and to the extent defined by the agreement on the cessation of hostilities," thus forbidding all military aid beyond the French presence of about 5,000 men. The declarations were especially satisfying to China and the DRV, because they meant that Laos would be not only kept out of the American-run Southeast Asia Treaty Organization (SEATO) but also protected against bilateral U.S. subversion.

These hopes proved illusory. An American-sponsored protocol to the SEATO pact (September, 1954) designated Laos, as well as Cambodia and South Vietnam, as areas that would come under the treaty's protective umbrella. Testifying on the treaty's implications for U.S. involvement, Secretary of State Dulles emphasized that the policy was not to build up a large local force to deter invasion; nor was it to commit the United States automatically to defend the RLG. But since Laos, along with several other countries, was having to deal with subversive "threats of the same character," it was important to make clear that they would be defended and "begin to think of ways and means that might be available to combat this threat of subversion."[188]

What Dulles chose to call subversion was a disciplined, politically effective, and socially beneficial movement in the Pathet Lao–held provinces that was in marked contrast to the inefficiency and repressiveness of the RLG armed forces. For the Lao people in these areas, Pathet Lao administration was a welcome change. "The people were simply being governed intelligently for the first time. The tragedy was that the government could offer no competition."[189] Although, reportedly,[190] DRV advisers worked with Pathet Lao officials, the reason for the movement's success lay primarily in its respect for the people, its initiation of new labor practices, and the education and other social benefits it made available to the hill people for the first time.[191]

The successes of the Pathet Lao posed a threat to American plans for Indochina. What would happen if elections were held and a coalition government of national unity formed, with the Pathet Lao emerging as a national power? Laos might become the first "domino" to fall to communism, followed inexorably by the rest of mainland Southeast Asia and then the entire region.[192] The first steps to counter this possibility started the United States down the road of intervention in contravention of the Geneva agreements.

Early in 1956, after much internal debate and against the advice of the Joint Chiefs of Staff, Washington began a program to increase the Royal Laotian Army to 25,000 men. It was a strictly political decision, based on the hope a large army (in Lao terms) would be better able to compete with the Pathet Lao for popular support. The momentum of this decision turned an essentially police force into a conventional army, "with the United States equipping it and financing it to the last penny."[193]

On the political side, the State Department worked to prevent a coalition government. In August, 1956, Prince Souvanna Phouma, the Prime Minister, and his half-brother, the Pathet Lao leader Prince Souphanouvong, agreed to conduct supplementary National Assembly elections (general elections not involving the Pathet Lao had been held in December, 1955) that would bring the communists into the government. American Ambassador J. Graham Parsons would later admit: "I struggled for sixteen months to prevent a coalition."[194] Souvanna ignored Parsons and went ahead. Agreements were signed in November, 1957, that gave two cabinet posts to Pathet Lao representatives (one was Souphanouvong), established a date for elections, legalized the Pathet Lao's party (the Neo Lao Hak Sat, NLHS), provided for the return of Sam Neua and Phong Saly to RLG authority, and set conditions for the reintegration of some and the demobilization of other Pathet Lao troops.

The supplementary elections held in May, 1958, went as the Americans had feared. The NLHS and an allied party won thirteen of the twenty contested seats; Souphanouvong was the top vote-getter, and later was elected chairman of the Assembly. In response, American economic aid, "now amounting to all but a fraction of the Laotian budget," was cut off in an effort "to force Prince Souvannaphouma out of office."[195] Souvanna lost on a vote of confidence in the Assembly and had to resign. The new Prime Minister, Phoui Sananikone, was more to the Americans' liking: His cabinet excluded the two NLHS ministers and included four members of the "Committee for the Defense of National Interests," a group of young army officers who evidently were financed by the CIA.[196] The United States had succeeded in swinging the RLG to the right.

In the events that followed during the remainder of Eisenhower's tenure—the inclusion of army officers in Phoui's government in January, 1959, Phoui's declaration the next month that Laos would no longer be bound by the pledge at Geneva to restrict foreign military aid, General Phoumi Nosavan's coup in December, and the countercoup in August, 1960, by Captain Kong Le to reinstall Souvanna Phouma—the United States became more openly aligned with the rightists. A military training mission was set up in Vientiane, the administrative capital, in the guise of a Programs Evaluation Office.[197] The CIA supported General Phoumi's December coup, which was then "legalized" by "elections" staged to remove NLHS competition.[198] American rural "civil action teams"—actually, CIA and Special Forces personnel—began arming and advising Meo tribesmen in anticommunist insurgency.[199] Soon afterward, the CIA also began supporting Thai clandestine operations in Laos and Chinese Nationalist bombing runs using Civil Air Transport planes.[200] When Kong Le staged his coup, Eisenhower, failing "to persuade Souvanna Phouma not to bring the Pathet Lao into his government," authorized expanded U.S. support of Phoumi, including U.S. and Thai aircraft.[201]

The fighting that occurred in this period, which continued until the next Geneva Conference in 1961–62, was the direct consequence of American intervention to deny the Pathet Lao a voice in Lao politics—a voice, it must be emphasized, that was accepted by Prime Minister Souvanna Phouma, confirmed in elections, and squelched by CIA support of a rightist takeover. Faced with a neutralist, all-Lao solution, Washington balked; as in

Vietnam, it would seek out those Lao willing to work toward an American solution, one that accepted the consequences of civil war. As Eisenhower said when he discussed Laos with President-elect Kennedy, the communists could not be permitted to take part in the government, and the fall of Laos to the communists would mean the loss of all Southeast Asia. He had to wonder, however, "why, in interventions of this kind, we always seem to find that the morale of the Communist forces was better than that of the democratic forces." There was more "dedication" on the communist side, he decided, and the morale problem "was a serious one and would have to be taken into consideration as we became more deeply involved."[202] Kennedy would accept a coalition in Laos a year later; but he, as well as Johnson and Nixon, would affirm the objective of a noncommunist Laos, accept Eisenhower's strategic assessment, and likewise decide that the morale problem would have to be dealt with in the course of deeper intervention.

Cambodia, 1970

Prince Norodom Sihanouk had led his country's struggle to gain independence from France, had been independent Cambodia's only leader, and had been the architect of a neutralist foreign policy based on accommodation to, and friendly relations with, China and the DRV. In foreign policy, his signal accomplishment was that he had preserved Cambodian sovereignty and kept the Vietnam war from ravaging his country. He accepted as the price of these benefits the use of Cambodian territory bordering on South Vietnam by Vietnamese communist forces as sanctuary and conduit for military equipment. Once the war ended, he hoped that, with China's help, he would obtain renewed promises by a victorious NLF government in Saigon to respect Cambodian independence and territorial integrity.

But on March 18, 1970, while Sihanouk was in Europe, the Cambodian National Assembly voted to depose him and to vest power in General Lon Nol.[203] Subsequent developments showed the wisdom of the prince's warning that a Cambodia aligned with the United States and South Vietnam against the DRV and NLF would convert his country into "a second Laos." During the remainder of March, talks in Phnom Penh between the new regime and DRV officials broke down; Lon Nol closed the port of Sihanoukville (Kompong Som) to communist-flag ships and abrogated a trade agreement with the NLF; and Cambodian border forces cooperated with South Vietnamese military units and U.S. advisers in attacking communist positions. In April, Lon Nol appealed to Washington for arms, which he received. As South Vietnamese penetrations of the sanctuary areas and U.S. involvement became more overt,[204] Vietnamese communist forces replied by moving west and south, closing in on Phnom Penh. Full-scale warfare was imminent in Cambodia as it had never been before.

In Washington, on April 20, President Nixon told the nation that over the next twelve months 150,000 Americans would be withdrawn from South Vietnam. He gave no hint of the intervention to come in Cambodia; only later would he reveal he "knew [then] that we might be at a crossroads in Cambodia."[205] Secretary Rogers, expressing (as it turned out) his personal conviction and not administration policy, told a House committee on April 23: "Our whole incentive is to de-escalate. We recognize that if we escalate and we get involved in Cambodia with our ground troops, that our whole program is defeated."[206] A week later, Nixon informed Congress and the people that a major force of American and South Vietnamese troops—eventually, about 80,000—was invading communist base areas in Cambodia in order, among other reasons, "to protect our men who are in Vietnam and to guarantee the continued success of our withdrawal and Vietnamization programs."[207]

From Nixon's April 30 speech, his follow-up report of June 30 on the operation, and other accounts, four basic motivations emerge for the decision to invade Cambodia.

First, Nixon evidently believed the deposition of Sihanouk afforded a political opportunity, and the westward movement of communist forces a military opportunity, to strike against the bothersome sanctuaries. As Defense Secretary Melvin R. Laird would later attest, "This was the time to hit them."[208] Nixon's notes on the decision, made available to correspondent Stewart Alsop, show the thought that "time running out" and that "military aid" to Lon Nol could be "only symbolic."[209]

Second, and closely related to the golden opportunity, was the consideration that Cambodia's survival as a noncommunist state "was needed to assure the defense of South Vietnam and the process of American withdrawal, to spare Saigon the blow of seeing a neighbor collapse while the United States did nothing."[210] If Cambodian resistance collapsed, a communist-controlled government would emerge, running "the risk of Cambodia's becoming one vast enemy staging area, a springboard for attacks on South Viet-Nam without fear of retaliation."[211] At the time of the decision, it would seem, Lon Nol's pro-Western stance was less important to the President than was the territory over which his authority was supposed to extend.

A third cluster of motives was strictly tactical. His military commander and ambassador in Vietnam argued that since the President was committed to further troop reductions (including two divisions based across the border from Cambodia), and given the opportunities previously cited, he should move to neutralize the sanctuaries while he had the forces to do so.[212] This was what Nixon apparently meant when he said, on April 30, that intervention in Cambodia would save American lives and be "indispensable for the continuing success of" Vietnamization. Henry Kissinger reportedly tacked on a diplomatic argument: "that, as long as American troops were being withdrawn and the Communist sanctuaries remained immune, there was no real inducement to the Communist side to negotiate seriously."[213]

Over and above all these factors, and perhaps more crucial than any of them at the moment of decision, was Nixon's belief that he could teach the communist world a lesson and improve his own and the nation's standing—in a word, avoid "humiliation"—by taking decisive action. Like his predecessors, he was "not going to be the first President to preside over an American defeat."[214] The enemy was unwilling to negotiate and was being aggressive on the battlefront; if the United States reacted only with protests, "the credibility of the United States would be destroyed" everywhere; the government "will not be humiliated," "will not be defeated," will not act "like a pitiful helpless giant" when threatened by "the forces of totalitarianism and anarchy"; the United States must prove itself "worthy" of world leadership and not "become a second-rate power."[215] With the communist world seemingly testing him on other fronts as well, Cambodia was an ideal spot to show his mettle. He would accept the "deep divisions" his action would precipitate at home; he was more concerned about the effects on Hanoi of such divisions.[216] "I would rather be a one-term President than to be a two-term President at the cost of seeing America become a second-rate power and see this nation accept the first defeat in its proud 190-year history," he concluded on April 30.

In the context of America's Asia policy, past and present, it is important to go beyond the tactical questions raised by the Cambodia decision. For the decision revealed much more than that the Vietnamization concept had failed, both as a military and as a diplomatic strategy; or how the logic of winning while "winding down" the war required expanding it; or how a "limited duration" intervention could become a full-fledged military and political commitment. The decision also said important things about U.S. priorities when intervening in the Third World and about the decision-making process on intervention.

In his April 30 speech, Nixon claimed that for five years the United States "did not wish to violate the territory of a neutral nation." In fact, as the Pentagon Papers show, while President Johnson rejected suggestions by the Joint Chiefs of Staff to make a major thrust into the sanctuary areas, he did authorize "hot pursuit" raids and occasional bombing missions in Cambodia. Nixon went further, as a Senate hearing discovered in 1973. In the fourteen months before the invasion, U.S. aircraft made over 3,600 B-52 sorties, all unreported, against targets in Cambodia. Nothing would stand in the way of a Vietnam victory. When it came down to an invasion, legality was immaterial: "State Department lawyers were not told to prepare the legal case for invasion until four days after it began."[217] So was the view of the Cambodian Government. Lon Nol acquiesced in the American intervention because it saved his regime, even at the cost of bringing in Vietnamese occupation troops.[218] The President decided that Cambodia, for America's sake, needed to be saved.

The decision itself, like the six Vietnam decisions on escalation, emerged from a prior Presidential determination to "do something." Nixon's April 30 presentation of three alternatives—doing nothing, doing more (massive aid to Cambodia), or doing what was done—was misleading. While doing nothing was a theoretical possibility, it was not a "live" option. The only kind of choice

Nixon was disposed to consider was one that called for an invasion.[219] Even the single reported high-level dissenter to the invasion, Secretary Rogers, favored sending in South Vietnamese troops,[220] which had to mean heavy U.S. logistical and air support. By portraying his decision as a middle-level, nonextremist alternative, Nixon, in the manner of his predecessors, tried to make an invasion appear to be modest and unavoidable.

All accounts are agreed that Nixon made the Cambodia decision alone. This meant that not only the Cambodians but also the Congress was not consulted. One informed report is that only two senators were briefed before the decision; and the day before Nixon's speech, the Senate Republican whip, Robert Griffin, called Kissinger to complain that he was getting word of South Vietnamese forays into Cambodia from the news wires.[221] Nixon clearly wished to insulate himself from congressional pressure—and from public damnation. His declaration on being a "one-term President," his concern about "deep divisions" in the nation because of their possible effects in Hanoi, and his remarks to journalists about not being influenced by polls and demonstrations[222] all reflected a well-entrenched Presidential denigration of public opinion and social tranquillity when making Indochina policy.

The Cambodian intervention in many ways was Vietnam in microcosm, an outgrowth both of the politics of escalation in the 1960's and, more broadly, of the antinationalism of American policy in Asia that emerged from the China experience. For a time, the intervention produced more concerted public upheaval than any previous single foreign-policy decision, probably because it came so suddenly, contrasted so strongly with public expectations, and was quickly followed by the killings of four Kent State University students. Yet, as blatant a form of intervention as the invasion was, it was consistent in motive and execution with other American interventions elsewhere in Asia.

6

The Case for
Nonintervention

The unpleasant but inescapable conclusion of this review of American interventions in the Third World is that, on balance, they have been highly effective instruments for attaining immediate U.S. foreign-policy objectives. While U.S. administrations have sustained setbacks, as in Indonesia, the Bay of Pigs, and Bangladesh, only one—in Vietnam—has had long-term domestic and international consequences. Elsewhere, movements representing opposition to the status quo have been thwarted, friendly governments have been buttressed and unpalatable ones overturned, and U.S. economic access and political influence have been preserved or expanded. The American record is sufficiently strong to justify, in the minds of decision-makers, continuation of interventionism where circumstances abroad appear to warrant it and where other means of exerting influence seem infeasible and/or ineffective.

The motives of these interventions go beyond simple anticommunism, as was revealed with particular clarity in Lebanon, in the initial stage of the Dominican intervention, and in the opposition to Bangladesh. U.S. policy-makers assumed that social revolutionary governments and political movements were dangerous if they disturbed, or seemed prepared to disturb, a status quo favorable to U.S. political, economic, and strategic interests. Beyond the question of these movements' or governments' ideological loyalties was the threat they were believed to pose to the existing boundaries of local politics, foreign policy, economic relationships, and balance of regional power. Preventive (or pre-emptive) intervention thus aimed not simply at restoring or preserving anticommunist authority, but more broadly at maintaining or creating a dependable, advantageous "stability."

This essentially imperial foreign-policy objective* inevitably conflicts with the oft-expressed official sympathy with nationalism, self-determination, and political change. The conflict may stem from the conviction of every President from Truman to Nixon that no people would freely choose a communist form of government. Nationalism and communism therefore cannot operate in concert; and nationalism, where it takes violent expression, as in civil wars and revolutions, must be opposed, because it involves or leads to the kind of chaos that communist forces, local and international, are believed bound to exploit. The American "tradition" of anticolonialism and revolution thus is set aside when change is brought about by other than nonviolent, nonradical means. Indeed, counterrevolution is the more recent American tradition—preventive action, or proxy intervention behind regimes receptive to U.S. influence and hostile to leftist ideologies, programs, and parties. And with that choice, the United States becomes the enemy of the "historical process" of disruptive change characteristic of Third World politics.[1]

An imperial foreign policy gives priority to the imposition of "law and order" on the international system. American administrations have been no more willing internationally than domestically to condone or accommodate disobedience, violence, civil strife, and insurgency. In both spheres, coercion of one kind or another has been the common response.[2] Whether one chooses to explain this compulsion in political, economic, or racial terms, the outcome is the same: intervention against nationalism. Both officials and academics[3] who have argued the need for a U.S. police function abroad, usually reasoning that it is vital to act sooner rather than later and thus prevent anarchy from spreading out of control, insist that the use of force should be discrete, pru-

---

* "Imperial" rather than "imperialistic" because the latter would mean that American interventions have been motivated mainly by the need for territory, bases, new markets, lines of communication, or corporate profits. Instead, the motivation has generally been to preserve or expand *dependency relationships* with Third World societies by insuring access to, and exerting predominant influence over, their politics, economies, and military affairs.

dent, detached, and timely. But these qualifications have affected only the mode of intervention; that the United States has preferred acting by proxy and with minimal force to becoming directly involved scarcely reduces the American role as an imperial power.

Nationalism has not been the only victim of the American interest in "stable" societies and alignment with reactionary partners. Elementary standards of humanitarianism and international law, and respect for supranational organizations, have also suffered. When the risks and costs of intervention are weighed, human life becomes totally politicized. The achievement of political and military objectives invariably has priority in American policymaking over prospects of destructiveness—as was the case, for example, in the Congo, Vietnam, Nigeria/Biafra, and Bangladesh. ("Atrocities" and "bloodbaths" tend to be condemned in Washington only when a hostile government or movement is the alleged perpetrator—as in China, 1949–50; Cuba after Castro's takeover; and by the NLF in Vietnam.) Adherence to treaty restrictions on the exercise of power has similarly been dependent on political judgments. U.S. policy in the three Latin American interventions, which showed utter disdain for the nonintervention principle, is illustrative. In those cases, as well as in policy toward Lebanon and Bangladesh, regional (the OAS) and international (the United Nations) organizations were ignored when they failed to serve or were believed unlikely to serve U.S. interests. (When the United Nations was prepared to work on behalf of U.S. objectives in the Congo, its cooperation was welcomed.) These aspects of American behavior are not, of course, peculiar to U.S. foreign policy; they are mentioned only to emphasize that the kinds of immoral, illegal, and manipulative practices for which socialist governments are usually condemned are standard components of American interventionism.

While it will not be surprising for most readers that U.S. interventions in the Third World have been motivated by power political considerations, the basic ingredients of that motivation may be more controversial. As was discussed in the first chapter, I believe that at the heart of American interventionism is an ideological consensus among postwar high-level policy-makers about the necessity of an activist U.S. role, and the presumption of U.S.

responsibilities, for projecting U.S. power and influence abroad. This ideology has been cloaked in a variety of strategic formulations—containment, the falling-domino principle, counterinsurgency, balance of power—all of which denote an expansionist interpretation of the national interest that has become policy-making dogma. Interventions, therefore, should be understood as resulting from the ideology's distorting effect on American officials' perception of Third World conditions.

The case studies point up a number of commonalities in the American perception that are worth recapitulating:

1. *Political or social instability in the Third World is a breeding ground for radical leftist forces.* Policy-making in Washington generally assumes the worst. Instability abroad is believed to be the result of international communist influences, to be amenable to direction by local procommunist organization (even though only a handful of communists may actually be identified), and to be detrimental to American political and economic interests. The consideration that an unstable situation abroad might enable the United States to identify with the nationalist, change-oriented objectives of those behind it, or refuse to identify with the government against which instability is directed, has been systematically ignored or downgraded. Radical nationalists like Nasser, Lumumba, Mossadegh, Castro, and Sukarno have been caricatured as communist dupes, while avowed communists (Mao, Ho) have been treated as antinationalists. Presumptions about the ultimate loyalty of these men have invariably forced them to reciprocate American hostility.

2. *History's "lessons" amply justify an imperial foreign policy.* Eisenhower's action in Lebanon, Kennedy's in the Congo, Johnson's in Vietnam—each of these, and others that have been studied, were prefaced by historical evaluation that "proved" the validity of concern about "another" communist takeover and "demonstrated" the wisdom of U.S. intervention. Analogies to the "loss" of China and Cuba, and to the "threat" to Greece and Korea, were useful ways for administrations to legitimize their interventions and rationalize them to the public. These experiences became models of communist behavior, distorting the intelligence

community's reporting (as in the Dominican case) as well as high-level perspectives. Rarely were such manipulations of history questioned among policy-makers; since instability and the communist threat are considered constants in international politics, there apparently was every reason to regard intervention as a responsible means of dealing with them. Previous interventions thus justified later ones; interventionism was historically consistent, and if, as in the Congo, Indochina, or Cuba, one administration succeeded to the interventionist policies of its predecessor, there was all the more justification for not reversing course and instead being prisoner to the past.

3. *Third World upheavals are foreign-policy crises having personal as well as national implications.* Not only does the ideology of national interests encourage American involvement in the domestic affairs of the developing countries, but also, for U.S. policy-makers, intervention becomes a personal test of nerve and will. The interaction of these two perspectives is well illustrated in the following statement by Walt W. Rostow:

> We must expect over the next decade recurrent turbulence in these [Third World] areas; we must expect systematic efforts by the Communists to exploit this turbulence; we must expect from time to time that crises will occur; and a great deal of skill, courage, and insight will be required to handle them in ways which do not damage—and if possible promote—the interests of the free world.[4]

A Third World crisis, from a crisis manager's viewpoint, is an expected event, since "turbulence" and communism will always be found together. The policy-making process puts a premium in such situations on toughness under fire, the ability to "see the thing through"—in other words, as in (among others) Laos, the Congo, Vietnam, and Cambodia, the attachment of higher priority to personal loyalty and strength of conviction than to intellectual sophistication and qualities of human understanding. Those persons who would make decisions on intervention hence were usually managers (of power) rather than area specialists, men who calculated costs and benefits in power-political rather than human, legal, or moral terms. They dealt with Third World problems as part of a global contest for ideological and military supremacy rather than as intractable events that are forever at the mercy of time and circumstance.*

THE CONDITIONS OF INTERVENTION

While it is not the purpose of this study to develop hypotheses about the precise circumstances and manner of American interventions in Third World countries,[5] the case studies do suggest the strategic and political factors that U.S. policy-makers did weigh when interventions were undertaken. These factors may be worth specifying because they show in another way how uninfluential considerations of Third World nationalism and principles of law and morality have been when U.S. administrations believed the national interest to be challenged.

There would seem to be two primary and three secondary conditions of Third World interventions:

Primary:
1. There must be a sociopolitical revolutionary milieu—either political violence in which a revolutionary movement (the so-called communist threat) is involved or radical domestic change that is being carried out by a revolutionary government.
2. The revolutionary movement's or government's policies and programs must be perceived as threatening "stability" beyond the country in which the movement or government is operating.

Secondary:
1. The risk of direct Soviet or Chinese intervention in response to U.S. involvement must be low.
2. U.S. intervention must be sanctioned by domestic (U.S.), regional, or international authority.

---

* I contend that area specialists are less likely than crisis managers to abuse the power of decision on Third World policy. Area specialists have an intellectual commitment to Third World cultures that usually enables them to empathize with non-Western peoples and accept their intrinsic worth as individuals. Crisis managers, with their interest in power rivalry, systems, cost-benefit calculations, and gamesmanship, typically lack such a commitment.

3. U.S. intervention must be invited by a "representative" of local political authority.

As already suggested, it is the perceived threat to stability rather than the communist threat alone that has consistently set the stage for decisions to intervene in the Third World. Radicalism must be coupled to chaos, or the likelihood of chaos. When that occurs—and it occurs quite often in Third World politics—there seems to be a visceral reaction among high U.S. policy-makers in the direction of a preventive intervention to stifle the threat before it gets out of hand.

But whether U.S. intervention in some form will actually take place seems to depend on a further condition, namely, that the American interest in stability be jeopardized beyond the specific country in which a revolutionary situation exists. There have, after all, been numerous instances of civil strife in the Third World that U.S. administrations ignored.[6] The common feature of the interventions examined in this study is that a social revolutionary movement or government was perceived from Washington to threaten a *regional* status quo. The success of the radical movement's opposition or the government's program would become infectious, in Washington's judgment, and therefore should be resisted. Recall, for instance, that the United States intervened in China mainly because a stable China under Chiang Kai-shek was deemed important to the maintenance of American predominance in postwar Asia's balance of power; intervened in Lebanon to cut short encirclement of the Middle East by radical Arab nationalist governments; intervened in Guatemala, Cuba, and the Dominican Republic to silence or prevent the spread of radical socialism in Latin America; intervened in Indochina initially to keep the "dominoes" from falling throughout Southeast Asia and later to preserve faith in America's willingness and ability to combat national liberation wars; and intervened in Bangladesh to re-establish a stable balance of power on the Indian subcontinent. *How far* the United States was prepared to pursue intervention was determined, as has been seen, by a variety of other circumstances, including domestic politics, bureaucratic bargaining, military assessments, and competing demands for attention and resources from other international problems. But the point to be emphasized here is that radicalism in Third World politics, when perceived to have more than local implications, incited the American will to intervene.

Secondary conditions of U.S. intervention are those that usually affect decisions on it but are not indispensable. Among them is the assessment of prospects for Soviet or Chinese counteraction. This consideration is considered secondary because U.S. policy-makers have, as in Laos, Vietnam, and the Congo, accepted the risk of counteraction weighed against the benefits of intervention. All the interventions discussed in this study were undertaken with great confidence, however, that such counteraction would not occur, or could be handled effectively if it unexpectedly did occur. The assessment invariably proved correct: Whereas the Americans were prepared to play for high stakes, the Russians or the Chinese were not. Had *their* evaluation of the relationship between Third World instability and their own national interests been equivalent to the Americans', one or another past "crisis" might easily have mushroomed into a direct confrontation of the major powers. Instead, the limited, hesitant, and carefully controlled character of Soviet and Chinese involvement in Third World political violence, and on behalf of Third World ideological allies, has given the United States free rein to intervene.* And the cumulative experience of these unopposed interventions has probably emboldened U.S. policy-makers to believe that the entire Third World, and not merely Latin America, is a low-risk area for applying American power.

Intervention usually has also been conditioned by sanction from various sources, most importantly from the Congress and from regional and international organizations. With the important exceptions of the Dominican, Cambodian, and Bangladesh interventions, all the others found U.S. administrations seeking, or referring to, authority for their actions from key congressmen, congressional resolutions, the United Nations, or regional associations.

---

* The major limitation that the United States has observed in these interventions is not to escalate to the point of threatening a major adversary's most security-sensitive areas. Having paid the price in Korea of insensitivity to Chinese security interests, U.S. intervention in Laos and over North Vietnam carefully avoided provoking the P.R.C. to counteract directly. No crisis in areas adjacent to the Soviet Union has yet occurred.

Sanction was rarely difficult to find, and opposition easy to avoid. Hurried "crisis" meetings with select congressional leaders almost always led to approval of interventionary actions (opposition in 1954 to U.S. involvement in Indochina being a notable exception). Public opinion could always be counted on to support the President in a time of national trial. Enabling documents such as the SEATO pact, the U.N. Charter, the OAS Charter, and the Tonkin Gulf Resolution were sufficiently ambiguous to be either stretched or distorted in order to serve the administration's purposes. But the three exceptions to these rules of procedure reduce the criticality of them. In the first case U.S. troops were landed, in the second U.S. forces invaded, and in the third aid was covertly sent and a naval task force dispatched, on each occasion without prior congressional or any other authority. The lack of domestic and supranational sanction thus will not deter administrations from using force or threat abroad if the "national interest" (incorporated in conditions 1 and 2) so dictates.

Finally, U.S. officials have also sought authorization of intervention from within the country that is the subject of intervention. Presidents value invitations for purely instrumental reasons: They lend legitimacy to the intervention by making it appear to be in response to a call for help from a lawful representative of a Third World society. On occasion, failure to find a credible local authority has played a part in preventing a U.S. intervention from occurring—for example, Eisenhower's unwillingness to intervene on behalf of Bao Dai's Vietnam in 1954, and the same administration's inability to find a suitable Cuban exile leader who would represent the Bay of Pigs invaders. But, as with the previous two conditions, this one generally has not needed to be promptly or fully satisfied to bring about intervention. Third World governments and opposition groups in whose behalf the United States intervened have clearly lacked popular credentials that would make their invitations credible (as in Laos, Vietnam, Cuba, and Guatemala). In addition, interventions have occurred where no government in fact existed (the military triumvirate that called on the U.S. Embassy in the Dominican Republic); where the national leader did not have control over his armed forces (Chamoun in Lebanon); and where no request to intervene was received or even made (Cambodia).

AN ALTERNATIVE TO INTERVENTION

The imperial persuasion in American foreign policy toward the Third World is not open to question only on moral, legal, and humanitarian grounds. In long-term perspective interventions do not serve the political, economic, and strategic interests that are usually cited to justify them. It is, in other words, in the interest of the United States, as that interest has been defined by American policy-makers, to make nonintervention the keystone of U.S. policy.

In the first place, interventions against nationalism confirm suspicions of, and hostility toward, the United States (and "U.S. imperialism"), thus limiting American access and influence in the Third World. This was or is the case, for example, in postwar China, in Sukarno's Indonesia, in Africa because of opposition to the nationalist movements in the Portuguese colonies, and throughout Latin America. American behavior in the Third World has conformed to the descriptions of it preferred by Moscow and Peking. The United States would today have far greater diplomatic latitude and economic opportunities abroad than it now enjoys had it chosen not to intervene against radical movements and governments.

Where the United States has chosen to intervene against revolutionary movements, moreover, it has often become entangled in commitments to governments that are inefficient, corrupt, lacking in popular authority, and oppressive. These regimes have been able to manipulate American commitments to acquire increased military and economic aid and to develop a U.S. interest in, and ultimate responsibility for, their very survival. U.S.-Cambodia relations after the April, 1970, invasion provide a recent illustration of this phenomenon. Should such regimes be overthrown, the American capacity to disengage its support and realign with a successor revolutionary government is weakened if not eliminated for years to come.

Intervention against radical governments does more than assure their lasting hostility toward the United States. For lack of any better alternative as much as because of ideological affinity, these governments are bound to move closer toward the socialist world, and may become politically and economically dependent on it. After U.S. interventions, the new government of China (from 1950 to 1959), Sukarno's Indonesia (from 1958 to 1965), and Cuba (after 1961) became active opponents of American foreign policy and accepted varying degrees of dependency on Soviet trade and aid. Interventions thus not only defy the concepts of state sovereignty and territorial integrity, they also weaken the capacity of radical governments to develop independent foreign and domestic policies. Had nonintervention been practiced, opportunities would probably have become available for Washington to work constructively with these governments, offering them the kind of technical help and diplomatic cushioning they needed to avoid being dependent on any one foreign power.

Intervention, often carried out in parts of the world that are as remote from the United States politically and strategically as they are geographically, makes defense of the "national interest" a world-wide responsibility. The arenas in which a direct confrontation of the major powers may occur become ever wider; the chance of war brought on by the momentum of conflict or miscalculation increases. The fact that, until now, the United States has been able to project its power into the Third World with relative impunity is no guarantee for the future, especially as both the U.S.S.R. and China are expanding their international engagements and the reach of their military power into traditionally American preserves. Nor can the United States be assured that new diplomatic understandings with those nations in the 1970's will remove Third World countries as potential points of conflict. As American conduct of the Indochina war has shown, the improvement of relations with Russia and China has not been allowed to impede the pursuit of objectives in Third World areas in which the socialist powers also have interests. The United States has proceeded with intervention at the cost of straining and setting back relations with its major international adversaries rather than abandon its minor allies.

Another long-term disadvantage of interventionism is that it confirms racial stereotypes, increases racial hatreds, and thus enhances the possibility of race conflict. American behavior broadens the global North-South conflict from an economic one (the "haves" versus the "have-nots") to a racial one (between the white and colored peoples). Rhetoric about social justice and self-determination, and technical assistance programs to Third World governments, cannot be of great help either to the American image or to American purposes when the U.S. Government assumes the right of intervention to ensure Third World stability. Only when nonintervention is the rule can American espousals of interest in assisting "have-not" peoples to be independent and self-reliant become credible.

With the American intervention on a massive scale in Indochina, the relationship became clear for the first time between an imperial policy abroad and domestic division. So costly and fruitless has U.S. policy been in Indochina since the early 1950's that widespread doubts have arisen at home about the sanity of American foreign-policy leadership generally, and about the usefulness of global involvement. Resort to the most sophisticated means of violence and terror have been seen in many quarters to have parallels at home; and the fact that, both at home and abroad, the targets have been colored peoples accentuates the sense of injustice and oppression among American minorities that had developed before the war reached its height. Less dramatic forms of intervention may well enable administrations to continue to use it without fear of vigorous public opposition. But so long as Vietnam remains recent history, interventions that previously would have raised no eyebrows now will be subjected to public and congressional scrutiny. At the least, the government will no longer be able to count on the traditionally large reservoir of support (or apathy) for foreign policies and programs that made endorsement of interventions so automatic in the past.

Noninterventionism can begin to restore confidence in the government's ability to manage foreign affairs with sense and decency. Its axioms would essentially be the reverse of those that I have proposed constitute U.S. foreign-policy ideology. America's domestic tranquillity depends on the quality of life at home, not on security and stability abroad. Security and stability abroad depend on the relationship of individual governments to their citizens, not on a moral or political responsibility that has been unwarrantedly assumed. Finally, the fullfillment of America's international role depends on the dynamism and openness of American society, the opportunities for individual growth afforded by American institutions, and the ability of the American Government to exercise restraint in its projection of power abroad. Refusing to become party to the domestic conflicts of other nations would not represent an abnegation of power and responsibility, but a realization of their limits.

The mood of the public and Congress, as reflected in the 1973 War Powers Resolution that restricts the President's use of force abroad, appears to be highly receptive to noninterventionism and the definition of a narrower, more manageable, and more purposeful range of foreign interests. Indeed, such a shift in over-all policy should facilitate an administration's argument in behalf of other international programs, including foreign economic assistance, defense budgets, and diplomacy with the Soviet Union and China. It should be as possible to "sell" noninterventionism today as it has been to "sell" interventionism; much depends on whether the American Government is prepared to do away with the ideological component of foreign policy-making.

Abroad, a policy of nonintervention must include above all a receptivity to radical change, regardless of the ideology or economic philosophy of the government or movement supporting such change. This suggestion is not for a simpleminded shift from systematically resisting to systematically supporting radicalism. What counts is the quality of economic and political life that radical change promises. The United States should be identifying with those groups or governments that are devoted to promoting national independence, enhancing their capacity for self-reliant economic growth, and working toward equality of social and economic justice and personal freedom. It should not give aid or comfort to a movement or regime—such as that in white Southern Africa or Pakistan during the Bangladesh revolution—that, as a matter of policy or practice, denies its people equal opportunity and violates common standards of humanitarian treatment. The American interest should lie in the realization of long-cherished and widely accepted values rather than in a particular (Western) structure of authority, pattern of politics, or ideological tendency in the cold war.[7]

American administrations must come to accept that a stable world order in which the danger of war is receding and the urge to predominance of the major powers is checked can be promoted more surely by aligning with (but not intervening behind) the forces of change than by opposing them. Intervention can, at most, only brake temporarily the momentum of revolution; it cannot, short of prolonged military occupation (and questionably even then), eradicate those governmental deficiencies or conflicts of political interest that give rise to civil strife. The lessons for future decisions on revolution abroad should come from unsuccessful interventions; those that have achieved U.S. objectives in the short run do not advance American interests in the long run, and in fact retard them.

If this perspective were put into practice, would there not be a danger of the Third World's eventual encirclement and political absorption by the socialist world? This question, posed by those who have long and successfully argued that noninterventionism is too risky, sees communism as a singular formula for satellization rather than for what it is, a modernizing ideology.[8] Proponents of the interventionist philosophy do not see how self-fulfilling it can be—how the act of intervention promotes the very instability, anti-American hostility, and attraction to radical ideologies that it seeks to prevent. Even if a hands-off American policy toward Third World civil strife should encourage the U.S.S.R. and China to increase their efforts to benefit from it, those powers have already found, most notably in Africa and the Middle East, that there are severe limits to their ability to control events in the Third World. Third World governments, including those receptive to socialism, jealously safeguard their sovereignty, with or without an American presence or the possibility of U.S. intervention. If history is any guide, the consequences of Soviet or Chinese attempts to manipulate Third World politics are more likely to be new Vietnams for them than the establishment of a new communist imperium.

Are there nevertheless circumstances under which U.S. intervention in Third World civil wars or revolutions can be "legitimate"? Two of the African cases—the Congolese civil war, in its initial phase, and the revolutions in the Portuguese colonies—suggest exceptions to a noninterventionist policy. Where a request for intervention is made by a government whose credentials are nowhere questioned, or by a revolutionary movement whose claims to represent nationalist sentiment are not in doubt; where that request is channeled through and action is authorized by the United Nations; and where the purpose of the intervention is to weaken or remove a clearly foreign presence—in such circumstances, American involvement would be morally, politically, and legally defensible.

Such a conjunction of circumstances warranting intervention, which would be in a multilateral framework, is highly improbable. The inviting authority is seldom a single voice representative of all major political factions' and the voice itself is not likely to be universally acknowledged. For these and other reasons, the U.N. membership will rarely be in agreement on the legitimacy of the request, much less the means of acting upon it. And there will be few cases in which the "foreign" character of the intruder is obvious to all.

Intervention, however, *should be* the rare exception and no longer the practiced tool of American foreign policy. When intervention occurs, it should be universally condoned. It should not serve specifically American purposes, whether those be in pursuit of traditional imperial objectives or, as is sometimes urged, in order actively to promote the interests of revolutionary movements. If proscriptions against unilateral intervention are to have meaning, they must be enforced with respect to both "good" and "bad" governments and "progressive" and "reactionary" movements. Nor should they leave open the alternative of intervening where success is likely and U.S. interests are clearly at stake.[9] Except under the unusual conditions just mentioned, U.S. policy in the Third World should proceed from the assumption that intervention cannot be ultimately profitable and that nonintervention is the most appropriate way to promote American influence and the American example.

Notes

Chapter 1: The Ideology of National Interest

1. Richard J. Barnet is prominent among those scholars who have drawn attention to the shared characteristics, in background, education, and career patterns, of what he calls the "National-Security Managers." This elite, which comprises officeholders of assistant secretary rank and up in the Executive, defense, and intelligence branches, numbered only about 400 individuals from 1945 to 1967. (Barnet, *Intervention and Revolution: The United States in the Third World* [New York: World, 1968], p. 25; and see his *Roots of War* [New York: Atheneum, 1972].)
2. Speech of March 23, 1962, in *Public Papers of the Presidents of the United States: John F. Kennedy, 1962* (Washington, D.C.: Government Printing Office, 1963), p. 265.
3. See, for instance, Hans J. Morgenthau, *A New Foreign Policy for the United States* (New York: Praeger, 1969), especially pp. 120 ff., where he discusses the Soviet-American competition in terms of "two hostile and incompatible ideologies," Communism versus anti-Communism. And see Michael Parenti, *The Anti-Communist Impulse* (New York: Random House, 1969), introductory chapter.
4. Eugene V. Rostow, *Law, Power, and the Pursuit of Peace* (New York: Harper & Row, 1968), p. 40.
5. McGeorge Bundy, "The End of Either/Or," *Foreign Affairs*, XLV, no. 2 (January, 1967), p. 190.
6. Harry S. Truman, *Years of Trial and Hope*, vol. II of *Memoirs* (Garden City, N.Y.: Doubleday, 1956), pp. 107–8.
7. In *Department of State Bulletin*, October 7, 1957, pp. 569–70.
8. Statement of November 22, 1963, quoted by Dean Rusk, *ibid.*, September 12, 1966, p. 363.
9. In a speech of February 12, 1965, quoted in Barnet, *Intervention and Revolution*, p. 12.
10. Quoted in Walt W. Rostow, *View from the Seventh Floor* (New York: Harper & Row, 1964), p. 53.
11. Inaugural address, January 20, 1965.
12. E. V. Rostow, p. 15.

13. Interview with C. L. Sulzberger, *New York Times*, March 10, 1971, p. 14.
14. *Department of State Bulletin*, October 7, 1957, p. 576.
15. *Ibid.*, March 22, 1965, p. 403. Compare the opinion of Harlan Cleveland, Assistant Secretary of State for International Organization Affairs under Kennedy and Johnson: "The price of power is involvement. . . . Because we do not want to have to use our ultimate power, we must constantly be using more limited forms of power, serving (sometimes without being invited) as the world's leading peacemakers and peacekeepers. . . ." *The Obligations of Power: American Diplomacy in the Search for Peace* (New York: Harper & Row, 1966), pp. 11, 14–15.
16. Walt W. Rostow, *The United States in the World Arena: An Essay in Recent History* (New York: Harper, 1960), pp. 544, 546.
17. Dean Rusk, *The Winds of Freedom: Selections from the Speeches and Statements of Secretary of State Dean Rusk, January 1961–August 1962* (ed. Ernest K. Lindley) (Boston, Mass.: Beacon Press, 1963), p. 227.
18. E. V. Rostow, p. 44.

CHAPTER 2: EISENHOWER AND THE MIDDLE EAST

1. Joseph Marion Jones, *The Fifteen Weeks (February 21–June 5, 1947)* (New York: Viking Press, 1955), p. 140.
2. *Ibid.*, p. 143.
3. Louis L. Gerson, *The American Secretaries of State and Their Diplomacy: John Foster Dulles* (New York: Cooper Square, 1967), pp. 252–57.
4. John C. Campbell, *Defense of the Middle East* (New York: Harper, 1958), pp. 66–67.
5. Malcolm Kerr, "American Policy Toward Egypt, 1955–1971: A Record of Failures," Southern California Arms Control and Foreign Policy Seminar, Los Angeles, March, 1973, p. 4. See also Richard H. Nolte, "United States Policy and the Middle East," in Georgiana Stevens (ed.), *The United States and the Middle East* (Englewood Cliffs, N.J.: Prentice-Hall, 1964), pp. 160–61.
6. John S. Badeau, *The American Approach to the Arab World* (New York: Harper, 1968), pp. 8–9.
7. Dwight D. Eisenhower, *Waging Peace, 1956–1961* (Garden City, N.Y.: Doubleday, 1965), p. 178.
8. *Ibid.*, pp. 182–83, for Eisenhower's view. For the State Department's assessment, see U.S. Senate, Committee on Foreign Relations and Committee on Armed Services, *Hearings: The President's Proposal on the Middle East*, 87th Cong., 2d Sess., pt. 1, January 14–February 4, 1957 (Washington, D.C.: Government Printing Office, 1957), p. 41.
9. Eisenhower, pp. 178–81; Campbell, pp. 123–24.
10. This section relies on material in John C. Campbell and Helen Caruso, *The West and the Middle East* (New York: Council on Foreign Relations, 1972), chap. 3; Charles Issawi, *Oil, the Middle East and the World* (New York: Library Press, 1972); and Michael Tanzer, *The Political Economy of International Oil and the Underdeveloped Countries* (Boston, Mass.: Beacon Press, 1969), pp. 42–45.
11. Tanzer, p. 54.
12. *Ibid.*, pp. 55–56. On this flow of personnel, Tanzer cites at length from

the intensive research of Robert Engler, *The Politics of Oil* (New York: Macmillan, 1961).

13. Issawi, pp. 51–52.
14. Joyce and Gabriel Kolko, *The Limits of Power: The World and United States Foreign Policy* (New York: Harper & Row, 1972), pp. 236–42; Dean Acheson, *Present at the Creation: My Years in the State Department* (New York: Signet, 1969), pp. 265–67.
15. Harry S. Truman, *Years of Trial and Hope*, vol. II of *Memoirs* (Garden City, N.Y.: Doubleday, 1956), p. 95.
16. Quoted in Dean Acheson, p. 267.
17. *Ibid.*, p. 651.
18. Cf. Sir Anthony Eden, *Full Circle* (Boston, Mass.: Houghton Mifflin, 1960), pp. 198, 201; and Acheson, pp. 652–53, 866.
19. *Ibid.*, p. 653; Eden, p. 195.
20. J. and G. Kolko, p. 417.
21. Eden, p. 208.
22. *Ibid.*, p. 212.
23. Text of Eisenhower's letter in *Public Papers of the Presidents of the United States: Dwight D. Eisenhower, 1953* (Washington, D.C.: Government Printing Office, 1960), pp. 482–84. Mossadegh's letter is *ibid.*, pp. 484–86.
24. Eisenhower, *Mandate for Change, 1953–1956* (Garden City, N.Y.: Doubleday, 1963), p. 163.
25. *Ibid.*
26. Richard W. Cattam, *Nationalism in Iran* (Pittsburgh, Pa.: University of Pittsburgh Press, 1964), pp. 198–99, 212–13, 216.
27. Eisenhower, *Mandate for Change*, p. 163.
28. *Ibid.*, p. 165.
29. Leonard M. Fanning, *Foreign Oil and the Free World* (New York: McGraw-Hill, 1954), pp. 296–97.
30. *Ibid.*, p. 302.
31. *Department of State Bulletin*, August 16, 1954, p. 230.
32. *Public Papers of the Presidents of the United States: Dwight D. Eisenhower, 1958* (Washington, D.C.: Government Printing Office, 1959), pp. 549–57.
33. Kerr, pp. 7–8.
34. Eisenhower, *Waging Peace*, p. 265.
35. Quoted in Leila M. T. Meo, *Lebanon: Improbable Nation* (Bloomington, Ind.: Indiana University Press, 1965), p. 111.
36. Eisenhower, *Waging Peace*, p. 262.
37. Anthony Nutting, *Nasser* (London: Constable, 1972), pp. 201, 211.
38. *Ibid.*, p. 201.
39. Eisenhower, *Waging Peace*, p. 196.
40. *Ibid.*, pp. 197–98.
41. *Ibid.*, pp. 198–99; Meo, p. 191.
42. Eisenhower, *Waging Peace*, p. 199.
43. *Ibid.*, p. 203.
44. *Ibid.*, p. 263.
45. Malcolm Kerr, "The Lebanese Civil War," in Evan Luard (ed.), *The International Regulation of Civil Wars* (London: Thames and Hudson, 1972), pp. 69–70.

46. Eisenhower, *Waging Peace*, p. 265.
47. Meo, p. 168.
48. *Ibid.*, p. 167.
49. Robert Murphy, *Diplomat Among Warriors* (London: Collins, 1964), p. 488.
50. David Wise and Thomas B. Ross, *The Invisible Government* (New York: Bantam, 1964), pp. 337–38.
51. Meo, p. 176.
52. Eisenhower, *Waging Peace*, p. 266.
53. *Ibid.*
54. Robert McClintock, *The Meaning of Limited War* (Boston, Mass.: Houghton Mifflin, 1967), pp. 101–2.
55. Meo, p. 195; McClintock, p. 102.
56. Eisenhower, *Waging Peace*, p. 266.
57. *Report of the United Nations Observation Group in Lebanon,* S/4069 (New York: U.N. Security Council, July 30, 1958), p. 21.
58. Eisenhower, *Waging Peace*, p. 269.
59. *Ibid.*, p. 268.
60. See his statement on the U.S. landing in Lebanon of July 15, 1958, in *Public Papers* (1958), p. 554.
61. *Report,* S/4069, *op. cit.* Murphy (p. 490) wrote: "The American troop landings had been a surprise and a shock to the U.N. group, which regarded our military action with mixed emotions, as it seemed to interfere with their own efforts to settle the civil war."
62. Nutting, pp. 212–21.
63. Eisenhower, *Waging Peace*, p. 263, n. 2.
64. Nutting, p. 227.
65. Eisenhower, *Waging Peace*, p. 264.
66. Nutting, p. 236.
67. Eisenhower, *Waging Peace*, p. 270.
68. *Ibid.*
69. *Ibid.*, p. 274.
70. *Ibid.*
71. Address of July 15, 1958, in *Public Papers* (1958), p. 555.
72. Murphy, p. 485.
73. As reported in *Time*, July 28, 1958, p. 12.
74. Nixon's speech of July 19, 1958, in Minneapolis; text in *Vital Speeches of the Day*, XXIV, no. 20 (August 1, 1958), 618.
75. *Time, op. cit.*
76. Murphy, p. 486.
77. Eisenhower, *Waging Peace*, p. 272.
78. Sherman Adams, *Firsthand Report: The Story of the Eisenhower Administration* (New York: Harper & Row, 1961), p. 290. Adams was Eisenhower's Special Assistant.
79. Murphy, p. 486.
80. McClintock, pp. 108–9.
81. *Ibid.*, pp. 110–14, and Charles W. Thayer, *Diplomat* (New York: Harper, 1959), pp. 33–36.
82. Murphy, p. 487.
83. Eisenhower, *Waging Peace*, p. 280.
84. Murphy, pp. 500–503.

85. Eisenhower, *Waging Peace*, p. 290.
86. *Ibid.*, p. 289.
87. See Kerr, in Luard, pp. 79–80.
88. Kerr, "American Policy Toward Egypt," p. 19.

CHAPTER 3: KENNEDY AND AFRICA

1. These conclusions emerge from a study by an economic adviser on Africa to the International Bank for Reconstruction and Development. See Andrew M. Kamarck, "The African Economy and International Trade," in Walter Goldschmidt (ed.), *The United States and Africa*, rev. ed. (New York: Praeger, 1963), pp. 157–59. The figures he provides (p. 157) indicate that prewar American imports from and exports to Africa totaled about $200 million; all forms of prewar U.S. investments were also about $200 million. By 1961, total trade was about $1.5 billion, and investments were about $1.4 billion.
2. See U.S. House of Representatives, Committee on Foreign Affairs, Subcommittee on Africa, *Report of the Special Study Mission to Africa, South and East of the Sahara*, 84th Cong. 2d Sess., July 27, 1956 (Washington, D.C.: Government Printing Office, 1956), pp. 12–13, 148–49.
3. Richard M. Nixon, "The Emergence of Africa: Report to President Eisenhower," *Department of State Bulletin*, April 22, 1957, p. 637.
4. Quoted in Rupert Emerson, *Africa and United States Policy* (Englewood Cliffs, N.J.: Prentice-Hall, 1967), p. 23.
5. Quoted *ibid.*
6. House, *Report of the Special Study Mission* . . . , p. 149.
7. *Ibid.*
8. Chester Bowles, *Africa's Challenge to America* (Berkeley: University of California Press, 1956), pp. 96–97.
9. Arthur M. Schlesinger, Jr., *A Thousand Days: John F. Kennedy in the White House* (Boston, Mass.: Houghton Mifflin, 1965), p. 551.
10. Speech in the Senate, July 2, 1954, in John F. Kennedy, *The Strategy of Peace* (ed. Allan Nevins) (New York: Harper, 1960), p. 71.
11. Speech of June 28, 1959, *ibid.*, p. 130.
12. Elsewhere in his Algeria speech, for instance, Kennedy lamented that the administration's policy "has endangered the continuation of some of our most strategic airbases, and threatened our geographical advantages over the Communist orbit. It has affected our standing in the eyes of the Free World, our leadership in the fight to keep that world free, our prestige, and our security; as well as our moral leadership in the fight against Soviet imperialism in the countries behind the Iron Curtain." *Ibid.*, p. 68.
13. Schlesinger, p. 553.
14. Kennedy, p. 131 (speech of October 13, 1959).
15. See, for example, a speech of June 28, 1959, *ibid.*, pp. 124–30.
16. *Ibid.*, p. 127.
17. *Ibid.*, p. 129.
18. *Ibid.*, pp. 126–27.
19. Schlesinger, p. 561.
20. *Ibid.*, p. 565.
21. These and other developments in U.S.-Algeria relations are concisely

treated by William B. Quandt, "United States Relations with Algeria: Learning to Do Business with Radical Nationalists," Southern California Arms Control and Foreign Policy Seminar, Los Angeles, October, 1971.

22. This paragraph draws on information in Schlesinger, pp. 567–73, and William Attwood (ambassador to Guinea under Kennedy and to Kenya under Johnson), *The Reds and the Blacks: A Personal Adventure* (New York: Harper & Row, 1967), chap. 3.

23. Robert Murphy, *Diplomat Among Warriors* (London: Collins, 1964), p. 405.

24. Dwight D. Eisenhower, *Waging Peace*, 1956–1961 (Garden City, N.Y.: Doubleday, 1965), pp. 574–75.

25. *Ibid.*, p. 572.

26. *Ibid.*, p. 573.

27. Murphy attended the inaugural ceremonies in Léopoldville at which Lumumba delivered a scathing attack on Belgian colonial rule. After meeting Lumumba, Murphy reported: "Full of zeal, hostile to the Belgians, caring little for amenities or accuracy, a new demagogue was making his appearance on the world scene. . . . I ascertained that Lumumba's knowledge of Communism was extremely vague, though his confusion made him as useful for the Soviet Government's purposes as an outright agent." Murphy, pp. 408–9.

28. Eisenhower, p. 572, n. 13.

29. Albert P. Disdier, "Economic Prospects at Independence: Myths and Realities," in Helen A. Kitchen (ed.), *Footnotes to the Congo Story* (New York: Walker, 1967), p. 3.

30. Smith Hempstone, *Rebels, Mercenaries, and Dividends: The Katanga Story* (New York: Praeger, 1962), pp. 51–52.

31. Conor Cruise O'Brien, *To Katanga and Back: A United Nations Case History* (New York: Grosset & Dunlap, 1962), p. 173.

32. U.S. House of Representatives, Committee on Foreign Affairs, Subcommittee on Africa, *Staff Memorandum on the Republic of the Congo*, 87th Cong., 1st Sess., April 13, 1961 (Washington, D.C.: Government Printing Office, 1961), p. 50.

33. *Ibid.*, p. 48.

34. See the testimony of ARMCO's president in U.S. House of Representatives, Committee on Foreign Affairs, Subcommittee on Africa, *Hearings: Activities of Private U.S. Organizations in Africa*, 87th Cong., 1st Sess., May 8–June 1, 1961 (Washington, D.C.: Government Printing Office, 1961), pp. 154 ff.

35. U.S. Army, *Area Handbook for the Republic of the Congo (Léopoldville)* (Washington, D.C.: Government Printing Office, 1962), p. 535, and Murphy, pp. 401–2.

36. Murphy, p. 412.

37. Patrice Lumumba, *Congo, My Country* (New York: Praeger, 1962), pp. 143, 174.

38. René Lemarchand, "Patrice Lumumba in Perspective," in Kitchen, p. 35.

39. Hempstone, p. 24.

40. U.N. Security Council Document S/143, in *Department of State Bulletin*, August 1, 1960, p. 161.

41. Document S/4405, in U.N. Security Council, *Official Records: Resolu-*

tions and Decisions of the Security Council 1960 (New York: United Nations, 1965), p. 6.

42. Robert C. Good, "The Congo Crisis: A Study of Postcolonial Politics," in Laurence W. Martin (ed.), *Neutralism and Nonalignment: The New States in World Affairs* (New York: Praeger, 1962), p. 41.

43. Helmut Sonnenfeldt, "The Soviet Union and China," in Kitchen, pp. 29–30; Eisenhower, p. 575; U.S. Army, *Handbook*, p. 361.

44. Later, on September 13, a joint session of the Chambers voted extraordinary powers to Lumumba, but the vote lacked a quorum. The complex constitutional issues are treated in Crawford Young, *Politics in the Congo* (Princeton, N.J.: Princeton University Press, 1965), pp. 176–78, 325–30, and Catherine Hoskyns, *The Congo Since Independence* (New York: Oxford University Press, 1965), pp. 208–10.

45. O'Brien, p. 60.

46. Cited *ibid.*

47. See the discussion *ibid.*, pp. 56–57. With the increasingly strident Soviet criticisms of the UNF's conduct in the Congo, and then Chairman Khrushchev's demand that the Secretary-General's position be made a "troika," or tripartite post, it was perhaps inevitable, as O'Brien notes, that no representative to the Secretariat from a socialist state should have been kept informed of U.N. activities, or even allowed access to the Congo files.

48. As Sorensen has written, "The Kennedy Congo policy was largely an extension of the Eisenhower policy." Theodore Sorensen, *Kennedy* (New York: Harper & Row, 1965), pp. 635–36.

49. See Schlesinger, p. 575.

50. George W. Ball, "The Elements in Our Congo Policy," Department of State Publication 7326, December, 1961, p. 2.

51. Sorensen, p. 636.

52. For Cleveland's remarks, see U.S. House of Representatives, Committee on Foreign Affairs, Subcommittee on International Organizations and Movements, *Hearings: United Nations Operations in the Congo*, 87th Cong., 1st Sess., April 13, 1961 (Washington, D.C.: Government Printing Office, 1961), pp. 19–21.

53. *Ibid.*, p. 20.

54. Ball, "The Elements in Our Congo Policy," p. 2.

55. See Sorensen, p. 636: "[Kennedy's] aim was the restoration of stability and order to a reunited, independent and viable Congo, free from Communist domination and free from both civil war and cold war conflicts."

56. See the testimony of G. Mennen Williams, Assistant Secretary of State for African Affairs, in U.S. House of Representatives, Committee on Foreign Affairs, Subcommittee on Africa, *Hearing: Africa Briefing*, 88th Cong., 1st Sess., February 23, 1963 (Washington, D.C.: Government Printing Office, 1963), pp. 11–12.

57. O'Brien, pp. 58–59.

58. Cleveland's testimony, *op. cit.*, pp. 2, 7.

59. U.N. Security Council document S/4741, in *Official Records: Resolutions and Decisions of the Security Council 1961* (New York: United Nations, 1965), pp. 2–3.

60. Roger Hilsman, *To Move a Nation: The Politics of Foreign Policy in the*

Administration of John F. Kennedy (Garden City, N.Y.: Doubleday, 1967), pp. 257–60.

61. Taking together all forms of U.S. aid to the Congo between July, 1960, and June, 1964, the total is over $400 million. The figure includes $168 million to the UNF; the remainder is technical assistance, bilateral military aid ($6.1 million), and economic aid to finance imports. See Hoskyns, p. 474, n. 4; Lefever, in Hilsman and Good (eds.), *Foreign Policy in the Sixties: The Issues and the Instruments* (Baltimore, Md.: Johns Hopkins Press, 1965), p. 143; Lefever, *Crisis in the Congo*, p. 131; Williams, in Kitchen, p. 147.

62. For instance, Dean Rusk testified in January, 1962, that the Congolese request was for the "urgent dispatch of United Nations forces to the Congo to protect the national territory of the country and avoid a threat to. international peace." (Dean Rusk, *The Winds of Freedom: Selections from the Speeches and Statements of Secretary of State Dean Rusk, January 1961–August 1962* [ed. Ernest K. Lindley] [Boston, Mass.: Beacon Press, 1963], p. 222); G. Mennen Williams asked an audience to "recall the United Nations was invited into the Congo by the Congolese Government to assist that new nation in overcoming postindependence disorders, in safeguarding Congolese unity, and in rebuilding the nation's administrative and economic health." (*Department of State Bulletin*, September 17, 1962, pp. 418–21).

63. Sorensen, p. 637.

64. From his speech on the Senate floor, January 25, 1962, in *Congressional Record* (Senate), 87th Cong., 2d Sess., 1962, pp. 894–97.

65. In the view of Harlan Cleveland, "The United States had a national security interest in what happened in the Congo." The United States could abstain from intervening "only at the ultimate peril of our own national security." Cleveland, in Kitchen, pp. 71, 75.

66. See Schlesinger, p. 577. Schlesinger writes that he, too, "inclined toward this view," but does not say he argued for it.

67. Cleveland's testimony, *op. cit.*, p. 2.

68. Said Under Secretary Ball: "Mr. Adoula is moderate in his views, firmly non-Communist and committed to genuine independence and progress for the Congo. . . . The Adoula government . . . is a broadly based coalition under the leadership of an outstanding non-Communist African nationalist. This government's objectives are fully consistent with ours." ("The Elements in Our Congo Policy," pp. 9–10.)

69. Hilsman, p. 265.

70. *Ibid.*, p. 266.

71. *Ibid.*, p. 267.

72. Lefever, in Hilsman and Good, pp. 147–48.

73. Lefever, *Crisis in the Congo*, p. 131; and Attwood, p. 197.

74. Lefever, in Hilsman and Good, p. 148.

75. Richard J. Barnet, *Intervention and Revolution* (New York: World, 1968), p. 249.

76. Attwood, p. 212.

77. Hilsman, p. 240.

78. This paragraph is based on the accounts in Arthur Agwuncha Nwankwo and Samuel Udochukwu Ifejika, *Biafra: The Making of a Nation* (New York: Praeger, 1970), pp. 146–250, and Charles R. Nixon, "Nigeria and

Biafra," in Steven L. Spiegel and Kenneth N. Waltz (eds.), *Conflict in World Politics* (Cambridge, Mass.: Winthrop, 1971), pp. 281–300.

79. Nixon, in Spiegel and Waltz, p. 295; John de St. Jorre, *The Brothers' War: Biafra and Nigeria* (Boston, Mass.: Houghton Mifflin, 1972), pp. 181–83, 302; and Laurie S. Wiseberg, "The Nigerian Civil War, 1967–1970: A Case Study in the Efficacy of International Law as a Regulator of Intrastate Violence," Southern California Arms Control and Foreign Policy Seminar, Los Angeles, May, 1972, pp. 12–13.

80. Wiseberg, pp. 18–19.

81. About three-fourths of Nigeria's oil was believed to be in the east. Over a billion dollars had been invested by American and European companies, including Shell, Gulf, and British Petroleum. See Robert Fitch and Mary Oppenheimer, "Let Them Eat Oil," *Ramparts* (September 7, 1968), pp. 34–38.

82. De St. Jorre, pp. 138–41.

83. John Marcum, *The Angolan Revolution* (Cambridge, Mass.: MIT Press, 1969), vol. I, p. 184.

84. *Ibid.*, p. 273.

85. *Ibid.*, pp. 184, 273.

86. Quoted in Emerson, p. 73.

87. Details of the equipment that has been diverted over the years may be found in S. J. Bosgra and C. Van Krimpen, "Origins of Portuguese Military Equipment—Portugal and NATO," in Colin Legum and John Drysdale (eds.), *Africa Contemporary Record: 1969–1970* (London: William Chudley & Son, 1970), pp. C117–C139, and Basil Davidson, "Arms and the Portuguese," *Africa Report*, XV, no. 5 (May, 1970), pp. 10–12. The U.N. report is in the U.N. General Assembly, *Official Records*, Seventeenth Session (1962), Annexes, vol. 2, "Report of the Special Committee on Territories Under Portuguese Administration," A/5160.

88. Institute for Strategic Studies, *The Military Balance, 1971–1972*, London, 1972, p. 21.

89. The figure represents only "operating costs," not the total U.S. investment in the Azores. See Senate, *Hearings: Spain and Portugal*, p. 2406.

90. *Department of State Bulletin*, January 3, 1972, pp. 7–9, and February 28, 1972, p. 280.

91. The quotation is from *Department of State Bulletin*, June 8, 1970, p. 718. See also the *Bulletin* of October 12, 1970, p. 421 and Jennifer Davis, "U.S. Economic Involvement," *Africa Today*, XVII, no. 4 (July–August, 1970), p. 6.

92. Davis, p. 7.

93. *Ibid.*, pp. 16–17.

94. Richard M. Nixon, *U.S. Foreign Policy for the 1970's: Building for Peace* (Washington, D.C.: Government Printing Office, February 25, 1971), p. 119. (Cited hereafter as *Nixon Report 1971*).

95. According to the U.S. Department of Commerce *Statistical Abstract* for 1971 (Washington, D.C.: Government Printing Office, 92d ed., p. 771), U.S. trade with Angola, Mozambique, and South Africa was about 38 per cent of trade with all of Africa in 1970. The book value of American corporate investments was about $900 million in South Africa (in 1971) and about $56 million in Rhodesia (in 1970). See National Council of Churches, Corporate Information Center, *Church Investments, Cor-*

porations, and Southern Africa (New York: Friendship Press, 1973), p. 35.
96. *Nixon Report 1971*, p. 116.
97. John Marcum, "Southern Africa and United States Policy: A Consideration of Alternatives," in George W. Shepard, Jr. (ed.), *Racial Influences on American Foreign Policy* (New York: Basic Books, 1970), p. 201; Richard L. Sklar, "On Sustaining an Oppressive Regime," *Los Angeles Times*, June 4, 1972, p. G7; and Ian Meckler, *Pattern for Profit in Southern Africa* (Lexington, Mass.: Heath, 1973).
98. Sklar, p. G7.
99. *Ibid.*

CHAPTER 4: JOHNSON AND LATIN AMERICA

1. Cited in C. Neale Ronning (ed.), *Intervention in Latin America* (New York: Knopf, 1970), p. 25.
2. See William Everett Kane, *Civil Strife in Latin America: A Legal History of U.S. Involvement* (Baltimore, Md.: Johns Hopkins Press, 1972), p. 7.
3. James Petras, *Politics and Social Structure in Latin America* (New York: Monthly Review Press, 1970), pp. 304–5.
4. Alonso Aguilar, *Pan-Americanism from Monroe to the Present*, trans. from the Spanish by Asa Zatz (New York: Monthly Review Press, 1968), pp. 74–76; Adolf A. Berle, *Latin America: Diplomacy and Reality* (New York: Harper & Row, 1962), p. 87.
5. See the discussion in Aguilar, pp. 87–98, and in Edwin Lieuwen, *United States Foreign Policy in Latin America* (New York: Praeger, 1965), p. 91.
6. Texts are in U.S. House of Representatives, Committee on Foreign Affairs, *Collective Defense Treaties*, 90th Cong., 1st Sess., April 10, 1967 (Washington, D.C.: Government Printing Office, 1967), pp. 21–47.
7. Aguilar, pp. 90–91.
8. Kane, pp. 152–53.
9. Berle, p. 92.
10. *Ibid.*, p. 94.
11. See the statement of John C. Dreier, U.S. Representative to the OAS Council, in *Department of State Bulletin*, May 31, 1954, p. 835.
12. From Kennedy's address on "The Lessons of Cuba" (April 20, 1961), in *Department of State Bulletin*, May 8, 1961, p. 659.
13. Total U.S. economic aid to Latin America between 1948 and 1970 was about $5.3 billion, of which $3.8 billion was in loans and $1.5 billion in grants. (U.S. *Statistical Abstract*, 92d ed., 1971, p. 763).
14. On the role of the unions in Latin America, see Ronald Radosh, *American Labor and United States Foreign Policy* (New York: Random House, 1969).
15. This collaboration is amply documented *ibid.*
16. Address to Congress, March 14, 1961, quoted in Edward J. Williams, *The Political Themes of Inter-American Relations* (Belmont, Calif.: Duxbury Press, 1971), p. 37.
17. Quoted in Arthur M. Schlesinger, Jr., *A Thousand Days: John F.*

Kennedy in the White House (Boston, Mass.: Houghton Mifflin, 1965), p. 195.
18. Rusk speech, in *Department of State Bulletin*, September 12, 1966, p. 367.
19. Walt W. Rostow, *View from the Seventh Floor* (New York: Harper & Row, 1964), p. 144.
20. Schlesinger, p. 791.
21. Petras, p. 232.
22. The Marshall Plan analogy and the quotation belong to Adolf A. Berle, head of the Latin America task force; see Schlesinger, p. 202.
23. See, for example, Petras, pp. 234–35, and North American Congress on Latin America, *Yanqui Dollar: The Contribution of U.S. Private Investment to Underdevelopment in Latin America* (New York: NACLA, 1971), p. 22.
24. K. H. Silvert, "A Hemispheric Perspective," in John Plank (ed.), *Cuba and the United States: Long-Range Perspectives* (Washington, D.C.: Brookings Institution, 1967), p. 139.
25. Abraham F. Lowenthal, "Alliance Rhetoric versus Latin American Reality," in Richard B. Gray (ed.), *Latin America and the United States in the 1970's* (Itasca, Ill.: Peacock, 1971), p. 116. Another excellent critique of the Alliance is by Lawrence E. Harrison, "Waking from the Pan-American Dream," *Foreign Policy*, no. 5 (Winter, 1971–72), 163–81.
26. See Nixon's speech of October 31, 1969, in Gray *op. cit.*, pp. 265–66.
27. *Ibid.*, p. 267. It was under Nixon that the Overseas Private Investment Corporation was set up in 1969 with a $20 million capitalization. The Corporation's purpose is to "mobilize and facilitate the participation of United States private capital and skills in the economic and social progress of less developed friendly countries and areas," and to insure investors against loss due to revolution, expropriation, and other causes. Text of the Corporation's charter is in U.S. House of Representatives, Committee on Foreign Affairs, *Inter-American Relations*, 92d Cong., 2d Sess., October 10, 1972 (Washington, D.C.: Government Printing Office, 1972), pp. 416–18.
28. William P. Rogers, *United States Foreign Policy, 1971*, Department of State Publication 8634, Washington, D.C., March, 1972, pp. 133, 446. (Hereafter cited as *Rogers Report 1971*.)
29. Speech of June 10, 1963, quoted in David Wise and Thomas B. Ross, *The Invisible Government* (New York: Bantam, 1964), p. 178.
30. John Gillin and K. H. Silvert, "Ambiguities in Guatemala," *Foreign Affairs*, XXXIV, no. 3 (April, 1956), 475–76.
31. Marta Cehelsky, "Guatemala's Frustrated Revolution: The Liberation of 1954," unpublished master's thesis (Columbia University, 1967), p. 38, n. 30.
32. Richard Allen LaBarge, "Impact of the United Fruit Company on the Economic Development of Guatemala, 1946–1954," in LaBarge *et al.*, *Studies in Middle American Economics* (New Orleans: Middle American Research Institute, Tulane University, 1968), p. 42; Cehelsky, p. 39, n. 32.
33. Ronald M. Schneider, *Communism in Guatemala, 1944–1954* (New York: Praeger, 1959), pp. 36–39, 44, 52, 302.

34. See Gillin and Silvert, pp. 471–72, and the official indictment of the Department of State, *Intervention of International Communism in Guatemala*, Department of State Publication 5556 (Washington, D.C.: Government Printing Office, 1954), pp. 39–40, 68–71.
35. Dwight D. Eisenhower, *Mandate for Change, 1953–1956* (Garden City, N.Y.: Doubleday, 1963), p. 421.
36. Speech of June 30, 1954, in *Department of State Bulletin*, July 12, 1954, p. 43.
37. Testimony before the U.S. House of Representatives, Select Committee on Communist Aggression, Subcommittee on Latin America, *Ninth Interim Report of Hearings Under Authority of H. Res. 346 and H. Res. 438*, 83d Cong., 2d Sess., September 27–29 and October 8, 14–15, 1954 (Washington, D.C.: Government Printing Office, 1954), p. 124.
38. *Ibid.*, pp. 125, 127.
39. See *Intervention of International Communism in Guatemala, op. cit.*, pp. 83–85.
40. News conference of May 25, 1954; *ibid.*, p. 12.
41. Wise and Ross, pp. 182–85.
42. See the testimony of William Willauer, at the time ambassador to Honduras. He referred to a diplomatic "team" consisting of Peurifoy, himself, and the ambassadors to Costa Rica and Nicaragua, all of whom worked closely with CIA personnel. U.S. Senate, Committee on the Judiciary, Subcommittee to Investigate the Administration of the Internal Security Act and Other Security Laws, *Communist Threat to the United States Through the Caribbean*, pt. 13, 87th Cong., 1st Sess., March 29, April 26, June 1, July 27, 1961 (Washington, D.C.: Government Printing Office, 1962), p. 866.
43. Ydigoras Fuentes, *My War with Communism* (Englewood Cliffs, N.J.: Prentice-Hall, 1963), pp. 50–51.
44. Willauer testimony, *op. cit.*
45. Text in *Department of State Bulletin*, April 26, 1954, p. 638.
46. Philip B. Taylor, "The Guatemalan Affair: A Critique of United States Foreign Policy," *American Political Science Review*, L, no. 3 (September, 1956), 791, 792. Mexican criticism of the declaration was especially intense, one distinguished international lawyer, Isidro Fabela, calling it a manifestation of "international McCarthyism." See J. Alvarez del Vayo, "Aggression Is the Word: The Guatemala Crisis," *The Nation*, June 26, 1954, p. 538.
47. Speech of March 8, 1954, in *Intervention of International Communism in Guatemala, op. cit.*, p. 6.
48. Speech of March 16, 1954; *ibid.*, p. 11.
49. Eisenhower, p. 426.
50. On June 25, 1954, the Senate passed Concurrent Resolution 91, which reiterated the State Department's case against Guatemala, supported the Caracas declaration, and urged the administration to "take all necessary and proper steps to support the Organization of American States in taking appropriate action to prevent any interference by the international Communist movement in the affairs of the States of the Western Hemisphere." Text in *Intervention of International Communism in Guatemala, op. cit.*, p. 24.
51. Wise and Ross, pp. 192–94.

52. Schneider, p. 310.
53. The best source on the Security Council debates is Taylor, pp. 798–803, from which much of the following discussion derives.
54. Statement of June 25, 1954, in *Intervention of International Communism in Guatemala, op. cit.*, p. 18.
55. Testimony of Raymond G. Leddy in House, *Ninth Interim Report*, p. 200.
56. *Ibid.*, p. 199.
57. In his speech of June 30, 1954, cited previously, n. 36.
58. John Foster Dulles was legal counsel to United Fruit when it drew up contracts with the Guatemalan Government in the 1930's. Allen Dulles had been company president, and Henry Cabot Lodge was a large stockholder. See Kane, p. 188, and Taylor, p. 791, n. 17.
59. Wise and Ross, pp. 22–27.
60. *Ibid.*, pp. 195–96. Eisenhower, in his *Waging Peace, 1956–1961* (Garden City, N.Y.: Doubleday, 1965), p. 613, reported his preparedness to intervene directly to prevent the coup from succeeding. The United States did send warships to patrol the Guatemalan coast after Ydigoras's government contacted Washington requesting help.
61. See the account of Jerome Levinson and Juan de Onis, *The Alliance That Lost Its Way* (Chicago: Quadrangle, 1970), pp. 84–85. The 1963 intervention of the military was its fourth in Guatemalan politics, the others having occurred in 1957, 1960, and 1962. It may be more than coincidental that all four came after the start of the U.S. military assistance program, in 1956, which greatly enhanced the capabilities and prestige of the armed forces.
62. John F. Kennedy, *The Strategy of Peace* (ed. Allan Nevins) (New York: Harper, 1960), p. 133.
63. *Ibid.*, pp. 136–37.
64. See U.S. Senate Committee on Commerce, Subcommittee on Freedom of Communications, *The Speeches of Senator John F. Kennedy, Presidential Campaign of 1960* (Washington, D.C.: Government Printing Office, 1961), pp. 476, 511, 515.
65. *Ibid.*, pp. 681, 726.
66. Wise and Ross, p. 24.
67. Richard M. Nixon, *Six Crises* (Garden City, N.Y.: Doubleday, 1962), p. 352.
68. *Public Papers of the Presidents: Dwight D. Eisenhower, 1960* (Washington, D.C.: Government Printing Office, 1961), p. 568.
69. *Ibid.*, p. 623.
70. Eisenhower, *Waging Peace*, pp. 613–14.
71. Schlesinger, pp. 175–85.
72. See Theodore Draper, *Castro's Revolution: Myths and Realities* (New York: Praeger, 1962), pp. 70–72, and Schlesinger, pp. 236–37.
73. Quoted in Schlesinger, p. 245.
74. Writes Schlesinger: "The President saw no obligation to protect the Castro regime from democratic Cubans. . . . If the expedition succeeded, the overthrow of Castro would greatly strengthen democratic prospects in the hemisphere; if he called it off, he would forever be haunted by the feeling that his scruples had preserved Castro in power." (*Ibid.*, p. 258.) Theodore C. Sorensen, *Kennedy* (New York: Harper

& Row, 1965), p. 296, makes similar remarks about Kennedy's attitude.

75. Ambassador Smith's memoir (*The Fourth Floor: An Account of the Castro Communist Revolution* [New York: Random House, 1962], chaps. 17–18) reveals his recommendation, backed by the U.S. business community in Cuba and eventually the State Department, to persuade Batista to leave office in December 1958 in favor of a military junta. Castro would thus have been pre-empted. A secret emissary was sent to Batista from Washington but could not persuade him to step down.

76. U.S. Department of State, *Cuba* (Washington, D.C.: n.p., April 3, 1961), pp. 1–2, 35.

77. Haynes Johnson and Bernard M. Gwertzman, *Fulbright the Dissenter* (Garden City, N.Y.: Doubleday, 1968), pp. 174–75.

78. Schlesinger, p. 252.

79. *Ibid.*, p. 233.

80. *Ibid.*, p. 252.

81. *Department of State Bulletin*, May 8, 1961, p. 660.

82. These were Senate Res. 388 (September 17, 1962) and Senate Joint Res. 230 (October 3, 1962).

83. Lester D. Langley, *The Cuban Policy of the United States: A Brief History* (New York: Wiley, 1968), p. 187.

84. *Department of State Bulletin*, December 9, 1963, p. 903.

85. Lyndon B. Johnson, *The Vantage Point: Perspectives of the Presidency, 1963–1969* (New York: Holt, Rinehart & Winston, 1971), p. 197.

86. Economic information in this paragraph is from Center for Research in Social Systems, *Area Handbook for the Dominican Republic* (Washington, D.C.: Government Printing Office, 1966), pp. 355–66:

87. Thus, of the Dominican situation after Trujillo's assassination, Kennedy is quoted as having said: "There are three possibilities in descending order of preference: a decent democratic regime, a continuation of the Trujillo regime or a Castro regime. We ought to aim at the first, but we really can't renounce the second until we are sure that we can avoid the third." Schlesinger, p. 769.

88. Abraham F. Lowenthal, *The Dominican Intervention* (Cambridge, Mass.: Harvard University Press, 1972), p. 20.

89. Eisenhower, *Waging Peace*, pp. 534–35.

90. *Ibid.*, p. 534.

91. See Lowenthal, p. 10.

92. Quoted in Schlesinger, p. 770.

93. De Lesseps S. Morrison, *Latin American Mission: An Adventure in Hemispheric Diplomacy* (New York: Simon & Schuster, 1965), pp. 116–17, 125.

94. Schlesinger, p. 771.

95. Lowenthal, pp. 12–13.

96. John Bartlow Martin, *Overtaken by Events* (Garden City, N.Y.: Doubleday, 1966), pp. 357–58, 476. See also Lowenthal, p. 14.

97. See Bosch's own account, *The Unfinished Experiment* (New York: Praeger, 1964), p. 141.

98. Theodore Draper, *The Dominican Revolt* (New York: Commentary Reports, 1968), p. 7; and Jerome Slater, *Intervention and Negotiation: The United States and the Dominican Revolution* (New York: Harper & Row, 1970), p. 14.

99. Lowenthal, pp. 16–17.
100. Slater, pp. 16–17.
101. Speech of October 12, 1965; text in *Congressional Record*, October 15, 1965, p. 27160.
102. Johnson, p. 189.
103. See his remarks quoted in Draper, "A Case of Defamation: US Intelligence versus Juan Bosch (I)," *The New Republic*, February 19, 1966, p. 15.
104. Johnson, pp. 180–87.
105. *Ibid.*, p. 188.
106. A secret CIA-sponsored poll taken at this time showed public opinion overwhelmingly against Reid. But Bosch was running second to Balaguer. See Lowenthal, p. 48.
107. *Ibid.*, p. 47.
108. Draper, "A Case of Defamation (I)," pp. 18–19.
109. See Thomas Halper, *Foreign Policy Crises: Appearance and Reality in Decision Making* (Columbus, Ohio: Merrill, 1971), p. 69.
110. Text in U.S. Senate, Committee on Foreign Relations, *Background Information Relating to the Dominican Republic* (Washington, D.C.: Government Printing Office, 1965), pp. 57–59.
111. My understanding of the issues in this first stage of the Dominican revolution follows that of Draper in *The Dominican Revolt* and "The Dominican Intervention Reconsidered," *Political Science Quarterly*, LXXXVI, no. 1 (March, 1971), 1–36. Jerome Slater's *Intervention and Negotiation* presents a different interpretation on pp. 26–31.
112. Johnson, p. 190.
113. Lowenthal, p. 70.
114. Draper, "The Dominican Intervention Reconsidered," p. 20.
115. The words are Slater's, p. 26.
116. Quoted in Draper, "The Dominican Intervention Reconsidered," p. 6.
117. The State Department version is in U.S. Senate, Committee on the Judiciary, Subcommittee to Investigate the Administration of the Internal Security Act and Other Internal Security Laws, *Hearing: Testimony of Brigadier General Elias Wessin y Wessin*, 89th Cong., 1st Sess., October 1, 1965 (Washington, D.C.: Government Printing Office, 1965), pp. 208–10. See also Johnson, pp. 191–92.
118. Philip L. Geyelin, *Lyndon B. Johnson and the World* (New York: Praeger, 1966), p. 247.
119. On these events, see Lowenthal, pp. 90–94; Slater, p. 29; the speech of Senator Fulbright in *Congressional Record*, September 15, 1965, p. 23857; and Draper, *The Dominican Revolt*, pp. 108–10.
120. Quoted in Draper, *The Dominican Revolt*, p. 101.
121. Lowenthal, pp. 100–105; Johnson, p. 197.
122. Johnson, pp. 194–95.
123. Lowenthal, pp. 99–104; Fulbright speech of September 15, 1965, *op. cit.*, p. 23857.
124. Lowenthal, pp. 104–5.
125. The President is quoted as having said: "The OAS couldn't pour———— out of a boot if the instructions were written on the heel." Geyelin, p. 254.
126. Johnson, p. 202.

127. Slater, "The Limits of Legitimization in International Organizations: The Organization of American States and the Dominican Crisis," *International Organization*, XXIII, no. 1 (Winter, 1969), 56.
128. *Ibid.*, 61–64.
129. Fulbright speech of September 15, 1965, *op. cit.*, p. 23860.
130. Lowenthal, pp. 146–50; Fulbright speech, *op. cit.*, p. 23855.
131. Lowenthal, p. 150.
132. The "liberal" view is summarized *ibid.*, pp. 133–36.
133. Slater, *Intervention and Negotiation*, pp. 48, 205.
134. Draper, "The Dominican Intervention Reconsidered," pp. 24–25.
135. See Fred Goff and Michael Locker, *The Violence of Domination: U.S. Power and the Dominican Republic* (mimeo.), cited in Petras, pp. 236–37.
136. Slater, *Intervention and Negotiation*, pp. 46–47; Lowenthal, pp. 18–19.
137. See Petras, p. 347.
138. Halper, p. 66.
139. Johnson, p. 200.
140. See Halper, p. 67.
141. See Slater, *Intervention and Negotiation*, pp. 192–93, and Halper, pp. 75–76.
142. Slater, *Intervention and Negotiation*, pp. 210–12.
143. Address at Baylor University, May 28, 1965, in *Public Papers of the Presidents: Lyndon B. Johnson, 1965* (Washington, D.C.: Government Printing Office, 1966), I, 595.
144. Documentation of the interventions in Chile is contained in two issues of *Latin America & Empire Report*, produced by the North American Congress on Latin America: "Secret Memos from ITT," VI, no. 4 (April, 1972), and "Chile: The Story Behind the Coup," VII, no. 8 (October, 1973).

Chapter 5: Nixon and Asia

1. Lyman P. Van Slyke (ed.), *The China White Paper: August 1949* (Stanford, Calif.: Stanford University Press, 1967), vol. I, pp. iii-iv. (Hereafter referred to as *White Paper*.)
2. Foster Rhea Dulles, *American Policy Toward Communist China, 1949–1969* (New York: Crowell, 1972), pp. 6–7.
3. Among the sources for this background that I have found especially stimulating, in addition to *ibid.* (chap. 2), are: Warren I. Cohen, *America's Response to China: An Interpretative History of Sino-American Relations* (New York: Wiley, 1971); Tang Tsou, *America's Failure in China, 1941–1950* (Chicago: University of Chicago Press, 1963) (see the introductory chapter); Akira Iriye, *Across the Pacific: An Inner History of American-East Asian Relations* (New York: Harcourt, Brace & World, 1967); and Lucien Bianco, *Origins of the Chinese Revolution, 1915–1949*, trans. from the French by Muriel Bell (Stanford, Calif.: Stanford University Press, 1971).
4. Truman speech of December 15, 1945, in *White Paper*, II, 607–8.
5. Michael Lindsay, "The United States and the Chinese Communists, 1937–1945," *Asia Quarterly*, no. 3 (1971), p. 231. Patrick J. Hurley had been appointed to China by President Roosevelt in August, 1944,

as his Personal Representative. In January, 1945, Hurley became ambassador, a post he held until his resignation in November, 1945.
6. Marshall statement of January 7, 1947, in *White Paper*, II, 688.
7. *Ibid.*, 689.
8. News conference of March 11, 1948, in *Public Papers of the Presidents of the United States: Harry S. Truman, 1948* (Washington, D.C.: Government Printing Office, 1964), pp. 180–81.
9. Acheson speech of January 12, 1950, in *Department of State Bulletin*, January 23, 1950, p. 113. Similar remarks are in his forwarding letter to the *White Paper*, I, xiv.
10. See *Department of State Bulletin*, March 27, 1950, p. 468.
11. Harry S. Truman, *Memoirs*, vol. II, *Years of Trial and Hope* (Garden City, N.Y.: Doubleday, 1956), 91.
12. On General Joseph Stilwell's ordeal in China, see the masterful study by Barbara Tuchman, *Stilwell and the American Experience in China, 1911–1945* (New York: Macmillan, 1971).
13. The quoted phrase is that of John Carter Vincent, Chief of the Division of Chinese Affairs in the State Department, in U.S. Department of State, *Foreign Relations of the United States, 1945: VII, The Far East, China* (Washington, D.C.: Government Printing Office, 1969), p. 248. (Hereafter, *FRUS 1945.*) For other views of Foreign Service officers in China, see the memorandum of the U.S. Embassy's third (later, second) secretary, John S. Service, in *FRUS, 1943a: China* (Washington, D.C.: Government Printing Office, 1957), pp. 193–99; a synopsis of Service's views in *FRUS, 1944: VI, China* (Washington, D.C.: Government Printing Office, 1967), pp. 599–602; and the memorandum of the embassy's chargé, George Atcheson, in February, 1945, *FRUS, 1945*, pp. 242–46.
14. The only regular official contact with Yenan occurred between July, 1944, and March, 1945. An American Army Advisory Group, invited by the communist authorities, finally received permission from Chiang to visit their base areas. The Group's political officer, John S. Service, later wrote that "there has never been a Communist society that has been so open to Americans as the Chinese Communists[']" during those eight months. (Service, *The Amerasia Papers: Some Problems in the History of US-China Relations* [Berkeley: Center for Chinese Studies, University of California, 1971], p. 166, n. 47).
15. Service's interview with Mao, in Service, pp. 167–69.
16. See Barbara W. Tuchman, "If Mao Had Come to Washington: An Essays in Alternatives," *Foreign Affairs*, LI, no. 1 (October, 1972), 44–64.
17. As General Marshall said: ". . . we have a vital interest in a stable government in China and I am using the word 'vital' in its accurate sense. The next few months are of tremendous importance to the Chinese people and, I think, to the future peace of the world. . . . Stable governments in Asia are of great importance to us, not to mention what they mean to the people who have suffered to a degree which the Chinese have during the past decade." In *Department of State Bulletin*, March 24, 1946, p. 484.
18. See the discussion and documents in Stuart R. Schram, *The Political Thought of Mao Tse-tung* (New York: Praeger, 1963), pp. 126–27, 400–404.
19. Examples of this reporting are in *White Paper*, II, 565 ff. Service re-

ported, for instance, in October, 1944, that the Communists' "total mobilization is based upon and has been made possible by what amounts to
an economic, political and social revolution. This revolution has been
moderate and democratic. It has improved the economic condition of
the peasants by rent and interest reduction, tax reform and good government. It has given them democratic self-government, political conscious-
ness and a sense of their rights. It has freed them from feudalistic bonds
and given them self-respect, self-reliance and a strong feeling of cooperative group interest. The common people, for the first time, have been
given something to fight for."

20. Tuchman, *Stilwell*, pp. 238–39.
21. *Ibid.*, p. 401.
22. Harry S. Truman, *Memoirs*, vol. I, *Year of Decisions* (Garden City, N.Y.:
    Doubleday, 1955), 102.
23. Truman, *Memoirs*, II, 63–64.
24. See Lindsay, p. 256.
25. See the interview with Mao in Service, pp. 173–75.
26. *White Paper*, II, 768, 779.
27. *Ibid.*, 609.
28. *Ibid.*, I, x.
29. Quoted in Lindsay, pp. 251–52.
30. Truman, *Memoirs*, II, 62.
31. See *ibid.*, 65, and Tuchman, *Stilwell*, p. 529.
32. The speech is in *White Paper*, II, 689–94.
33. *Ibid.*, 694.
34. These lower figures reflect the withdrawal of the Marines in the first half
    of 1947. The Army and Navy Advisory Groups stayed on.
35. As dramatically described by Theodore H. White and Annalee Jacoby in
    Thunder Out of China (New York: William Sloane Associates, 1961),
    p. 289: "The United States marines, the Kuomintang, the former
    [Chinese] puppets, and the Japanese army, in one of the most curious alli-
    ances ever fashioned, jointly guarded the railways against the Chinese
    partisans. . . . In this area Communists now sniped at marine trains;
    marines shelled a village in retaliation. Our flag flew in the cockpit of a
    civil war."
36. *White Paper*, I, 354.
37. *Ibid.*, 356.
38. See Robert Payne, *Chinese Diaries, 1941–1946* (New York: Weybright
    & Talley, 1970), p. 336.
39. *Ibid.*, pp. 364–65.
40. *White Paper*, I, 180–81.
41. *Ibid.*, xvi–xvii.
42. See Seymour Topping, *Journey Between Two Chinas* (New York: Harper
    & Row, 1972), pp. 83–87.
43. *Department of State Bulletin*, March 27, 1950, pp. 468–69.
44. John Foster Dulles, *War or Peace* (New York: Macmillan, 1950), p.
    245.
45. See Milovan Djilas, *Conversations with Stalin* (New York: Harcourt,
    Brace & World, 1962), p. 182.
46. See John Service's report of June, 1945, in Lindsay, p. 229. If the
    United States had provided the bulk of aid and investment in China, it
    is possible that the radicalism of China's land reform, treatment of capi-

talists, and industrial program would have been meliorated. (Whether that development would have been "good" or "bad" for China is, however, a separate question.)

47. See *White Paper*, I, 280–85, and Dean Acheson, *Present at the Creation: My Years in the State Department* (New York: Signet, 1969), pp. 950–52.
48. *Department of State Bulletin*, January 23, 1950, p. 114.
49. This section is an expanded version of the author's "Beyond the Pentagon Papers," *Ramparts*, X, no. 8 (February, 1972), 49, 59–62. Reprinted by permission.
50. George Ball, *The Discipline of Power: Essentials of a Modern World Structure* (Boston, Mass.: Little, Brown, 1968), pp. 332–33.
51. Arthur M. Schlesinger, Jr., *The Bitter Heritage: Vietnam and American Democracy, 1941–1968*, rev. ed. (Greenwich, Conn.: Fawcett, 1968), p. 47.
52. Roger Hilsman, *To Move a Nation: The Politics of Foreign Policy in the Administration of John F. Kennedy* (New York: Holt, Rinehart & Winston, 1971), pp. 528 ff.
53. Leslie H. Gelb, "Vietnam: The System Worked," *Foreign Policy*, no. 3 (Spring, 1971), 140–67.
54. See the essay, "The Quagmire Myth and the Stalemate Machine," in Daniel Ellsberg's *Papers on the War* (New York: Simon & Schuster, 1972).
55. Taylor to Kennedy, November 1, 1961: "In fact, I do not believe that our program to save SVN will succeed without it [a combat task force]." Neil Sheehan *et al.*, *The Pentagon Papers* (New York: Bantam, 1971), p. 143. (Cited hereafter as *PP* (*Bantam*).)
56. *Ibid.*, p. 149.
57. Hilsman, pp. 486–87.
58. *PP* (*Bantam*), p. 218.
59. *The Senator Gravel Edition, The Pentagon Papers: The Defense Department History of United States Decisionmaking on Vietnam*, 5 vols. (Boston, Mass.: Beacon Press, 1972), vol. III, pp. 689–90. (Cited hereafter as *PP* (*Gravel*).)
60. *Ibid.*, IV, 252–53.
61. See, for example, Chester L. Cooper, *The Lost Crusade: America in Vietnam* (New York: Dodd, Mead, 1970), p. 393.
62. On the meetings of these "Wise Men," see *PP* (*Gravel*), IV, 266–68.
63. *Ibid.*, 270.
64. Rusk's testimony before the Senate Foreign Relations Committee on March 11: "It is quite clear from our recent contacts with Hanoi that they would not accept a partial cessation of the bombing as a step toward peace in any way, shape, or form." For the CIA analyses, see *PP* (*Gravel*), IV, 241.
65. Rusk's recommendations are recounted *ibid.*, 259.
66. NBC interview of September 9, 1963, *ibid.*, II, 828.
67. Quoted in Cooper, p. 168.
68. News conference of July 17, 1963, in *PP* (*Gravel*), II, 824.
69. CBS interview of September 2, 1963, in U.S. Senate, Committee on Foreign Relations, *Background Information Relating to Southeast Asia and Vietnam*, 3d rev. ed., July, 1967 (Washington, D.C.: Government Printing Office, 1967), pp. 112–13.

70. Speech at Johns Hopkins University, April 17, 1965, in Senate, *Background Information*, p. 149.
71. CBS interview of August 9, 1965, PP *(Gravel)*, IV, 636.
72. PP *(Bantam)*, p. 284. Nearly identical language was used by McNamara in a memorandum of March 16, 1964, *ibid.*, p. 278.
73. For instance, see PP *(Gravel)*, IV, 643, 660.
74. *Ibid.*, 677.
75. PP *(Bantam)*, p. 421.
76. *Ibid.*, p. 422.
77. General Taylor, before the Senate Foreign Relations Committee, February 17, 1966, in Senate, *Background Information*, p. 209. See also McGeorge Bundy in PP *(Gravel)*, III, 311.
78. Assistant Secretary of State Roger Hilsman, June 14, 1963, PP *(Gravel)*, II, 823.
79. Arthur M. Schlesinger, Jr., *A Thousand Days: John F. Kennedy in the White House* (Boston, Mass.: Houghton Mifflin, 1965), pp. 537–38.
80. See William Bundy to Rusk, January 6, 1965, in PP *(Gravel)*, III, 685.
81. Memorandum to McNamara, March 24, 1965, in PP *(Bantam)*, p. 438.
82. *Ibid.*, p. 432.
83. Ball, pp. 336–37.
84. Cooper, p. 416.
85. NBC interview of September 9, 1963, PP *(Gravel)*, II, 828.
86. Tom Wicker, *JFK and LBJ: The Influence of Personality Upon Politics* (New York: Morrow, 1968), p. 244.
87. See *ibid.*, p. 248. For LBJ, anticommunism was "the obvious shield against the kind of domestic political savagery McCarthyism had loosed on America, and which might come again."
88. See Ellsberg, pp. 97–98. Kennedy's actions in 1963 were "reflections of his judgment that 1963 was a worse time than 1965 [after the Presidential election] for him to lose a war to Communists, so that he would just have to keep it going till then."
89. On these points, see Gelb, p. 149.
90. See PP *(Bantam)*, pp. 204–5.
91. Cf. Bundy's account in "The Path to Viet Nam: Ten Decisions," *Orbis*, XI, no. 1 (Spring, 1967), 658, and the discussion in PP *(Bantam)*, pp. 323–26.
92. James C. Thomson, Jr., "How Could Vietnam Happen? An Autopsy," *Atlantic*, April, 1968, pp. 47–53.
93. Walt W. Rostow, *View from the Seventh Floor* (New York: Harper & Row, 1964), p. 120.
94. Douglas Pike, *Viet Cong: The Organization and Technique of the National Liberation Front of South Vietnam* (Cambridge, Mass.: MIT Press, 1966), pp. 376 ff.
95. PP *(Gravel)*, III, 668.
96. *Ibid.*, 311.
97. A concise summary of these findings is presented by Konrad Kellen, "1971 and Beyond: The View from Hanoi," in Joseph J. Zasloff and Allan E. Goodman (eds.), *Indochina in Conflict: A Political Assessment* (Lexington, Mass.: Heath, 1972), pp. 99–112. The remainder of the paragraph draws upon Kellen's essay and his, as well as my own, RAND studies.

98. Lodge cable to Kennedy, September 19, 1963, in *PP (Bantam)*, p. 209.
99. *PP (Gravel)*, II, 828.
100. See Nixon's interview with C. L. Sulzberger, *New York Times*, March 10, 1971, p. 14. (Cited hereafter as Sulzberger interview.)
101. Nixon's remarks on Guam, which were not for quotation, are *ibid.*, July 26, 1969, p. 8.
102. Sulzberger interview.
103. Richard M. Nixon, *U.S. Foreign Policy for the 1970's: Building for Peace* (Washington, D.C.: Government Printing Office, February 25, 1971), pp. 92, 94. (Cited hereafter as *Nixon Report 1971*.)
104. "Asia After Viet-Nam," *Foreign Affairs*, XLVI, no. 1 (October, 1967), 117.
105. Sulzberger interview.
106. Peggy Durdin, "The Political Tidal Wave That Struck East Pakistan," *New York Times Magazine*, May 2, 1971, p. 90.
107. Wayne Wilcox, "Political Change in Pakistan: Structures, Functions, Constraints and Goals," Paper P–3865, Rand Corporation, Santa Monica, Calif., June, 1968, p. 13.
108. See Aijaz Ahmad, " 'Law and Order' in Pakistan," *The Nation*, April 14, 1969, pp. 455–58, and W. H. Morris-Jones, "Pakistan Post-Mortem and the Roots of Bangladesh," *Political Quarterly*, XLIII, no. 2 (April–June, 1972), 192–94.
109. See the testimony of Professor Robert Dorfman of Harvard in U.S. House of Representatives, Committee on Foreign Affairs, Subcommittee on Asian and Pacific Affairs, *Hearings: Crisis in East Pakistan*, 92d Cong., 1st Sess., May 11, 25, 1971 (Washington, D.C.: Government Printing Office, 1971), pp. 27, 29–31; Aijaz Ahmad, "The Bloody Surgery of Pakistan," *The Nation*, June 28, 1971, pp. 815–16; Center for New Corporate Priorities, " 'We Merely Make Loans' (2)," Los Angeles, 1972, pp. 24–25.
110. Ahmad, "The Bloody Surgery of Pakistan," p. 816.
111. See U.S. Senate, Committee on the Judiciary, Subcommittee to Investigate Problems Connected with Refugees and Escapees, *Hearings: Relief Problems in East Pakistan and India*, 92d Cong., 1st Sess., pt. 1, June 28, 1971 (Washington, D.C.: Government Printing Office, 1971), pp. 41–47, 50–51, 53–69.
112. *New York Times*, April 10, 1971, p. 1. U.S. military aid to India did not begin until 1962, at the time of the Sino-Indian border conflict.
113. William J. Barnds, *India, Pakistan, and the Great Powers* (New York: Praeger, 1972), p. 104.
114. See Richard M. Nixon, *U.S. Foreign Policy for the 1970's: The Emerging Structure of Peace* (Washington, D.C.: Government Printing Office, February 9, 1972), p. 147. (Cited hereafter as *Nixon Report 1972*.)
115. *Nixon Report 1971*, p. 150.
116. *Ibid.*, p. 112: "India continues to follow a policy of non-alignment but of a cast significantly changed since the Chinese attack of 1962." This statement, it should be recalled, preceded India's signing of a friendship treaty with the Soviet Union (August 9, 1971).
117. Letters of David M. Abshire, Assistant Secretary of State for Congressional Relations, to Sen. J. William Fulbright, April 23 and May 6, 1971,

in U.S. Senate, Committee on Foreign Relations, *Suspension of Military Assistance to Pakistan*, Report No. 92–105, 92d Cong., 1st Sess., May 13, 1971 (Washington, D.C.: Government Printing Office, 1971), pp. 8, 16; *New York Times*, April 14, 1971, p. 13.

118. Testimony of Christopher Van Hollen, Deputy Assistant Secretary of State for Near Eastern and South Asian Affairs, in Senate, *Hearings: Relief Problems in East Pakistan and India*, pt. 3, October 4, 1971 (Washington, D.C.: Government Printing Office, 1971), p. 379.

119. *New York Times*, June 22, 1971, p. 1.

120. *Nixon Report 1972*, p. 142.

121. On the exception, see William P. Rogers, *United States Foreign Policy, 1969–1970* (Washington, D.C.: Government Printing Office, March, 1971), p. 93 (cited hereafter as *Rogers Report 1969–1970*); *Nixon Report 1971*, p. 113; Abshire letter to Fulbright of April 23, 1971, *op. cit.*, p. 8; Szulc article cited in n. 119.

122. Barnds, Table I-B, p. 227.

123. Dorfman testimony, *op. cit.*, p. 27.

124. Center for New Corporate Priorities, pp. 25–26.

125. *New York Times*, April 10, 1971, p. 1.

126. Dorfman testimony, *op. cit.*, p. 28.

127. Statements of Secretary Rogers, April 2 and 6, 1971, reprinted in Senate, *Suspension of Military Assistance to Pakistan*, p. 9. On the fact that U.S. weapons were being used in the repression, see Abshire's letter to Fulbright of April 23, 1971, *ibid.*, p. 7.

128. Background news conference of Henry Kissinger, December 7, 1971, in *New York Times*, January 6, 1972, p. 18. The normally unpublished transcript was made available by Senator Barry Goldwater when he inserted it in the *Congressional Record*. (Cited hereafter as Kissinger news conference.)

129. *Nixon Report 1972*, p. 143.

130. *Ibid.*, pp. 143–44.

131. Kissinger news conference.

132. *Nixon Report 1972*, p. 146.

133. Kissinger news conference.

134. Abshire letters to Fulbright of April 23 and May 6, 1971, *op. cit.*

135. Van Hollen testimony, *op. cit.*, p. 24.

136. *Nixon Report 1972*, p. 147. Two previous cease-fire resolutions were vetoed by the Soviet delegate in the Security Council.

137. *Ibid.*

138. Kissinger news conference.

139. *Nixon Report 1972*, p. 148.

140. *Ibid.*, pp. 148–49. On the last point, the President meant the Soviets might be led to believe their "expansionism" was tolerable to the United States, and that Chinese leaders might believe "force and threat" rather than restraint governed international relations.

141. Jack Anderson, "U.S. Show of Force in Bay of Bengal," *Washington Post*, December 31, 1971.

142. Testifying before a House subcommittee, Professor Gideon Gottlieb of the New York University School of Law pointed out that under provisions of the Fourth Geneva Convention, to which Pakistan was

a party, the international community was entitled to ensure that all non-combatants, even in a so-called civil conflict, received humane treatment. There was sufficient evidence that the Convention's provisions were being violated by Pakistani forces to justify investigation and relief efforts, Gottlieb argued, despite Islamabad's protest. See House, *Hearings: Crisis in East Pakistan*, pp. 13–14.

143. When the refugee flow swelled to approximately 9 million in late summer, 1971, India's cost was estimated at between $765.5 million and $1.3 billion a year. (U.S. Senate, Committee on the Judiciary, Subcommittee to Investigate Problems Connected with Refugees and Escapees, *Crisis in South Asia: A Report by Senator Edward M. Kennedy*, November 1, 1971 [Washington, D.C.: Government Printing Office, 1971], p. 33. [Cited hereafter as *Kennedy Report*.])

144. *Nixon Report 1972*, p. 145.

145. These deliberations, recorded in classified memoranda, are naturally only a partial record. But they provide valuable glimpses into the decision-making process. The documents, published in full in the *New York Times* on January 6 and 15, 1972, include memoranda of the WSAG meetings of December 3, 4, 6, and 8, 1971, and a cable to the Secretary of State by Kenneth B. Keating, U.S. Ambassador to India, on December 8. References to these documents will cite their dates, not the dates of publication.

146. To the contrary, the administration wanted to stay away from the whole question of the Sheikh's imprisonment. "We will go along in general terms [at the United Nations] with reference to political accommodation in East Pakistan," the WSAG minutes of December 4 read, "but we will certainly not imply or suggest any specifics, such as the release of 'Mujib."

147. *Washington Post*, September 3, 1971.

148. Abshire letter to Fulbright of April 23, 1971, *op. cit.*, p. 7.

149. *Rogers Report 1969–1970*, p. 93. "Washington" officials need to be distinguished from U.S. officials in Dacca, East Pakistan, who accurately reported the atrocities and apparently criticized the State Department's refusal to publicize and condemn them. The Department also refused to supply these cabled reports to the Senate Foreign Relations Committee. (Senate, *Suspension of Military Assistance to Pakistan*, p. 3.)

150. Abshire letter to Fulbright of May 6, 1971, *op. cit.*, p. 17.

151. See the WSAG minutes of December 6, 1971.

152. The figure of ten ships is from a statement by Senator Kennedy in Senate, *Hearing: Relief Problems in East Pakistan and India*, pt. 3, p. 356. The approximate value of $5 million in "spare parts" does not square with Van Hollen's testimony, which was that $6.1 million in arms had either been shipped or was "in the pipeline" as of October 1, 1971. (*Ibid.*, p. 373.)

153. *Ibid.*, pt. 3, pp. 374–76, 394.

154. William P. Rogers, *United States Foreign Policy, 1971*, Department of State Publication 8634, Washington, D.C., March, 1972, p. 115. Cited hereafter as *Rogers Report 1971*.)

155. When, at the same meeting, the Deputy Secretary of Defense, David Packard, observed that Pakistan could only receive jets through a third country if it were determined that Pakistan was eligible for direct

assistance, Kissinger, according to the minutes, "reiterated that he desired to keep Hussein in a 'holding pattern' . . . and that he should not be turned off."

156. Jack Anderson, "Secret Cables on Pakistan Quoted," *Washington Post*, January 12, 1972.

157. Malcolm Browne in *New York Times*, March 29, 1972, p. 1. The aircraft sales to Pakistan would be consistent with the fact that the Pakistani Government had long supported the Arab states' policies on Israel, and that after the fighting no Arab nation recognized Bangladesh.

158. *Nixon Report 1972*, p. 145.

159. Keating cable of December 8, 1971. As it was, the U.N. Relief Mission could only post 70 men and 38 observers in East Pakistan. See Senate, *Hearing: Relief Problems in East Pakistan and India*, pt. 3, pp. 358, 467.

160. *Kennedy Report*, pp. 60–61.

161. *Los Angeles Times*, June 9, 1972, p. 14.

162. See *New York Times*, March 12, 1972, p. 8, and a supplemental statement by Maurice Williams, deputy administrator of AID, in U.S. House of Representatives, *Hearing on H.R. 13759 to Amend the Foreign Assistance Act of 1961, and for Other Purposes*, 92d Cong., 2d Sess., pt. 2, March 28–29, April 11, 1972 (Washington, D.C.: Government Printing Office, 1972), pp. 361–62.

163. WSAG minutes of December 4, 1971.

164. The words in quotations are attributed to the President in the WSAG documents of December 3 and 8, 1971. It was at the first of these meetings that Kissinger reported the now famous line, "He [Nixon] wants to tilt in favor of Pakistan."

165. WSAG minutes of December 8, 1971.

166. Quoted in Jack Anderson, "Protesters Leak Their Own Secrets," *Washington Post*, January 18, 1972.

167. Minutes of December 6 and 8, 1971.

168. Quoted in the Anderson column of January 18, 1972.

169. Quoted in Jack Anderson, "Bay of Bengal and Tonkin Gulf," *Washington Post*, January 10, 1972.

170. Nixon, "Asia After Viet-Nam," p. 120.

171. WSAG minutes of December 6, 1971.

172. *New York Times*, December 29, 1971, p. 7.

173. The memorandum is in *PP* (*Gravel*), II, 643–48.

174. Wise and Ross, *The Invisible Government*, p. 145.

175. See Ambassador Howard Palfrey Jones's valuable account, *Indonesia: The Possible Dream* (New York: Harcourt Brace Jovanovich, 1971), p. 143.

176. During the rebellion, Dulles wrote to Ambassador Jones: "The Communists are taking advantage of the fact that President Sukarno feels a need for greater authority at the top in the situation that confronts him. They are seeking to impose upon Indonesia a Communist-type 'dictatorship of the proletariat' which will end up by taking the Indonesian Republic into the Communist camp and making Sukarno in effect a prisoner." *Ibid.*, p. 139.

177. Goodyear and U.S. Rubber had huge rubber estates in Indonesia, among the world's largest. Oil interests were held by Standard Oil, Caltex, and Shell. (*Ibid.*, p. 131, n. 4.) The Communist Party dominated the unions of both industries; indeed, its electoral gains in 1957 in

South Sumatra were largely due to the vote of oil-field workers. *Ibid.*, pp. 113, 132.

178. See Herbert Feith, "Dynamics of Guided Democracy," in Ruth T. Mc-Vey (ed.), *Indonesia* (New Haven, Conn.: HRAF Press, 1963), pp. 319–20, 337–38.

179. *New York Times*, February 12, 1958, cited in Jones, p. 68.

180. Testimony before U.S. House of Representatives, Committee on Foreign Affairs, *Hearings on H.R. 12181: Mutual Security Act of 1958*, 85th Cong., 2d Sess., pts. 1–8, vol. I, February 18–28 and March 8–13, 1958 (Washington, D.C.: Government Printing Office, 1958), p. 219.

181. Jones, p. 77.

182. The issues in the rebellion are discussed by Feith, in McVey, pp. 317–21, and Jones, p. 72.

183. Jones, p. 78.

184. See *ibid.*, p. 71.

185. *Ibid.* pp. 78, 118–27.

186. *Ibid.*, p. 78.

187. *Ibid.*, p. 135.

188. Quoted in Arthur J. Dommen, *Conflict in Laos: The Politics of Neutralization* (New York: Praeger, 1964), p. 66; see also p. 62.

189. Hugh Toye, *Laos: Buffer State or Battleground* (London: Oxford University Press, 1968), p. 116.

190. Paul F. Langer and Joseph J. Zasloff, *North Vietnam and the Pathet Lao: Partners in the Struggle for Laos* (Cambridge, Mass.: Harvard University Press, 1970), p. 62.

191. Toye, pp. 114–15.

192. Eisenhower, *Waging Peace*, p. 607.

193. Dommen, p. 101.

194. Quoted *ibid.*, p. 85. n. 19.

195. Toye, p. 118.

196. Hilsman, p. 115; Toye, p. 111.

197. Toye, p. 124.

198. Dommen, pp. 127–29; Toye, p. 133.

199. See the Lansdale memorandum, *PP* (*Gravel*), II, 646.

200. *Ibid.*, 645.

201. Eisenhower, *Waging Peace*, pp. 608–9.

202. See the memorandum written by Clark Clifford on the meeting, held January 19, 1961, in *PP* (*Gravel*), II, 635–37.

203. This paragraph draws on material in my *China and Southeast Asia—The Politics of Survival: A Study of Foreign Policy Interaction* (Lexington, Mass.: Heath, 1971), pp. 137–45.

204. See, in addition to *ibid.*, Hedrick Smith, "Nixon's Decision to Invade Cambodia," *New York Times*, June 30, 1970, pp. 1, 14.

205. In his June 30 "Report on the Conclusion of the Cambodian Operation," *Department of State Bulletin*, July 20, 1970, p. 69. Smith's account (*op. cit.*) indicates that Nixon purposely used a one-year withdrawal plan in his April 20 speech to hide his intention not to withdraw any troops for the next two months, thus giving him forces to deploy near or in Cambodia.

206. Quoted in "Richard Nixon's Ten Days," *Newsweek*, May 18, 1970, p. 41.

207. Speech of April 30, 1970; text in *Los Angeles Times,* May 1, 1970, pp. 30–31.
208. *Washington Post,* May 15, 1970.
209. Stewart Alsop, "On the President's Yellow Pad," *Newsweek,* June 1, 1970, p. 106.
210. Smith, *op. cit.*
211. Nixon, June 30 report, *op. cit.,* p. 70.
212. Smith, *op. cit.,* and Alsop, "The Timing of the Gamble," *Newsweek,* May 11, 1970, p. 112.
213. As paraphrased by Alsop "The Timing of the Gamble."
214. Quoted in Alsop, "The President on Vietnam," *Newsweek,* October 13, 1969, p. 33.
215. All these phrases are from his April 30, 1970, speech.
216. Alsop, "On the President's Yellow Pad."
217. Smith, *op. cit.*
218. *Ibid.:* "Notice of the President's speech reached Premier Lon Nol only after it was over, because the Pnompenh cable office was closed. . . . The White House believed if he said 'no' [to the major part of the operation], it was in trouble; if he said 'yes,' he might be." Nixon obscured the question when he referred on April 30 to Cambodian appeals for "assistance." The appeal was for arms and ammunition, not for troops.
219. See, in addition to the *Newsweek* account cited above (n. 206), David R. Maxey, "How Nixon Decided to Invade Cambodia," *Look,* August 11, 1970, pp. 22–25.
220. Smith, *op. cit.*
221. Maxey, pp. 24–25.
222. See Alsop, "The President on Vietnam," and Sulzberger interview.

Chapter 6: The Case for Nonintervention

1. See the discussion in Herbert S. Dinerstein, *Intervention Against Communism* (Baltimore, Md.: Johns Hopkins University, 1967), pp. 33–37.
2. On the domestic and international parallels of intervention to preserve order, see Bernard P. Kiernan, *The United States, Communism, and the Emergent World* (Bloomington: Indiana University Press, 1973), pp. 173–76. A recent illustration of this parrallel is Richard Nixon's equation of the containment of China with the containment of "outlaw" elements in America's ghettos. See his "Asia After Viet-Nam," *Foreign Affairs,* XLVI, no. 1 (October, 1967), 123.
3. See, for instance, George Liska, *War and Order: Reflections on Vietnam and History* (Baltimore, Md.: Johns Hopkins University, 1968), especially pp. 15–29.
4. Walt W. Rostow, *View from the Seventh Floor* (New York: Harper & Row, 1964), p. 22.
5. One stimulating effort in this direction is Herbert K. Tillema's *Appeal to Force: American Military Intervention in the Era of Containment* (New York: Crowell, 1973), which offers an empirical and theoretical examination of the conditions that promote and restrain U.S. military intervention abroad.

6. See *ibid.*, chap. 5.
7. Concerning these values, see Robert A. Packenham, *Liberal America and the Third World* (Princeton, N.J.: Princeton University Press, 1973).
8. See Kiernan, chap. 1.
9. These are the two criteria suggested by Hans Morgenthau, *A New Foreign Policy for the United States* (New York: Praeger, 1969), p. 128.

Bibliography of Major Sources

Rather than include here every source used, I have instead listed only those books and articles that I have consulted frequently and that are readily available to other readers. Additional sources are cited in the footnotes.

GENERAL SOURCES

ACHESON, DEAN, *Present at the Creation: My Years in the State Department* (New York: Signet Books, 1969).

BARNET, RICHARD J., *Intervention and Revolution: The United States in the Third World* (New York: World, 1968).

EISENHOWER, DWIGHT D., *Mandate for Change, 1953–1956* (Garden City, N.Y.: Doubleday, 1963).

———, *Waging Peace, 1956–1961* (Garden City, N.Y.: Doubleday, 1965).

HILSMAN, ROGER, *To Move a Nation: The Politics of Foreign Policy in the Administration of John F. Kennedy* (New York: Doubleday, 1967).

JOHNSON, LYNDON BAINES, *The Vantage Point: Perspectives of the Presidency, 1963–1969* (New York: Holt, Rinehart & Winston, 1971).

KENNEDY, JOHN F., *The Strategy of Peace* (ed. Allan Nevins) (New York: Harper, 1960).

KIERNAN, BERNARD P., *The United States, Communism, and the Emergent World* (Bloomington, Ind.: Indiana University Press, 1973).

MURPHY, ROBERT, *Diplomat Among Warriors* (London: Collins, 1964).

ROSTOW, WALT W., *View from the Seventh Floor* (New York: Harper & Row, 1964).

SCHLESINGER, ARTHUR M., JR., *A Thousand Days: John F. Kennedy in the White House* (Boston, Mass.: Houghton Mifflin, 1965).

SORENSEN, THEODORE C., *Kennedy* (New York: Harper & Row, 1965).

TRUMAN, HARRY S., *Memoirs*. 2 vols. (Garden City, N.Y.: Doubleday, 1956). Vol. I: *Year of Decisions*. Vol. II: *Years of Trial and Hope*.

WISE, DAVID, and THOMAS B. ROSS, *The Invisible Government* (New York: Bantam, 1964).

THE MIDDLE EAST

BADEAU, JOHN S., *The American Approach to the Arab World* (New York: Harper & Row, 1968).

CAMPBELL, JOHN C., *Defense of the Middle East* (New York: Harper, 1958).

CAMPBELL, JOHN C., and HELEN CARUSO, *The West and the Middle East* (New York: Council on Foreign Relations, 1972).

CATTAM, RICHARD W., *Nationalism in Iran* (Pittsburgh, Pa.: University of Pittsburgh Press, 1964).

EDEN, SIR ANTHONY, *Full Circle* (Boston, Mass.: Houghton Mifflin, 1960).

ISSAWI, CHARLES, *Oil, the Middle East and the World* (New York: Library Press, 1972).

KERR, MALCOLM, "American Policy Toward Egypt, 1955–1971: A Record of Failures" (Los Angeles: Southern California Arms Control and Foreign Policy Seminar, March, 1973).

LUARD, EVAN (ed.), *The International Regulation of Civil Wars* (London: Thames & Hudson, 1972).

McCLINTOCK, ROBERT, *The Meaning of Limited War* (Boston, Mass.: Houghton Mifflin, 1967).

MEO, LEILA M. T., *Lebanon: Improbable Nation* (Bloomington, Ind.: Indiana University Press, 1965).

NUTTING, ANTHONY, *Nasser* (London: Constable, 1972).

TANZER, MICHAEL, *The Political Economy of International Oil and the Underdeveloped Countries* (Boston, Mass.: Beacon Press, 1969).

THAYER, CHARLES W., *Diplomat* (New York: Harper, 1959).

AFRICA

ATTWOOD, WILLIAM, *The Reds and the Blacks: A Personal Adventure* (New York: Harper & Row, 1967).

BOWLES, CHESTER, *Africa's Challenge to America* (Berkeley: University of California Press, 1956).

CHILCOTE, RONALD H., *Portuguese Africa* (Englewood Cliffs, N.J.: Prentice-Hall, 1967).

EMERSON, RUPERT, *Africa and United States Policy* (Englewood Cliffs, N.J.: Prentice-Hall, 1967).

GOLDSCHMIDT, WALTER (ed.), *The United States and Africa,* rev. ed. (New York: Praeger, 1963).

HEMPSTONE, SMITH, *Rebels, Mercenaries, and Dividends: The Katanga Story* (New York: Praeger, 1962).

HILSMAN, ROGER, and ROBERT C. GOOD (eds.), *Foreign Policy in the Sixties: The Issues and the Instruments* (Baltimore, Md.: Johns Hopkins Press, 1965).

HOSKYNS, CATHERINE, *The Congo Since Independence* (New York: Oxford University Press, 1965).

KITCHEN, HELEN (ed.), *Footnotes to the Congo Story* (New York: Walker, 1967).

LEFEVER, ERNEST W., *Crisis in the Congo* (Washington, D.C.: Brookings Institution, 1965).

LEGUM, COLIN, and JOHN DRYSDALE (eds.), *Africa Contemporary Record: 1969–1970* (London: Chudley, 1970).

LUMUMBA, PATRICE, *Congo, My Country* (New York: Praeger, 1962).

MARCUM, JOHN, *The Angolan Revolution,* 2 vols. (Cambridge, Mass.: MIT Press, 1969). Vol. I: *The Anatomy of an Explosion, 1950–1962.*

MARTIN, LAURENCE W. (ed.), *Neutralism and Nonalignment: The New States in World Affairs* (New York: Praeger, 1962).

NWANKWO, ARTHUR AGWUNCHA, and SAMUEL UDOCHUKWU IFEJIKA, *Biafra: The Making of a Nation* (New York: Praeger, 1970).

O'BRIEN, CONOR CRUISE, *To Katanga and Back: A United Nations Case History* (New York: Grosset & Dunlap, 1962).

ST. JORRE, JOHN DE, *The Brothers' War: Biafra and Nigeria* (Boston, Mass.: Houghton Mifflin, 1972).

SPIEGEL, STEVEN L., and KENNETH N. WALTZ (eds.), *Conflict in World Politics* (Cambridge, Mass.: Winthrop, 1971).

U.S. Army, *Area Handbook for the Republic of the Congo (Léopoldville)* (Washington, D.C.: Government Printing Office, 1962).

WISEBERG, LAURIE S., "The Nigerian Civil War, 1967–1970: A Case Study in the Efficacy of International Law as a Regulator of Intrastate Violence" (Los Angeles: Southern California Arms Control and Foreign Policy Seminar, May, 1972).

YOUNG, CRAWFORD, *Politics in the Congo* (Princeton, N.J.: Princeton University Press, 1965).

LATIN AMERICA

AGUILAR, ALONSO, *Pan-Americanism from Monroe to the Present,* trans. from the Spanish by Asa Zatz (New York: Monthly Review Press, 1968).

BERLE, ADOLF A., *Latin America: Diplomacy and Reality* (New York: Harper & Row, 1962).

BONSAL, PHILIP W., *Cuba, Castro, and the United States* (Pittsburgh, Pa.: University of Pittsburgh Press, 1971).

BOSCH, JUAN, *The Unfinished Experiment* (New York: Praeger, 1964).

DRAPER, THEODORE, *Castro's Revolution: Myths and Realities* (New York: Praeger, 1962).

———, "The Dominican Intervention Reconsidered," *Political Science Quarterly*, LXXXVI, no. 1 (March, 1971), 1–36.

———, *The Dominican Revolt* (New York: Commentary Reports, 1968).

FITZSIMONS, LOUISE, *The Kennedy Doctrine* (New York: Random House, 1972).

GRAY, RICHARD B. (ed.), *Latin America and the United States in the 1970's* (Itasca, Ill.: Peacock, 1971).

HALPER, THOMAS, *Foreign Policy Crises: Appearance and Reality in Decision Making* (Columbus, Ohio: Merrill, 1971).

JOHNSON, HAYNES, and BERNARD M. GWERTZMAN, *Fulbright the Dissenter* (New York: Doubleday, 1968).

KANE, WILLIAM EVERETT, *Civil Strife in Latin America: A Legal History of U.S. Involvement* (Baltimore, Md.: Johns Hopkins Press, 1972).

LANGLEY, LESTER D., *The Cuban Policy of the United States: A Brief History* (New York: Wiley, 1968).

LIEUWEN, EDWIN, *U.S. Policy in Latin America: A Short History* (New York: Praeger, 1965).

LOWENTHAL, ABRAHAM F., *The Dominican Intervention* (Cambridge, Mass.: Harvard University Press, 1972).

MARTIN, JOHN BARTLOW, *Overtaken by Events* (New York: Doubleday, 1966).

PETRAS, JAMES, *Politics and Social Structure in Latin America* (New York: Monthly Review Press, 1970).

PLANK, JOHN (ed.), *Cuba and the United States: Long-Range Perspectives* (Washington, D.C.: Brookings Institution, 1967).

RADOSH, RONALD, *American Labor and United States Foreign Policy* (New York: Random House, 1969).

RONNING, C. NEALE (ed.), *Intervention in Latin America* (New York: Knopf, 1970).

SCHNEIDER, RONALD M., *Communism in Guatemala, 1944–1954* (New York: Praeger, 1959).

SLATER, JEROME, *Intervention and Negotiation: The United States and the Dominican Revolution* (New York: Harper & Row, 1970).

SMITH, EARL E. T., *The Fourth Floor: An Account of the Castro Communist Revolution* (New York: Random House, 1962).

TAYLOR, PHILIP B., "The Guatemalan Affair: A Critique of United

States Foreign Policy," *American Political Science Review*, L, no. 3 (September, 1956), 787–806.

YDIGORAS FUENTES, MIGUEL, *My War with Communism* (as told to Mario Rosenthal) (Englewood Cliffs, N.J.: Prentice-Hall, 1963).

ASIA

ADAMS, NINA S., and ALFRED W. McCOY (eds.), *Laos: War and Revolution* (New York: Harper, 1970).

BARNDS, WILLIAM J., *India, Pakistan, and the Great Powers* (New York: Praeger, 1972).

COHEN, WARREN I., *America's Response to China: An Interpretative History of Sino-American Relations* (New York: Wiley, 1971).

COOPER, CHESTER L., *The Lost Crusade: America in Vietnam* (New York: Dodd, Mead, 1970).

DOMMEN, ARTHUR J., *Conflict in Laos: The Politics of Neutralization* (New York: Praeger, 1964).

DULLES, FOSTER RHEA, *American Policy Toward Communist China, 1949–1969* (New York: Crowell, 1972).

ELLSBERG, DANIEL, *Papers on the War* (New York: Simon & Schuster, 1972).

The Senator Gravel Edition, The Pentagon Papers: The Defense Department History of United States Decisionmaking on Vietnam. 5 vols. (Boston, Mass.: Beacon Press, 1972).

IRIYE, AKIRA, *Across the Pacific: An Inner History of American–East Asian Relations* (New York: Harcourt, Brace & World, 1967).

JONES, HOWARD PALFREY, *Indonesia: The Possible Dream* (New York: Harcourt Brace Jovanovich, 1971).

LINDSAY, MICHAEL, "The United States and the Chinese Communists, 1937–1945," *Asia Quarterly*, no. 3, 1971, pp. 215–56.

McVEY, RUTH T. (ed.), *Indonesia* (New Haven, Conn.: HRAF Press, 1963).

MAXEY, DAVID R., "How Nixon Decided to Invade Cambodia," *Look*, August 11, 1970, pp. 22–25.

NIXON, RICHARD M., "Asia After Viet-Nam," *Foreign Affairs*, XLVI, no. 1 (October, 1967), 111–25.

PIKE, DOUGLAS, *Viet Cong: The Organization and Technique of the National Liberation Front of South Vietnam* (Cambridge, Mass.: MIT Press, 1966).

SERVICE, JOHN S. *The Amerasia Papers: Some Problems in the History of US-China Relations* (Berkeley: University of California, Center for Chinese Studies, 1971).

SHAPLEN, ROBERT, *The Lost Revolution: The U.S. in Vietnam, 1946–1966*, rev. ed. (New York: Harper, 1966).

SHEEHAN, NEIL et al., *The Pentagon Papers* (New York: Bantam, 1971).

THOMSON, JAMES C., JR., "How Could Vietnam Happen? An Autopsy," *Atlantic*, April, 1968, pp. 47–53.

TOYE, HUGH, *Laos: Buffer State or Battleground* (London: Oxford University Press, 1968).

TSOU, TANG, *America's Failure in China, 1941–1950* (Chicago: University of Chicago Press, 1963).

TUCHMAN, BARBARA W., "If Mao Had Come to Washington: An Essay in Alternatives," *Foreign Affairs*, LI, no. 1 (October, 1972), 44–64.

————, *Stilwell and the American Experience in China, 1911–1945* (New York: Macmillan, 1971).

VAN SLYKE, LYMAN P. (ed.), *The China White Paper: August 1949*, 2 vols. (Stanford, California: Stanford University Press, 1967).

WHITE, THEODORE H., and ANNALEE JACOBY, *Thunder Out of China* (New York: William Sloane Associates, 1961).

WHITWORTH, WILLIAM, *Naive Questions About War and Peace* (New York: Norton, 1970).

Index

Acheson, Dean, 11, 34, 87; and China, 128–29, 132, 138, 140–41, 143–44; and Iran, 18
Adoula, Cyrille, 60–61, 63
Africa: Chinese policy in, 42, 79, 214; colonialism in, 41, 42, 44, 45, 62; decolonization in, 41; importance of, to U.S., 42–43, 47–48; nationalism in, 45, 63–64, 67; politics in, 42–43, 67; Soviet policy in, 42, 49, 79, 214; troops from, in Congo, 51; U.S. aid to, 43, 48; U.S. bases in, 43–45; U.S. influence in, 210
Afro-Asian nations, 42, 80; and colonialism, 48, 51, 74, 79; Conference of, in Bandung, 42; and Congo, 63
AID, 77, 93n, 180
Algeria, 46–50, 58
Allende, Salvador, 93n, 125
Alliance for Progress, 88–90, 92, 124
Alsop, Stewart, 197
Anderson, Jack, 177–79
Anglo-Iranian Oil Company, 18–19, 22
Angola, 48, 73–78. (See also Portugal)
Anticolonialism (see Colonialism)
Anticommunism in U.S. policy, 4, 23, 28, 59, 89, 97, 108, 148, 201
Antinationalism: in Bangladesh policy, 186; in Cambodia policy, 200; in China policy, 143; in Cuba policy, 104; defined, 2; in Indonesia policy, 191; in Middle East policy, 23, 38–39; in U.S. foreign policy, 2, 204, 210; in Vietnam policy, 162–63
Arab Union, 32
Arabian American Oil Company, 19

Arbenz Guzman, Jacobo, 93–103, 189
Arevalo, Juan José, 94, 103
ARMCO International Corporation, 53
Asia: balance of power in, 135, 166, 170, 188, 207; "loss" of, 154; pattern of U.S. interventions in, 127, 199–200; revolutionary nationalism in, 127, 166; self-reliance in, 165–66; U.S. commitments to, 165; U.S. interests in, 165; U.S. military aid to, 165
Aswan Dam, 13, 49
Awami League, 167, 174, 175, 178; election victory of, 169, 176; outlawed, 170; program of, 167–68
Ayub Khan, Mohammad, 167, 168
Azores, U.S. bases in, 44, 48, 73, 74, 76, 77, 78n

Baath party, 25, 32
Baghdad Pact, 12, 22, 25, 170
Balaguer, Joaquin, 114, 122, 124
Balance of power, 202, 204; in Asia, 135, 166, 170, 188, 207; in China, 129; in South Asia, 171, 177, 181, 183, 185, 207; worldwide, 159, 164, 165
Ball, George W., 59, 64, 145, 154, 158
Bangladesh, 73, 167, 201, 203, 207; Bengalis in, 166–68, 170, 173, 179, 184; Bihari minority in, 178; humanitarian relief in, 173, 179, 180; independence of, 166, 178, 185–87; and Mukti Bahini (Liberation Army), 170, 174, 180; nationalism in, 184, 185; Nixon Administration's policies toward,

251

POLITICAL SCIENCE

PRAEGER UNIVERSITY SERIES

The United States Against the Third World

Antinationalism and Intervention

MELVIN GURTOV

America was the first nation successfully to rebel against a colonial government. Yet, paradoxically, in the post–World War II era it has invariably opposed the forces of nationalism in the developing areas of the world. What accounts for America's failure to translate its ideals into sympathy for national movements seeking radical change?

In THE UNITED STATES AGAINST THE THIRD WORLD, Melvin Gurtov traces the methods and motives of American administrations from Truman through Nixon in dealing with political violence, rebellion, and revolution in the Third World. Examining fifteen cases of intervention since 1945, when cold-war attitudes first took hold, he marshals convincing evidence to indict the United States for a short-sighted foreign policy that has served to thwart two major and related forces in the world nationalism and radical change to accomplish modernization. This essentially imperial policy, Gurtov charges, seems designed to protect any status quo that is favorable to U.S. interests, while it ignores, more often than not, the wishes of the weaker nations, elementary standards of humanitarianism, international law, and respect for international organizations.

Gurtov traces the development of interventionism through each administration since World War II: Eisenhower in the Middle East, Kennedy in Africa, Johnson in Latin America, and Nixon in Asia. He not only analyzes the particular crisis in each region—Lebanon, the Congo, the Dominican Republic, and Bangladesh—but also relates that crisis to the evolution of U.S. policy in other areas of tension and conflict in the same region. Without neglecting economic factors, Gurtov focuses on U.S. domestic decision-making processes and their international political impact.

The book concludes by pointing out the long-term advantages of an American policy of nonintervention under international auspices and other restricted conditions.

MELVIN GURTOV is Associate Professor of Political Science at the University of California at Riverside. His most recent book is *China and Southeast Asia—The Politics of Survival: A Study of Foreign-Policy Interaction.*

Cover design by Roy Kuhlman

Our political science catalogue is available on request.

PRAEGER PUBLISHERS
111 Fourth Avenue, New York, N.Y. 10003